PRINCIPLES

of

FUNDRAISING

THEORY AND PRACTICE

WESLEY E. LINDAHL, PHD

Nils Axelson Professor of Nonprofit Management
Dean, School of Business and Nonprofit Management
North Park University

JONES AND BARTLETT PUBLISHERS

Sudbury, Massachusetts

BOSTON   TORONTO   LONDON   SINGAPORE

World Headquarters
Jones and Bartlett Publishers
40 Tall Pine Drive
Sudbury, MA 01776
978-443-5000
info@jbpub.com
www.jbpub.com

Jones and Bartlett Publishers
Canada
6339 Ormindale Way
Mississauga, Ontario L5V 1J2
Canada

Jones and Bartlett Publishers
International
Barb House, Barb Mews
London W6 7PA
United Kingdom

Jones and Bartlett's books and products are available through most bookstores and online booksellers. To contact Jones and Bartlett Publishers directly, call 800-832-0034, fax 978-443-8000, or visit our website www.jbpub.com.

Substantial discounts on bulk quantities of Jones and Bartlett's publications are available to corporations, professional associations, and other qualified organizations. For details and specific discount information, contact the special sales department at Jones and Bartlett via the above contact information or send an email to specialsales@jbpub.com.

Production Credits
Acquisitions Editor: Jeremy Spiegel
Production Director: Amy Rose
Production Assistant: Julia Waugaman
Senior Marketing Manager: Barb Bartoszek
Manufacturing and Inventory Control Supervisor: Amy Bacus
Composition: Achorn International
Cover Design: Brian Moore/Kristin E. Parker
Cover and Title Page Image: © Andreas Guskos/ShutterStock, Inc.
Printing and Binding: Malloy Incorporated
Cover Printing: Malloy Incorporated

Library of Congress Cataloging-in-Publication Data

Lindahl, Wesley E., 1954–
    Principles of fundraising : theory and practice / by Wesley E. Lindahl.
        p. cm.
    Includes bibliographical references and index.
    ISBN 978-0-7637-5914-8 (pbk.)
    1. Fund raising. 2. Nonprofit organizations—Finance. I. Title.
    HG177.L55 2010
    658.15′224—dc22
                                                                            2008055381

6048
Printed in the United States of America
13 12 11 10 09   10 9 8 7 6 5 4 3 2 1

In memory of Anita Hillin, my fundraising colleague for 18 years at Northwestern University and most recently a teaching colleague at North Park University, whose positive attitude and optimistic outlook on life was contagious.

Contents

Record keeping?

Preface

For close to 20 years, I developed and taught courses in the area of fundraising and nonprofit organizations. The idea for this textbook came from my years of teaching this topic.

In the early 2000s, I joined the faculty full-time at North Park University and soon began thinking of a possible new textbook: one that would combine theory and practice and be based within a marketing orientation.

My students played a role in helping to draft this textbook. Developed as a part of the introductory course in fundraising at North Park University's School of Business and Nonprofit Management, students from the Fall 2004, 2005, and 2006 on-campus sections of SBNM 5770 (Principles of Fundraising for Nonprofit Organizations) helped by drafting or rewriting sections of chapters as part of their course work. Students from the Summer 2006 class provided helpful suggestions for improvement. Since 2006 I have revised and rewritten many sections of the book. I have used the text constantly over this time. Hundreds of students have used the material and the constant updating has provided a well-crafted textbook for students new to the field of nonprofit fundraising.

The book is organized using a core of basic background chapters (1–7) along with a series of chapters that could be read or used in class in any order (8–12). The core starts with an introduction to the field of fundraising within a marketing orientation. Chapter 2 discusses the theories behind why people give to nonprofit organizations. It combines theory with the results of surveys from many different sources. It concludes with a summary of motivations for elite donors. Chapter 3 continues the motivation discussion for non-individual donors, such as corporations and foundations. Chapter 4 provides a historical account of fundraising, demonstrating a growing profession that developed in the United States over the past 100 years. The theory of fundraising is covered in Chapter 5. It includes theories from economics, psychology, sociology, and organizational management, and applies them to fundraising practice. Government regulations are discussed in Chapter 6, including non-profit status, IRS Form 990, receipting regulations, and accountability issues. International students will find the need to supplement the United States-based material with references to their own country's tax rules for charitable giving. The core of the textbook is completed within Chapter 7. Here the practice of fundraising is laid out within the following structure: Research, Planning, Cultivation, Solicitation, Stewardship, and Evaluation.

Following the seven core chapters are five chapters on special topics of interest to students in the field of fundraising. Any discussion of fundraising tends to gravitate to the boards of trustees. How do you involve the board members in fundraising? This question is explored in Chapter 8. Religious fundraising is approached in Chapter 9. This topic is often short-changed within our increasingly secular world. However, approximately one-third of all giving in the United States goes to religious organizations. To really understand giving and fundraising, you need to understand religious motivations. Diverse populations and fundraising is discussed in Chapter 10. Organizations attempting to increase the diversity of donors need to consider the structural and historic issues involved. Chapter 11 covers ethics, which is important to fundraisers because they work to build relationships with donors centered on trust. I have included a methodology developed by Marilyn Fischer in her book *Ethical Decision Making in Fundraising*. The final discussion, Chapter 12, talks about how to structure an organization to achieve success in fundraising. Included in this chapter is a discussion of budgeting and resource allocation for fundraising based on concepts developed in my award-winning book *Strategic Planning for Fundraising*.

This textbook will be enormously useful for teachers and students at the upper-level undergraduate or graduate level. The combination of theory and practice sets it apart from other textbooks in this field. Students will be able to put fundraising within context and allow for further practical learning. At North Park University, for example, the Principles of Fundraising for Nonprofit Organizations course is followed by four specific fundraising courses (Grant Writing, Annual and Major Gifts, Capital Campaigns, and Planned Giving) that build on the basic materials found in this textbook.

Acknowledgments

The preparation of this book was partially funded by the Nils Axelson Endowed Professorship Fund and the Axelson Center for Nonprofit Management at North Park University. I thank my faculty colleagues in the School of Business and Nonprofit Management at North Park who provided comments, feedback, and general support throughout the writing process. Particular mention should be made of the current full-time faculty at the school: Michael Avramovich, John Bonie, Gianfranco Farruggia, Ann Ownby Hicks, Robert Hirsch, Al Kamienski, Catherine Marsh, Crendalyn McMath, Tim O'Brien, and Lee Sundholm. Thanks as well to the North Park staff and part-time nonprofit management instructors who supported me in many different ways: Jimmie Alford, Meta Anderson, Noelle Baker, Don Cassiday, Nicole Daniels, Christa Beall Diefenbach, Lisa Dietlin, Sarah Fodor, Stacy French Reynolds, Gary Grace, Colette Hands, Anita Hillin, Penelope Hunt, Chiku Jallah, Trevor James, Joseph Jones, Richard Lies, Melissa Morris Olson, Chris Nicholson, Melissa Patterson, Martin Paulson, Charles Peterson, Kurt H. Peterson, Deborah Popely, Pamela Ransom, Pier Rogers, Ken Schaefle, Robert Shafis, Tracey Starkovich, Shannon Stubblefield, Andrew Tiebert, Rick Yngve, and Dayle Zelenka.

I owe a big debt of gratitude to authors Kathleen S. Kelly and Joseph R. Mixer whose earlier textbooks on fundraising helped to guide and inspire me to write *Principles of Fundraising: Theory and Practice*. As pioneers in the field, they have led the way and shown me the path ahead. Thank you both for your labor in this developing academic area.

I would like to thank Michael O'Neill who inspired me to keep working on the book during the early years of drafting. We had talked at the ARNOVA conference in 2003, the year his new edition of *Nonprofit Nation* was released. He gave me the encouragement to turn a concept into reality.

Many thanks to the students who have helped to draft sections of this textbook or give suggestions for improvement, including the following individuals: Mo Aburmishan, Dan Boehlje, Emilio C. Bracho, Matthew Braun, Donna Catalano, Sharon Diaz, Kara Fagan, Jennifer G. Gorman, Ceasar Jauraidez, Scott E. Kaplan, Erin Kato, Elizabeth A. Kehoe, Casey Klarich, Dana L. Labrose, Britta Larson, Rebecca Lopez, Sara A. McGrath, Sarah A. Miller, Laura Lynn Millner Salameh, Tanya Pashkuleua, Eric Pement, Andrea Ridenour, Sarah Satterberg, Jennifer Schack, Susannah Schwarcz, Andre Sergeyev, Sejal Shah, Jennifer Smith, John R. Stodden, Valerie A. Stodden, Daniel Stutz, Joshua Swenson, Christine Villas, and Milan Vydareny. I would like to thank each one for their successful efforts.

I would like to thank Jeremy Spiegel, acquisitions editor, and the entire marketing, production, and manufacturing teams at Jones and Bartlett Publishers, including Barb Bartoszek, Amy Rose, Julia Waugaman, Amy Bacus, and Kristin E. Parker, for their help in making this book come to life.

Thanks, too, to my wife, Deb Lindahl, who put up with my hours in front of the computer screen—preventing her from using our only computer for blogging, checking emails, and surfing the Internet.

Finally, I am thankful to have a very capable graduate assistant, Debbie Dahlgren, to help me draft, edit, and organize the materials for inclusion in the final text. She did an outstanding job. Thank you for all of your hard work.

chapter one

Principles of Fundraising: Theory and Practice

Most seasoned fundraising professionals learned the theory and practice of their profession through on-the-job experiences, finding mentors along the way, and attending many (perhaps too many) professional conferences and workshops. Most concentrated on the practical side of learning, and perhaps some developed their own theories based on the patterns they found. A few of us—and I consider myself in that group—have wavered between theory and practice in both professional and academic settings. We have thought of fundraising principles as developing out of several different contexts—legal, sociological, economic, public relations, and marketing. We have researched and written, worked in the profession, and experienced the annual fund and major gift fundraising firsthand. We have discovered the power of theory to inform practice and the need to incorporate "best practices" into our understanding of the principles of fundraising.

I first learned the practice of reunion giving, for example, from John Birkholz, the former associate director of development at the Northwestern University Law School. The school's reunion giving program was the best at the university. They raised over $1 million consistently each year during the 1990s. Over lunch, John explained to me the mechanics of how to select co-chairs for each reunion class. How they should be asked up front to give their gift first before asking others, how the reunion giving committees should be set up, and how the alumni from each class should be asked for their gifts. It was a well-oiled process, explained entirely from a practical perspective, and it lacked a theoretical basis.

But since that lunch I have come across theory from psychology to help provide a context for why the reunion program works. Robert Cialdini's rule of consistency (see Chapter 5) fits nicely within the context of reunion giving. When people join committees they tend to take on the roles assigned to the committee. Therefore, when a member of the class of 1964 joins the reunion giving committee, he or she understands that asking others for gifts is a part of the committee responsibilities and takes up the role of solicitation. Alumni are much more receptive to giving within the context of a reunion rather than being asked out of the blue, "Hey, Joe, would you donate $1,000 unrestricted to the Law School?" Understanding the principles of fundraising requires knowledge of both the theory (the rule of consistency) and the practice (how to run a successful reunion giving campaign). The integration of theory and practice is the basic underlying concept in this book.

MARKETING ORIENTATION: FOCUSING ON DONOR RELATIONSHIPS

The field of marketing models fundraising in several ways. All involve relationships. Marketing is more than just promotion or sales, just as donor relationships with a nonprofit organization involve more than just asking. Marketing seeks to understand the customer and develop products to meet the customer's needs and wants. Fundraisers help guide and direct donors' philanthropic impulses. They discuss the impact of a major gift on the organization, and they report back on use of the funds for charitable purposes. They need to understand the donor's need for making an impact on society. Fundraising professionals generally think of fundraising as falling within a marketing orientation. In 1992 Kelly conducted a national study and found that "only 27% of the 296 practitioners participating in that quantitative study disagreed with the statement, 'Fund raising is analogous to marketing in the for-profit sector'" (1998, p. 12). Let us discuss more specifically how fundraising fits into the discipline of marketing.

Marketing should always start by keeping the "customer" in mind. Who is the customer in fundraising? Certainly the donor is the primary customer, but there are other stakeholders as well. The clients that are being served and the general public are two of the secondary components of the customer concept in fundraising. One of the concerns of using marketing as the framework for fundraising is that the donor, unlike the customer in a corporate setting, provides resources but is not given benefits equal to the resources. Part of the benefits goes to the other "customers" in the equation. Clients get access to services, and society generally improves as a result of these clients being served. If the marketing attention is focused strictly on the donor, there is a tendency to bend the mission (a phenomenon known as "mission creep") toward the need of the donor. Mission creep can be avoided if fundraisers realize that the donor is only a part of the customer equation (Kelly, 1998).

A second component of marketing is the use of segmentation to better relate to customers. This concept is very helpful in thinking about fundraising and developing relationships with donors. In direct mail fundraising, for example, a segmentation approach allows the staff to create an appropriate message for various donor categories. The typical segmentation strategy calls for sending a different message to those who have given in the past versus those being asked to give for the first time. A thank-you note is appropriate for the past givers and not for the yet-to-give group. Beyond the basic strategy, staff can analyze databases statistically to determine the best segmentation strategy.

Finally, those who take a marketing approach must listen to their customers and be willing to modify the "product" to adjust to the needs of the customers. For example, when providing a proposal to a major gift prospect, a fundraiser with a marketing orientation might be willing to adjust to the donor. Perhaps an organization is interested in a new health clinic program that doesn't include dental care. A major donor may have an interest in dental care. The organization adds the dental clinic program into the health clinic, and the donor funds the additional cost. Without the agreement to add the dental care, the donor may not have given at all or at a different level. Although this concept could be taken too far in a fundraising context, understanding donors by listening to them as funding proposals are developed makes a lot of sense and is a useful strategy in major gift fundraising to build ongoing relationships with donors. Back to the example, if the donor had suggested setting up an art museum within the health clinic, the organization may not have wanted to modify their "product." Organizations need to look to their mission and make sure that any modification to their program fits within their agreed-to framework of operation.

Now we move on to define fundraising as the term will be used throughout this book. Within a marketing framework, charitable fundraising can be thought of as the creation and ongoing development of relationships between a nonprofit organization and its various donors for the purpose of increasing gift revenue to the organization. Fundraising involves the careful development of donor relationships. It is not a one-way process; it is a two-way process that involves the donor as a key partner in an effort to better serve society.

PHILANTHROPY

If you start with a marketing orientation and focus on the "customer," you will quickly begin to understand donor philanthropy. The *Oxford English Dictionary* (2007, s.v. "philanthropy") defines philanthropy as "Love of mankind; the disposition or active effort to promote the happiness and well-being of others; practical benevolence, now esp. as expressed by the generous donation of money to good causes." Another definition of philanthropy is "Love of humankind, usually expressed by an effort to enhance the well-being of humanity through personal acts of practical kindness or by financial support of a cause or causes" (Levy, 1996–2003, p. 93). Philanthropy today provides broad support for almost every aspect of human endeavor, encompassing art, culture, museums, poetry, fighting hunger and poverty, religious institutions, health care facilities, schools, and universities.

According to Eugene Tempel, "We can identify at least seven significant roles that nonprofit organizations and philanthropy play in a civil society: They reduce human suffering, enhance human potential, promote private equity and justice, build community, provide human fulfillment, support experimentation and change, and foster pluralism" (2003, pp. 3–4). The form of philanthropy that concerns us will exclude the direct efforts of the federal, state, and local governments, even though they contribute to the same themes and serve many of the same publics. The exception is support of those nonprofit organizations that advocate for change in government policy. They are included in our discussion.

Robert Payton has coined the term *voluntary action for the public good* as defining philanthropy. Within this definition, he considers two parts: *community* and *compassion*. Compassion involves soup kitchens, homeless shelters, and health care clinics. Community involves hospitals, universities, schools, museums, and theater. A further complication in the definition is the fact that the Internal Revenue Service (IRS) uses the term "charitable" when describing the broad range of philanthropic organizations, when the average person tends to think of charitable as being just those organizations dealing directly with compassion. One should look carefully at how these terms are used (Payton, 1988).

The *independent sector* and *third sector* are two other terms used to describe the nonprofit sector—as distinct from the business and government sectors of society. Of the 36 categories that the IRS recognizes as tax exempt (see **Table 1-1**), the independent or third sector consists of "two major groups of tax-exempt organizations: 501(c)(3) charitable organizations and religious congregations and organizations; and 510(c)(4) social welfare organizations" (Weitzman, 2002, p. xxvii). I estimate that the total number of such nonprofit organizations in 2009 approaches 2 million. Not all nonprofit organizations are required to register with the government through the IRS, so the exact number is not known. In this book I concentrate on fundraising for charitable organizations, which represent almost 70% of all nonprofit organizations, or 1.4 million. Of those, the Giving USA Foundation (2008) reports that 1,128,367 are registered with the IRS. Religious congregations and very small organizations make up the balance. Chapter 6 describes the legal definitions of the different types of charitable organizations.

Roger Lohmann presents the theory of the commons to explain the domain into which nonprofits should be placed. According to Lohmann, nonprofits can provide neither purely public nor private goods. He says, "*A private good* is one whose benefits can be restricted to those who have paid for it" and "a *public good* is one that, if available at all, must be available to everyone" (1992, p. 168). Nonprofits do not provide services only to those who pay for them, nor do they provide services to everyone. Instead, they meet the needs of specific subsections of individuals whose interests and/or needs match the services provided by the nonprofit. The theory of the commons explains why there is an abundance of nonprofits in the world, yet there is no common belief structure for them all. More basically, it explains how two nonprofits with opposing points of view can coexist.

This theory is significant because it highlights the many choices that a donor has in determining where to allocate his or her resources. Rather than vaguely donating money to an organization that the donor hopes has his or her best interests in mind, the donor can give to the specific nonprofit with which he or she most closely identifies. Lohmann says, "Commons have been defined here as collectivities in which uncoerced participation, sharing, mutuality, and fairness play an important part" (1992, p. 254). In a democratic

Table 1-1 Types of Tax-Exempt Organizations by Internal Revenue Code Section

Code Section	Description of Organization	General Nature of Activities
220(e)	Medical Saving Accounts (MSAs)	Fiduciary agent for accounts used in conjunction with high-deductible health plans to save funds for future medical expenses
401(a)	Qualified pension, profit-sharing, or stock bonus plans	Fiduciary agent for pension, profit-sharing, or stock bonus plans
408(e)	Individual Retirement Arrangements (IRAs)	Fiduciary agent for retirement funds
501(c)(1)	Government Instrumentality; corporations organized under Act of Congress	Activities of a nature implied by the description of the class of organization
(2)	Title-holding corporations for exempt organizations	Holding title to property for exempt organizations
(3)	Religious, educational, charitable, scientific, or literary organizations; testing for public safety organizations. Also, organizations preventing cruelty to children or animals, or fostering national or international amateur sports competition	Activities of a nature implied by the description of the class of organization
(4)	Civic leagues, social welfare organizations, and local associations of employees	Promotion of community welfare and activities from which net earnings are devoted to charitable, educational, or recreational purposes
(5)	Labor, agricultural, and horticultural organizations	Educational or instructive groups whose purpose is to improve conditions of work, products, and efficiency
(6)	Business leagues, chambers of commerce, real estate boards, and like organizations	Improving conditions in one or more lines of business
(7)	Social and recreational clubs	Pleasure, recreation, and social activities
(8)	Fraternal beneficiary societies and associations	Lodge providing for payment of life, health, accident, or other insurance benefits to members

Code Section	Description of Organization	General Nature of Activities
(9)	Voluntary employees' beneficiary associations (including federal employees' voluntary beneficiary associations formerly covered by section 501(c)(10))	Providing for payment of life, health, accident, or other insurance benefits to members
(10)	Domestic fraternal societies and associations	Lodges, societies, or associations devoting their net earnings to charitable, fraternal, and other specified purposes, without life, health, accident benefits or other insurance to members
(11)	Teachers' retirement fund associations	Fiduciary association providing for payment of retirement benefits
(12)	Benevolent life insurance associations, mutual ditch or irrigation companies, mutual or cooperative telephone companies, and like organizations	Activities of a mutually beneficial nature implied by the description of the class of organization
(13)	Cemetery companies	Arranging for burials and incidental related activities
(14)	State-chartered credit unions and mutual insurance or reserve funds	Providing loans to members or providing insurance of, or reserve funds for, shares or deposits in certain banks or loan associations
(15)	Mutual insurance companies or associations other than life, if written premiums for the year do not exceed $350,000	Providing insurance to members, substantially at cost
(16)	Corporations organized to finance crop operations	Financing crop operations in conjunction with activities of a marketing or purchasing association
(17)	Supplemental unemployment benefit trusts	Fiduciary agent for payment of supplemental unemployment compensation benefits
(18)	Employee funded pension trusts (created before June 25, 1959)	Providing for payments of benefits under a pension plan funded by employees
(19)	Posts or organizations of past or present members of the armed forces	Activities implied by the nature of the organization

(*continues*)

Table 1-1 Continued

Code Section	Description of Organization	General Nature of Activities
(21)	Black Lung Benefit Trusts	Created by coal mine operators to satisfy their liability for disability or death due to black lung disease
(22)	Withdrawal liability payment funds	Providing funds to meet the liability of employers withdrawing from a multi-employer pension fund
(23)	Associations of past and present members of the armed forces founded before 1880	Providing insurance and other benefits to veterans or their dependents
(24)	Trusts described in section 4049 of the Employee Retirement Income Security Act of 1974	Providing funds for employee retirement income
(25)	Title-holding corporations or trusts with no more than 35 shareholders or beneficiaries and only one class of stock or beneficial interest	Acquiring real property and remitting all income earned from such property to one or more exempt organizations; pension, profit-sharing, or stock bonus plans; or governmental units
(26)	State-sponsored high-risk health insurance organizations	Activities of a nature implied by the description of the class of organization
(27)	State-sponsored workers' compensation reinsurance organizations	Activities of a nature implied by the description of the class of organization
501(d)	Apostolic and religious organizations	Activities of a nature implied by the description of the class of organization
501(e)	Cooperative hospital service organizations	Activities of a nature implied by the description of the class of organization
501(f)	Cooperative service organizations of operating educational organizations	Activities of a nature implied by the description of the class of organization
501(k)	Child care organizations	Activities of a nature implied by the description of the class of organization
501(n)	Charitable risk pools	Activities of a nature implied by the description of the class of organization

Code Section	Description of Organization	General Nature of Activities
521	Farmers' cooperatives	Activities of a nature implied by the description of the class of organization
529	Qualified state-sponsored tuition programs	Activities of a nature implied by the description of the class of organization

NOTE: Prepaid legal service funds, described in section 501(c)(20) of the Internal Revenue Code, were no longer tax exempt beginning with tax years after June 30, 1992.
Source: Internal Revenue Service (2004).

society, nonprofits fill the void that private and public institutions leave. Donors ✕ have the opportunity to give where they feel the biggest need exists. The theory of the commons factors freedom of choice into the giving equation.

In today's society, philanthropic organizations usually operate by obtaining support of needed resources in the form of cash grants, volunteer efforts, technical support, in-kind donations, and other approaches in order to accomplish their mission. Upon receiving donations, nonprofits in turn facilitate programs and services that change communities, provide health care, protect the environment, support art, and foster religious beliefs. Charitable giving can be expressed in different ways: a direct gift to a nonprofit, creation of a private foundation, establishing a corporate foundation, or the formation of a donor-advised fund at a community foundation. "Regardless of the size or type of the gift . . . there are a variety of vehicles through which philanthropic resources can be directed" (Delaware Valley GrantMakers, 2006).

GIVING USA DATA AND TRENDS IN GIVING

Since the mid-1950s, the Giving USA Foundation has produced its annual *Giving USA* report, which is considered the definitive source of giving information in the United States. It is important to reference the most recent edition of this publication to supplement the following description of national trends in philanthropy.

Figure 1-1 classifies contributions by source, according to the Giving USA Foundation. In 2007, corporations, the source of only 5.1% of all contributions, gave a total of $15.69 billion. Foundations, in contrast, representing 12.6% of the total giving, gave $38.52 billion, and bequests constituted

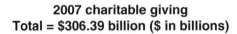

2007 charitable giving
Total = $306.39 billion ($ in billions)

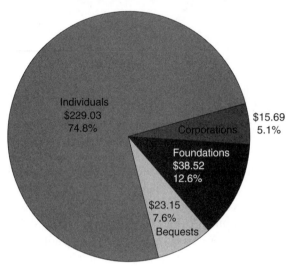

Figure 1-1. 2007 charitable giving. Total = $306.39 billion. *Source:* Giving USA Foundation (2008)

7.6%, or $23.15 billion. The trend in bequests is most challenging to predict because of the volatility in the number of bequests written as well as changes that occur in a donor's lifetime. Indisputably, most gifts come from individuals, supporting an avowed statistic that most of the support to any philanthropic organization comes from individuals. Living individuals represented an overwhelming 74.8%, or $229.03 billion, of the total giving in 2007 (Giving USA Foundation, 2008).

Individual giving can be measured as a percentage of personal income (before taxes are deducted) or as a percentage of disposable personal income (after taxes have been deducted). The 2006 *Giving USA* report estimates personal giving to charities and religious groups to be about 2.0% of personal income and 2.3% of disposable personal income (Giving USA Foundation, 2007, p. 34). The average giving of personal income between 1966 and 2006 was 1.8%, and the average giving of disposable personal income was 2.1%, so the most recent figures (this information was not updated in 2007 *Giving USA*) are very close to the 40-year average (p. 34). **Figure 1-2** shows details of individual giving as a share of income between 1966 and 2006.

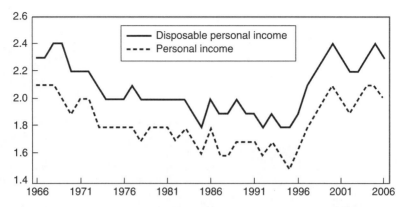

Figure 1-2. Individual giving as a share of income, 1966–2006.
Source: Giving USA Foundation (2007)

Between 1967 and 2007, total giving grew 190% (adjusted for inflation). **Figure 1-3** shows the 40-year trend of total giving between 1967 and 2007. During recessions, giving grows more slowly or declines when adjusted for inflation, and when the stock market rises, giving grows rapidly (Giving USA Foundation, 2008, p. 20). Giving as a percentage of gross domestic product (GDP) was at 2.2% in 2007. Giving as a percentage of GDP has ranged from 1.7% to 2.3% between 1967 and 2007 (Giving USA Foundation, 2008, p. 28).

Between 1967 and 2007, giving has increased annually (adjusted for inflation) at different rates during different periods. For individual giving, real rates from 1967 to 1990 were 2.5% annual growth and 3.5% growth from 1990 going forward. For bequests, real rates from before 1990 were 0.8%, and 5.9% from 1990 forward. For foundations, real rates were under 1.0% up until 1990, and 9.5% from 1990 forward. For corporations, real rates have been consistently averaging between 3.1% and 3.5% over the entire 40-year period (Giving USA Foundation, 2008, pp. 24–27).

Religion is the largest single recipient of contributions, receiving about $102.32 billion in 2007, or about 33.4% of all giving (Giving USA Foundation, 2008, p. 14). How much is $102.32 billion? To give some idea for comparison, annual spending in the United States on lawn and garden supplies was $85 billion in 2000, soft drink sales were $64 billion in 2003, and fast food restaurant sales were $110 billion in 1999 (empty tomb, inc., 2007). Giving to religious causes has increased over time, but it is still far below

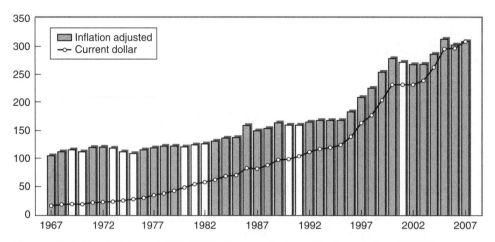

Figure 1-3. Total giving, 1967–2007. *Source:* Giving USA Foundation (2008)

what had typically been the case for decades. For instance, contributions to religious causes in 1966 were 45.7% of all giving (Giving USA Foundation, 2007, p. 38).

According to a report by the President's Council of Economic Advisers, most people try to make a donation of some kind. "Even among those with incomes under $10,000, almost half (48 percent) made a donation" to charity (Council of Economic Advisers, 2000, p. 6). However, the wealthy provide the lion's share of philanthropic giving. The 10% of the population who made the largest gifts accounted for "74 percent of the total of all philanthropic contributions" (p. 7). Yet, as wealth increased, the proportion given decreased. The Council of Economic Advisers goes on to say, "Families in the 20–40 percent range of the wealth distribution gave 1 percent of their wealth to charitable organizations, while the wealthiest gave just 0.4 percent" (p. 7).

Giving USA reports that 40% of all U.S. income and 85% of all publicly traded stocks and mutual funds (by value) are owned by just 10% of the U.S. population. Granted, this 10% constitutes 11 million households, so it is a significant number of people. The average net worth of each of these households is $2.7 million, and the average annual household income is $270,000 (Giving USA Foundation, 2004, p. 60).

As with all economic analyses, such as the *Giving USA* annual reports, there is room for a minority opinion that challenges us to be wary of hidden biases and slanted presentations even while using accurate data sets. A dissenting voice is represented by empty tomb, inc., a Christian research ministry in Champaign, Illinois. Researchers John and Sylvia Ronsvalle point out that the Giving USA Foundation is supported by for-profit fundraising consulting firms, who may want to show giving data in the best possible light. In particular, they say, Giving USA does not adjust its figures for increases in both population and income. For example, Giving USA reported a 2.80% increase in U.S. giving between 2002 and 2003. Thus, it appears that Americans became more generous over two consecutive years. However, when the numbers are adjusted for the increase in population and for income, giving as a percentage of disposable personal income (income after taxes) actually *declined* 2.00% (Ronsvalle & Ronsvalle, 2004).

Criticism aside, it is quite evident from the sheer level of total giving that the citizens of the United States participate strongly in philanthropy. They care about donating to charity. It is a part of their culture. Fundraisers need to understand that they don't need to necessarily convince Americans to give to charitable causes. Instead, fundraisers need to make the case for support of their particular organization's mission and associated programs.

GLOBAL PHILANTHROPY

Simmons and Nielsen define global philanthropy as "the use of financial and other resources to target underdevelopment around the world. This includes investments traveling over borders (donors in wealthier nations investing in poorer countries) and funds traveling within borders where the investors' goal is increasing the prosperity of an underdeveloped region or group of people" (2004, ¶ 3). According to an article in the *Chronicle of Philanthropy*, "Americans send more than $70 billion a year to aid people in developing countries, more than three times as much as the federal government provides in overseas aid" (Hall, 2006, p. 14). This figure includes donations from foundations, corporations, nonprofits, and other groups, and money that people in the United States send to relatives and friends in other countries (Hall, p. 14). According to Simmons and Nielsen (2004): "Global philanthropy, or global social investing, is expanding rapidly, a byproduct of the world's increasingly mobile workforce, the explosion of wealth in the 1990s, and improvements in telecommunications" (¶ 1).

For several decades, global philanthropy was found in only a small number of foundations, but because of the involvement of individuals such as Bill Gates, Ted Turner, George Soros, and Stephan Schmidheiny, individual global giving has received a great deal of attention (Simmons & Nielsen, 2004, ¶ 3).

In 1994 Stephan Schmidheiny created the AVINA Foundation, which partners with civil society and business leaders to work toward sustainable development in Latin America (Fuchs, 2004). George Soros is the founder of a network of philanthropic organizations that is active on a global basis. "Based primarily in Central and Eastern Europe and the former Soviet Union—but also in Africa, Latin America, Asia, and the United States—these foundations are dedicated to building and maintaining the infrastructure and institutions of an open society" (Open Society Institute and Soros Foundation Network, n.d.). Both Ted Turner, through the United Nations Foundation, and Bill Gates, through the Bill and Melinda Gates Foundation, have targeted global health issues such as AIDS, tuberculosis, and malaria (The Global Fund, n.d.). With the focus of these four philanthropists and their foundations, major global issues have received a lot of attention. Other international entrepreneurs and foundations have hopped on the bandwagon to give emphasis to these various global issues (Simmons & Nielsen, 2004, ¶ 3).

More statistics support the fact that global philanthropy has been expanding in recent years. "Foundation giving to international causes rose to $3.8 billion last year, the largest amount American grant makers have ever awarded overseas, says a new report. Such giving grew by $300 million from 2004, an 8-percent increase, not adjusting for inflation" (Wilhelm, 2006, p. 10). According to Wilhelm (2006), "Giving abroad has grown steadily during the last few years. Such giving has more than doubled since 1998, when international grants equaled $1.6 billion. But the substantial growth in the amount of money going abroad is largely attributed to the emergence of two wealthy funds, the Bill & Melinda Gates Foundation, which focuses on global health, and the Gordon and Betty Moore Foundation, which finances international conservation" (p. 10).

The health industry saw its share of giving nearly double to 32% between 1998 and 2002. By and large, the Bill and Melinda Gates Foundation was a major contributor to this area with its philanthropic response to the global AIDS crisis and other global pandemics. Public affairs, environmental issues, science and technology, and religion all showed record gains in this time as well, although not as large an increase as the health care industry (Atienza, Seidler, & Renz, 2004, ¶ 10).

It is unclear if this growth in global philanthropy will continue. The international philanthropic environment has been bombarded by a series of events since 2000—some of which, such as the tsunami in Thailand in 2005, translated into record-setting levels of support—others, such as the mishandling of contributions made following the 9/11 attacks, caused a drop in the level of trust for nonprofits supporting global initiatives. In a 2004 survey of grant makers, nearly 56% stated that with all of the external changes, there is definitely a greater urgency for global concerns to be at the forefront of the issues that are being addressed (Atienza, Seidler, & Renz, 2004, ¶ 15). Most respondents to the 2004 survey were more cautious about the future outlook in the field of international philanthropy. Nearly three-quarters of the respondents stated that the success of the U.S. economy in the 1990s created a large pool of potential philanthropists with a greater global perspective, while at the same time 78% agreed that it is now much more difficult to fund international programs due to the uncertainty of demands and regulations that are being put upon them. Finally, more than two-thirds of these funders believed that the "war on terrorism" has made funding more difficult (2004, ¶ 18).

RESOURCES

This chapter concludes with a description of key resources for the nonprofit sector and those interested in fundraising. We look at the organizations and publications providing support, information, and communications for the profession. The growth of resources over the years provides an indicator of growth in the sector overall and in the fundraising profession more specifically.

Associations and Affiliated Publications

Several organizations are committed to advancing the field of philanthropy, investigating research, and continuing to promote philanthropy as well as fundraising. The Association for Research on Nonprofit Organizations and Voluntary Action (ARNOVA) is the most prominent organization in the nonprofit sector that is committed to research in this field. Created in 1971 at Boston College as the Association for Voluntary Action Scholars, ARNOVA is "a community of people dedicated to fostering through research the creation, application and dissemination of knowledge on voluntary action, nonprofit organizations and philanthropy" (ARNOVA, 2008). ARNOVA's annual conference provides facilitation of the discussion of new principles, advocates new research agendas, and provides access to cutting-edge presentations and publications—all serving the purpose of enhancing the philanthropic field and strengthening the body of participants nationwide. ARNOVA's numerous publications, including *ARNOVA News*, *ARNOVA Abstracts*, *ARNOVA E-News*, and its most famous journal, *Nonprofit and Voluntary Sector Quarterly*, help equip professionals in the philanthropy field as well as build alliances and discover new principles in philanthropy and voluntary action (ARNOVA, n.d.). ARNOVA also provides electronic discussion groups and an employment network.

ARNOVA doesn't operate in isolation, however—it has formed a multitude of partnerships and alliances with other organizations that are committed to similar purposes. The Association of Fundraising Professionals (AFP), for example, is one of ARNOVA's premier partners. "One sign of fund raising's growing power and prominence came in 1960, when the National Society of Fund Raisers, the forerunner of the . . . [Association of Fundraising Professionals], was founded" (Billitteri, 2000, ¶ 32). For more than 40 years, AFP has also facilitated ideas to help advance philanthropy and assist organizations and other entities that are involved in that field. AFP represents nearly 28,000 members in more than 190 chapters throughout the United States, Mexico, Canada, and China. Independent Sector (IS), the Nonprofit Academic Centers Council, and the Urban Institute are some other close partners of ARNOVA.

Independent Sector is a coalition of major nonprofits and foundations interested in strengthening philanthropic activity and cooperation within the independent sector. In 1980 John Gardner "created the I.S. to forge a self-consciousness among grant-making and voluntary organizations—a sense that they occupied a distinct third space between government and market economy" (Friedman, 2003, p. 14). Their goals are to increase research on nonprofit issues, influence public policy, strengthen relationships within the nonprofit sector, grow relationships outside the sector, and increase diversity of its membership (Burlingame, 2004, p. 256).

Independent Sector releases a variety of books, publications, reports, and some quarterlies. Notable publications include a book series on giving and volunteering; *The New Nonprofit Almanac and Desk Reference* (Weitzman, 2002), published in cooperation with the Urban Institute; and the *Nonprofit Sector Yellow Book*, a directory of some 45,000 officers, trustees, department heads, administrators, and personnel of over a thousand major nonprofit organizations. The *Almanac and Desk Reference* blends the research of both IS and the Urban Institute, creating a compact, statistical digest of data derived from IRS Form 990, the National Center for Charitable Statistics, and a variety of other sources.

The Association for Healthcare Philanthropy (AHP) is dedicated to advancing fundraising in the healthcare field and providing research, publications, and education to healthcare fundraisers. Founded in 1967, AHP was created in a time when fundraising numbers in health care were soaring. Over 1,900 healthcare organizations are represented in the membership.

The Council for the Advancement and Support of Education (CASE) was formed in 1974 when two organizations merged to create an organization for professionals in education, fundraising, alumni relations, and communications. Over 55,000 professionals are represented among the CASE member institutions.

Other Non-Affiliated Publications

There are several other publications, not affiliated with specific associations, that cover the topics of philanthropy and fundraising. The *Chronicle of Philanthropy* is an oversized full-color newspaper published by the *Chronicle of Higher Education*. It appears every two weeks (except for the Fourth of July and Christmas holidays), and focuses on news items, employment opportunities, workshop listings, and some investigative reporting on fundraising, gifts and giving, nonprofit management, grants, and technology. It provides data from annual surveys on the following topics:

- Largest gifts for the preceding year, by individuals (January)
- Largest gifts for the preceding year, overall (February)
- Online fundraising (June)
- Charitable giving by big companies (July)
- Highest-paid salaries for chief executive officers (CEOs) of charities and foundations (September)
- "Philanthropy 400": the charities that raise the most money (November)

The leading annual publication on the charitable giving habits of Americans is *Giving USA,* published by the Giving USA Foundation, with research done by the Center on Philanthropy at Indiana University Purdue University at Indianapolis (IUPUI). The Giving USA Foundation is sponsored by about 40 for-profit counselors and fundraising firms that serve as consultants to nonprofit institutions and to philanthropic entities who intend to contribute to such organizations. The annual volumes of *Giving USA* are the most widely quoted and accessible tabulation of donors and nonprofit recipients. Results are divided by source or donor, type of recipient, and location.

There is a wealth of other literature, including academic journals like *Nonprofit Management and Leadership,* and full-color magazines oriented toward development officers who prefer a hands-on approach to writing,

Exhibit 1-1 Web Sites Useful in Philanthropic Research

Association of Fundraising Professionals, http://www.afpnet.org

Changing Our World (New York, NY), http://www.changingourworld.com

Chronicle of Philanthropy (Washington, DC), http://www.philanthropy.com

Foundation Center (New York, NY), http://www.fdncenter.org

Giving Institute (formerly AAFRC)/*Giving USA* (Glenview, IL), http://www.givinginstitute.org

Independent Sector (Washington, DC), http://www.independentsector.org

Internal Revenue Service, Statistics on Income (Kansas City, KS), http://www.irs.gov/taxstats/

The Nonprofit Quarterly (Boston, MA), http://www.nonprofitquarterly.org

Nonprofit Sector Research Fund, the Aspen Institute (Washington, DC), http://www.nonprofitresearch.org

The NonProfit Times (Parsipanny, NJ), http://www.nptimes.com

onPhilanthropy.com, published by Changing Our World (New York, NY), http://www.onphilanthropy.com

Philanthropy News Digest, published by the Foundation Center (Washington, DC), http://www.fdncenter.org/pnd/

Philanthropy News Network Online (Richmond, VA), http://www.pnnonline.org

---

such as *Nonprofit Times, Nonprofit Quarterly*, and *Nonprofit World*. The latter publications are geared more toward practical techniques of management. None of the academic journals or general serials sponsors annually updated, comprehensive reports quantifying donors and recipients in the independent sector on par with *Giving USA*. **Exhibit 1-1** provides a list of useful Web sites to refer to when researching philanthropy.

The federal government releases annually updated data on philanthropy in the *Statistical Abstract of the United States*, published by the U.S. Census Bureau. Especially interesting are the Social Insurance and Human Services tables, which cover charitable contributions, private philanthropy, foundations, grants, and volunteer efforts. The tables used here rely on data provided by the IRS, the U.S. Bureau of Labor Statistics, *Giving USA*, IS, and the Foundation Center in Washington, DC.

CONCLUSION

This chapter has introduced the concept of learning fundraising as a combination of theory and practice. We have looked at fundraising within the model of marketing and provided an overview of giving in the United States. We continue now by considering why donors make gifts to nonprofit organizations in the first place. Chapter 2 presents the latest theory and research in this area. It will help fundraisers to better understand motivations for giving and allow them to be more successful as they put these ideas into practice.

REFERENCES

American Red Cross. (2000). *Turning compassion into action: Donor dollars at work*. Retrieved April 19, 2006, from http://www.redcross.org/news/ds/hurricanes/support05/report.html

American Red Cross. (2005). *International services*. Retrieved April 19, 2006, from http://www.redcross.org/news/ds/profiles/disaster_profilei-sasia.earthquake.htm

ARNOVA. *Association overview*. (n.d.). Retrieved April 18, 2006, from http://www.arnova.org/?section=about&subsection=overview

ARNOVA. *Mission statement*. (2008). Retrieved February 9, 2008, from http://www.arnova.org/?section=about&subsection=mission

Atienza, J., Seidler, H., & Renz, L. (Eds.). (2004). *International grantmaking III: An update on U.S. foundation trends* (3rd ed.). New York: Foundation Center. Retrieved April 19, 2006, from http://www.fdncenter.org/gainknowledge/research/internationaltrends.html

Billitteri, T. J. (2000, January 13). Donors big and small propelled philanthropy in the 20th century. *Chronicle of Philanthropy* [electronic version]. Retrieved September 19, 2006, from http://philanthropy.com/premium/articles/v12/i06/06002901.htm

Burlingame, D. F. (Ed.). (2004). *Philanthropy in America: A comprehensive historical encyclopedia*. Vol. 1 and 2. Santa Barbara, CA: ABC-CLIO.

Council of Economic Advisers, Office of the President. (2000). *Philanthropy in the American economy*. (2000). Retrieved December 9, 2008, from http://clinton4.nara.gov/media/pdf/philanthropy.pdf

Delaware Valley GrantMakers. (n.d.) Retrieved April 18, 2006, from http://www.dvg.org/aboutgp/types_grantmakers.htm

empty tomb, inc. (2007). *Lifestyle spending table*. Retrieved on June 29, 2005, from http://www.emptytomb.org/lifestylestat.html

Friedman, L. J. (2003). Philanthropy in America: Historicism and its discontents. In L. J. Friedman & M. D. McGarvie (Eds.), *Charity, philanthropy, and civility in American history*. New York: Cambridge University Press.

Fuchs, P. (2004, July). Towards a virtuous cycle for sustainable development. Retrieved April 20, 2006, from http://www.avina.com/web/siteavina.nsf/PantallaCompleta/C36DBF87E878CFFC032573B000719C36?opendocument&idioma=eng

Giving USA Foundation. (2004). *Giving USA 2004*. Glenview, IL: AAFRC Trust for Philanthropy.

Giving USA Foundation. (2007). *Giving USA 2007*. Glenview, IL: Giving USA Foundation.

Giving USA Foundation. (2008). *Giving USA 2008*. Glenview, IL: Giving USA Foundation.

The Global Fund. (n.d.). Retrieved April 20, 2006, from http://www.theglobalfund.org/en

Hall, H. (2006, May 4). Americans send $70 billion to poor countries, far more than U.S. government spends. *Chronicle of Philanthropy, 18*(14). Retrieved February 9, 2008, from Academic Search Premier database.

Internal Revenue Service. (2004). Types of tax-exempt organizations by Internal Revenue Code Section. Excel v4.0 spreadsheet, retrieved on June 29, 2004, from http://www.irs.gov/pub/irs-soi/eoappdix.xls

Kelly, K. S. (1998). *Effective fund-raising management.* Mahwah, NJ: Lawrence Erlbaum Associates.

Levy, B. R. (Ed.). (1996–2003). *The AFP fundraising dictionary online.* Retrieved January 4, 2007, from the Association of Fundraising Professionals Web site, www.afpnet.org/content_documents/AFP_Dictionary_A-Z_final_6-9-03.pdf

Lohmann, R. A. (1992). *The commons: New perspectives on nonprofit organizations and voluntary action.* San Francisco, CA: Jossey-Bass.

Minnesota Council on Foundations. (2006). *What is philanthropy?* Retrieved April 11, 2006, from http://www.mcf.org/mcf/whatis/index.html

Open Society Institute and Soros Foundation Network. (n.d.) *About us: Executive bios.* Retrieved April 20, 2006, from http://www.soros.org/about/bios/a_soros

Payton, R. L. (1988). Philanthropy: Voluntary action for the public good. New York: American Council on Education/Macmillan. Retrieved April 18, 2006, from http://www.paytonpapers.org/output/ESS0025_1.shtm and http://www.paytonpapers.org/output/ESS0025_2.shtm

Ronsvalle, J. L., & Ronsvalle, S. (2004). *The state of church giving through 2002.* Champaign, IL: empty tomb.

Simmons, A., & Nielsen, D. (2004, December). Promoting global giving: An overview. *Alliance, 9*(4). Retrieved April 20, 2006, from http://www.allavida.org/alliance/dec04f.html

Simpson, J. A., & Weiner, E. S. C. (Eds.). (2007). *The Oxford English Dictionary.* New York: Oxford University Press.

Tempel, E. R. (2003). Contemporary dynamics of philanthropy. In H. A. Rosso & Associates, *Achieving excellence in fund raising* (pp. 3–13). San Francisco, CA: Jossey-Bass.

U.S. Census Bureau. (2003). *Statistical abstract of the United States: 2003* (123rd ed.). Washington, DC: Government Printing Office.

Weitzman, M. S., et al. (2002). *The new nonprofit almanac and desk reference: The essential facts and figures for managers and volunteers.* San Francisco, CA: Jossey-Bass.

Wilhelm, I. (2006, October 26). International grants rose by 8% last year. *Chronicle of Philanthropy, 19*(10). Retrieved January 6, 2007, from http://philanthropy.com/premium/articles/v19/i02/02004001.htm

chapter two

Individual Donor Motivations

A central question to the study of fundraising is, what motivates an individual donor to make a gift? If you consider a marketing orientation as the most appropriate for fundraising, then understanding donor motivation is simply the application of marketing concepts—of understanding your customer—to the field of fundraising. A wealth of information exists on donor motivation, from Andrew Carnegie's 1889 treatise "The Gospel of Wealth" to the Independent Sector's Web site (http://www.independentsector.org/programs/research/GV01main.html) showing the results of national surveys.

The 2008 television show *Oprah's Big Give* brought the whole discussion of giving and getting to the national consciousness. Contestants on the show traveled to a different city each week and were given some amount of money and an assignment. Sometimes they were asked to help a particular individual organization, while other times they were simply asked to find people in need. What motivated participants to go out and raise dollars after receiving their special instructions for the week? Was it just the good feeling they were getting from helping? Was it their need for publicity? Was it the hope that Oprah would reward them with some big gift at the end? What was the motivation of the donors contributing money to the cause? Did they align with the mission? Did they feel sorry for the sick children or needy people? Or did they just want the publicity of giving to one of Oprah's causes? While this program was an entertaining look at the drama of giving and getting, fundraisers need to have a firm grasp of why people give, how much they might give, and how they decide where to give their money and time.

COMPLEX MOTIVATIONS

Experts in the field notice that determining donor motivation is not always easy. "Motives for giving are much more complex than many observers or students of philanthropy have assumed" (Bremner, 1990, p. xiv). Each year, fundraising students in the School of Business and Nonprofit Management at North Park University have been asked what motivates them to make a gift. The in-class exercise is always a lively exchange as students reveal and debate the relative importance they assign to the reasons why they have made charitable gifts in the past. The list usually consists of the following: to help those less fortunate, religious reasons, involvement with a nonprofit organization, tax deductibility, guilt, peer pressure, because they are asked, because they know the person who is asking, for recognition, for benefits received, because of habit, or because they are expected to give. The conclusion is always drawn that motivations for giving are quite complex and certainly do not revolve around two or three "silver bullets" that fundraisers can use to inspire and cajole their prospects into becoming donors to their charitable organizations.

Joseph Mixer does an excellent job organizing survey data regarding donor motivations, starting with two main categories, internal and external. "Internal motivations arise when something is desired, satisfies a need, relieves tension, or feels good" (Mixer, 1993, p. 13), and "external influences come from persons, events, or conditions in the environment" (p. 13). Both internal and external factors have three subcategories. Internal reasons include "I," "we," and "they" factors. Significantly, both altruism ("we" factor) and self-interest ("I" factor) are included in the internal reasons. The third internal subcategory, "they" factors, includes negative reasons for giving. "'They' cause or may cause difficulties; 'they' are to blame, not the individual, even when the situation is of the individual's own making" (p. 20). Some examples of "they" factors are frustration, unknown situations, and insecurity. External motivations include rewards, stimulations, and situations, such as naming a building, being asked, and personal involvement with a nonprofit organization. **Exhibit 2-1** is a chart of motivations for giving.

Exhibit 2-1 Framework for Determining Why People Give

Internal Motivations	External Influences
Personal or "I" factors	**Rewards**
Acceptance of self or self-esteem	Recognition
Achievement	Personal
Cognitive interest	Social
Growth	
Guilt reduction or avoidance	**Stimulations**
Meaning or purpose of life	Human needs
Personal gain or benefit	Personal request
Spirituality	Vision
Immortality	Private initiative
Survival	Efficiency and effectiveness
	Tax deductions
Social or "we" factors	
Status	**Situations**
Affiliation	Personal involvement
Group endeavor	Planning and decision making
Interdependence	Peer pressure
Altruism	Networks
Family and progeny	Family involvement
Power	Culture
	Tradition
Negative or "they" factors	Role identity
Frustration	Disposable income
Unknown situations	
Insecurity	
Fear and anxiety	
Complexity	

Source: Mixer (1993, p. 14). Reprinted with permission of John Wiley & Sons, Inc.

Mixer also has asked people why they do not give (see **Exhibit 2-2**). This way of looking at motivations appears reversed but actually is helpful in understanding a potential donor more clearly. From this list a fundraiser can identify those negative situations that can be completely or partially compensated for by the organization. For example, problems such as lack of information, ineffective communication, or undesirable manner of asking can be researched and resolved or improved.

Exhibit 2-2 Framework for Determining Why People Do Not Give

*Personal Characteristic and
Situation Problems*

Personal preferences
Higher priorities*
Not concerned
Not interested*
Not involved
Stinginess

Contrary beliefs
Don't agree on policies*
Don't believe in cause*
Don't like programs
Different work ethic

Communication Problems

Lack of information
Mission not known
Organization unknown
Others not supporting
Need not shown*
No record of service
No real case
No results seen*

Ineffective communication
Negative publicity
Publications too slick
Unclear need
Promotion too costly

Reactions to Solicitations

Manner of asking
Asked too often*
Asked wrong way
Manipulation
Too many mailings*

Solicitor
Don't like the asker
No obligation to asker
Used paid solicitors
Wrong person asking*

Finances
Can't afford to give*
Fear of reciprocity
Economic conditions
Tax rates

Situations
Complexity of life
Competition
Changing environment
Outside local area

Relations with prospect
No personal contact
No recognition
Not appreciated
Not asked*
No tradition to give

Timing
Already gave
Asked too late
Wrong time

Organizational Image Problems

**Perceptions of poor
organizational behavior**
Active mistrust
High administrative costs
Agency too rich
Bad experience
Poor reputation
Services cost too much

Organizational Image Problems	**Management**
	Misuse of gifts
Perceptions of poor	Poor policies and rules
organizational behavior	High fundraising costs
Duplication of services	Poor management
Government involvement	
Taxes pay for services	

* Indicates most frequently mentioned.
Source: Mixer (1993, pp. 29–30). Reprinted with permission of John Wiley & Sons, Inc.

Independent Sector (IS) sponsors a telephone survey every few years that includes several questions on donor motivations. When asked why they give to charitable organizations, people typically respond: those with more should help those with less; they gained a feeling of personal satisfaction; religious belief; they want to give back to society or repay; they were asked; they want to continue activities of family; and they want to serve as an example to others, such as board members (Independent Sector, 2001).

ALTRUISTIC GIVING

Whether or not a gift can be given through a purely altruistic motivation has been debated over the years. An altruistic donor, in theory, should not receive anything back from the giving process—not even a good feeling. Is this even possible? Thomas Jeavons has written extensively on this dilemma. He concludes that donors do not give strictly based on either a desire to help or an interest in self-advancement; they give due to mixed motives. "Mixed motives are the rule, not the exception, of our experiences in philanthropy" (Jeavons, 1991, p. 55). This idea portrays donors as complex; they give both because they are interested in helping others *and* in meeting their own personal goals.

Odendahl developed a similar idea to Jeavons's but applied it only to elite donors. In the beginning of her controversial book *Charity Begins at Home,* Odendahl (1990) asserts: "Paradoxically, although people of all classes participate in nonprofit groups, most of these organizations are controlled by a few, and many charities benefit the rich more than they do the poor. The vast majority of nonprofit agencies and programs do not primarily serve the needy. Many elite philanthropists are civic-minded and sincere, but the system they help to maintain may actually reduce the extent to which basic human services are provided on a democratic basis" (p. 3).

Her position explains that donors may have the best intentions when they give, yet they still give out of a desire to receive something in return. Odendahl's position is more aggressive than that of Jeavons. While Jeavons notes that donors have complex intentions in their giving habits, Odendahl suggests that these intentions serve to maintain the position of the elite within American society and to prevent those who are not in the elite group from vertical mobility. "The general tendency of the wealthy to contribute to upper-class-specific programs and institutions aggravates the problems of inequality" (Odendahl, 1990, p. 16). The result is a castelike system where philanthropy does more harm than good for society.

In the twelfth century, the Jewish scholar Maimonides wrote a treatise on giving that provided a "ladder" of giving motivations. As people's giving reflects more and more altruism, they move up the ladder. The highest levels reflect the best reasons for giving (see **Exhibit 2-3**).

Exhibit 2-3 Maimonides' Ladder

A high level, of which none is higher, is where one takes the hand of an Israelite and gives him a gift or loan, or makes a partnership with him or finds him employment, in order to strengthen him until he needs to ask help of no one.

Below this is one who gives *tzedakah* to the poor, not knowing to whom he gives, while the poor person does not know from whom he takes.

Below this, the giver knows to whom he gives, and the poor person does not know from whom he takes.

Below this, the poor person knows from whom he takes, and the giver does not know.

Below this, one puts into another's hand before [the latter] asks.

Below this, one gives [to] another after [the latter] asks.

Below this, one gives another less than is appropriate, in a pleasant manner.

Below this, one gives sorrowfully.

Source: Kass (2002, p. xx). Courtesy of Amy Kass. Translated by Judah Mandelbaum.

Exhibit 2-4 Conceptual Domains

1. *communities of participation* are the networks of formal and informal relationships to which people are associated;
2. *frameworks of consciousness* are the ways of thinking and feeling that are rooted deeply enough in one's awareness to induce a commitment to a cause;
3. *direct requests* made to individuals for contributions of time and money;
4. *models and experiences from one's youth* which animate adult philanthropy;
5. *urgency for and effectiveness* of one's philanthropic involvement;
6. *discretionary resources,* primarily the level [of] one's time and money available after maintaining a comfortable standard of living;
7. *demographic characteristics.*

Source: P. G. Schervish (1997). Reprinted with permission of John Wiley & Sons, Inc.

IDENTIFICATION THEORY

In the 1990s Paul Schervish and John Havens developed the Identification Theory of Care, one of the most well-known theories of giving. Set within the conceptual domains of giving that Schervish found through his research (1997; see **Exhibit 2-4**), the Identification Theory seeks to integrate the complexities of human behavior in explaining where, why, and how much people choose to give. Intuitively, it suggests that individuals are most likely to give to issues with which they identify. The stronger the identification is, the greater the level of care and the greater the level of commitment will be (Schervish & Havens, 2002).

LISTENING TO DONORS

Each individual is unique, and therefore it is important to spend time listening to donors and finding out why they feel motivated to support any social cause. Schervish and Havens describe this complexity when referring to the rationale behind their Identification Theory, saying that their participants "typically could recall a specific moment in time when the identification with another was a life-changing event, motivating a caring response, and leading to a longer term commitment to philanthropy" (Schervish & Havens, 2002, p. 49). Listening to donors while keeping the basic ideas of donor motivation in mind will allow fundraisers to connect personally and professionally with donors and will result in more committed donors and greater success in the overall fundraising process.

Exhibit 2-5 BADS and the Hawthorne Effect

At first glance, the BADS study seems ineffective. After reading about it, you think, "I bet people are reporting to give at much higher levels than they actually do." Your theory has been previously documented; it is called the Hawthorne effect. The Hawthorne effect is defined as "the stimulation to output or accomplishment that results from the mere fact of being under observation" (Merriam-Webster, 2003, s.v. "Hawthorne effect"). It originated from a factory study conducted in 1927 to determine the environmental changes that caused an increase in worker productivity. Researchers determined that the environmental changes had no effect, but the presence of researchers at the Hawthorne plant was the cause of the increase in productivity. When participants know somebody is studying them, they are likely to alter their behavior. Schervish and Havens anticipated this possibility. Because of it, they designed their study to last 13 months. If the giving percentages were significantly larger in January 1996 than they were in January 1995, Schervish and Havens would know that the Hawthorne effect could be the reason. They noticed that the average giving and volunteering levels decreased rather than increased between 1995 and 1996, although the difference is not statistically significant (Schervish & Havens, 2001). They conclude: "When the period over which repeated interviewing takes place is lengthy and when respondents are coached to be accurate, the potential for a Hawthorne effect is dissipated" (Schervish and Havens, 2001, p. 542).

BOSTON AREA DIARY STUDY

Schervish and Havens initiated their work on the Boston Area Diary Study (BADS) to get a more accurate portrayal of the significance of giving in people's lives (see **Exhibit 2-5**). Instead of creating categories for individuals to mark off after handing out a survey or simply doing a standard phone survey, they decided to conduct a yearlong project to discover why individuals give, based on open-ended responses from the donors themselves. Their study went from January 1995 until January 1996 and involved 44 participants from the Boston area. This study came as a natural next step for Schervish, who had published a book the year before this study began in which he conducted open-ended interviews with 130 American millionaires in order to determine their "moral biographies," or the "set of moral obligations to which they respond in charting their daily lives" (Schervish, Coutsoukis, & Lewis, 1994, p. x). In the BADS study, Schervish and Havens elected to include both formal and informal giving and volunteering. They contacted participants on a weekly basis and recorded giving and volunteering patterns from the previous week.

Schervish and Havens found two theories helpful in making sense from data collected in their yearlong study. The first theory is the Identification Theory of Care mentioned above, which rejects the forced choice between "the ethical ideal of pure selflessness and that of pragmatic self-interest" (Schervish & Havens, 2002, p. 49). This theory suggests that "caring behavior is motivated by identification with the needs of others" (2002, p. 49). The second theory is the Moral Citizenship of Care. This theory provides "a theoretical framework for understanding and making broader interpretive sense of the full range of practical social relations of assistance" (2002, p. 65). Just as political and civic citizenship relate to how an individual perceives his or her responsibilities within the political and civic realms of society, moral citizenship relates to how an individual perceives his or her responsibilities within the moral realms of society. This realm is not exclusive to nonprofits; rather, it provides for formal and informal activities of care. Schervish and Havens (2001) assert: "The respondents were more inclined to feel and forge a unified fabric of care. What mattered to their senses and sensibilities was not whether an act was narrowly defined as formal giving and volunteering, nor whether it took place in and around the nonprofit sector; what mattered was whether there was an intentional and voluntary decision to respond to the needs of others as these needs arose in daily life" (p. 535).

ELITE GIVING

What exactly constitutes the elite? According to Merriam-Webster, *elite* means "a group of persons who by virtue of position or education exercise much power or influence" (2003, s.v. "elite"). Elite philanthropists have a history of giving that is perpetuated by their families, and they enjoy recognition associated with their family name. For most, the act of giving is a kind of legacy. The definition of elite giving is one that encompasses a number of subgroups (e.g., social elites, Jewish elite), but most important, two tenets hold true: first, true elite givers are "old money," and second, it is the responsibility of the elite to take care of and give back to the masses. This section seeks to demonstrate how the decisions, desires, motivations, patterns, and satisfaction associated with elite giving are distinct from other types of giving. Some of the studies cited involve very wealthy individuals, rather than just the elite. We assume that the very rich and the elite are highly overlapping populations.

History of Elite Giving

The American tradition of philanthropy as it is known today is just over 150 years old. One of its earliest supporters and notable millionaire, Andrew

Carnegie, was a trailblazer in elite philanthropy. "Although the etymology of 'millionaire' dates back to Disraeli in 1826, the word didn't come into common usage until the end of the 19th century—there simply weren't enough reasons to use the term until moguls like J. P. Morgan and Andrew Carnegie entered the popular consciousness" (Kafka & Pappas, 1999, ¶ 2). Carnegie's early assertions on why the wealthy should give still hold true today and are described below.

Though Andrew Carnegie was born into modest means, his legacy is important because he was among the first prolific philanthropists. It is the way in which he spent his wealth that makes Andrew Carnegie among the first elite givers. Andrew Carnegie has very distinct ideas on how elite givers should dispense their wealth and exactly who should be the beneficiary of their philanthropy. He believed it was the duty of the rich to shape the philanthropic process because the rich were more learned and would best know how to dispense their wealth and for what causes. His preference was that people of means have a hand in administering their contributions because others would most likely be wasteful. He reasoned that while alive, a philanthropist could make the decisions that will best provide for the masses, and that major gifts intended for public betterment serve the community better than small gifts to other ancillary institutions or directly to individuals who are in need. "Even the poorest can be made to see this, and to agree that great sums gathered by some of their fellow-citizens and spent for public purposes, from which the masses reap the principal benefit, are more valuable to them than if scattered among themselves in trifling amounts through the course of many years" (Carnegie, 1889, p. 7).

Where Carnegie differs from his contemporaries and even current elite givers is in the notion of *conspicuous consumption*, a term coined in 1899 by Thorstein Veblen (Kafka & Pappas, 1999, ¶ 5). Carnegie was clear in his beliefs. Living a modest life is the true mark of a wealthy, learned man with class. He would have emphatically disapproved of the extravagant lifestyles synonymous with today's elite class. Carnegie was very particular with regard to what he financed. He gave away almost his entire $350 million fortune to create 2,800 free libraries worldwide, among many other institutions (Chernow, 1998). He placed high importance on giving to institutions that would benefit the masses such as institutions of higher learning and libraries. According to Carnegie (1889): "The best means of benefiting the community is to place within its reach the ladders upon which the aspiring can rise—free libraries, parks, and means of recreation, by which men are helped in body and mind; works of art, certain to give pleasure and improve the public taste;

and public institutions of various kinds, which will improve the general condition of the people" (p. 10). For example, one of the institutions he had built, New York's Carnegie Hall, has stood for over a century as a temple of musical excellence and provides a benefit for the society at large—not for just a few individuals.

A prolific writer and opinionated man, Carnegie also had his own philosophy on the topic of inheritances. Andrew Carnegie's giving stems from the fact that he believed he should share what he had accumulated for the greater good. What makes his giving elite is that he assumed that his wealth was also a sign of intelligence. It was a good indication that he would be best equipped to make philanthropic decisions. How have his nearly 100-year-old ideas of philanthropy held up against the modern-day philanthropist? The next section seeks to compare the two.

The New Elites

In 2004 there were more than five million millionaires and nearly 500 billionaires in the world. Not all of these people are from "old money." A new group of wealthy and therefore influential people is called the "nouveau riche." Without a tradition of giving and a set of norms from which to work, members of this group are without a road map to establish their own set of philanthropic objectives. "The nouveau riche use charities to legitimize their place" (Yu, 1999, p. 45).

The technology boom of the 1990s and the initial public offerings (IPOs) and mergers associated with it made many people millionaires overnight. Silicon Valley, known as the "Land of the Cyberstingy" (Streisand, 2001, p. 40), is the home of many new elites who decided they wanted to use their newfound wealth to make a difference, now. They began giving money to every cause that came their way. In California, newly minted millionaires made gifts related to education at twice the national rate in a desperate bid to be agents for change. New elite givers were sometimes so personally invested that they quit their jobs to oversee their latest project (Streisand, 2001). Though Carnegie and the new elite both agree on being the primary administrators of their wealth disbursement while alive, the practice of hands-on, direct administration is distinctly new elite.

Often steeped in the language of measurable results and accountability that governs the technology sector, new elites were disheartened to find out it is difficult to measure results in the nonprofit sector. Replacing the wisdom of generations of philanthropic activities, the new elites are now seeking the

Exhibit 2-6 Elite Giving Practices

Despite recent dramatic changes in giving practices, the early philanthropists were in many respects very similar to the modern philanthropists in their approach. They gave money, but they also gave their time and expertise to causes they believed in. "Engaged" philanthropy applied as much to railroad baron Leland Stanford as it does today to software billionaire Bill Gates (Wason, 2004, p. 9).

counsel of philanthropic advisers. Large companies such as TimeWarner and Cisco Systems, which created many "dot.com" millionaires, have such professionals on staff. The new elite's lessons for responsible philanthropy were learned the hard way by the sector's star student—Microsoft co-founder Bill Gates (Streisand, 2001).

When Gates began his charitable work about 10 years ago, like most of his technology-minded counterparts, he was determined to make education and technology his areas of interest. However, when it began to dawn on him that children in Africa did not have food or medicine, never mind access to the Internet, his focus and that of the Bill and Melinda Gates Foundation shifted to global health care. Interestingly, Gates is also seeking counsel to guide his giving initiatives, but not in the form of professional advice. "With the help of his father, who is from a generation that had a very different view of its responsibilities, Gates is now coming to a point where he sees that there's more to life than gathering patents and making billions" (Is success a sin? 2001, p. 67).

A perfect example of a modern-day philanthropist who understands the duties and responsibilities that are synonymous with elite giving is David Rockefeller, Sr., the grandson of the great Standard Oil magnate John D. Rockefeller, who was responsible for creating the family fortune. It is from that generation that David Rockefeller (born in 1915) was taught the fundamental principle of noblesse oblige (Lenzer & Ebeling, 2000)—"the obligation of honorable, generous, and responsible behavior associated with high rank or birth" (Merriam-Webster, 2003, s.v. "noblesse oblige").

The new elite are in the process of supplementing the current rules of philanthropic engagement. The thought process is still distinctly elite—that giving is a duty. However, issues of measurable outcomes and watching today's new money turn into old gives way to a new generation of elite. Are the new elite truly elite? (See **Exhibit 2-6**.) Perhaps not, but as they continue to engage in thoughtful philanthropy, become catalysts for change that have positive repercussions for the masses, continue to grow their fortunes, develop their own set of guidelines for philanthropy, and teach them to the next generation, they are well on their way.

Motivations for Elite Giving

It is often said that fundraising is both an art and a science. The motivations for elite giving are exactly that, art and science. The science portion is that there are identified reasons behind the way elite givers tend to give and why. The art portion is that more often than not, elite donors are motivated by a variety of reasons, at the same time and to varying degrees. Together, the motivations and reasons behind them paint a donor's giving portrait. Because so much is dependent on an individual's beliefs and experiences, the combinations of motivations are as varied as the individuals. That said, several motivations can be used to frame the questions of what motivates elite giving.

The Seven Faces of Philanthropy

Several researchers have developed frameworks for better understanding why wealthy individuals give gifts. Russ Alan Prince and Karen Maru File used research among the wealthy to develop the "Seven Faces of Philanthropy" framework. The perspective of this research is that wealthy donors fall into one of seven basic motivational categories in their philanthropic efforts. These categories are *Communitarian, Devout, Investor, Socialite, Altruist, Repayer,* and *Dynast* (Prince & File, 1994). In addition to explaining the seven types of donors, Prince and File provide information in their book *The Seven Faces of Philanthropy* that helps fundraisers determine how to appeal to each type of donor. **Exhibit 2-7** illustrates all seven prototypes.

Prince and File anticipate objections to their theory in the beginning of their book and defend against accusations that their theory is overly simplistic by saying: "The Seven Faces form of segmentation is revealing because one set of motivations tends to dominate people's decisions, even though close questioning will reveal that any individual donor will also feel additional motivations. Experienced fundraisers will recognize that the Seven Faces approach has limits and constraints. Motivational segmentation methodologies such as these simplify human motivations to some degree in order to provide a useful and easily applied framework" (1994, p. 13). Essentially, they want readers to know that the information contained in their text is helpful for professional fundraisers but should be used in conjunction

Exhibit 2-7 Prince and File's (1994) Seven Donor Types

Type: **Communitarian**

Definition: "Believe their fortune is intertwined with that of their community" (pp. 17–18)

Description: Tied to the community, have strong inclination to give, desire to be involved on a greater level than just giving

Type: **Devout**

Definition: "Believe that it is God's will for them to help others" (p. 31)

Description: Regular church attendees, frequently mention God's blessings in their lives

Type: **Investor**

Definition: "Giving is something personally rewarding that is sanctioned by the IRS" (p. 47)

Description: Give based on financial ability, take tax exemptions on their donations

Type: **Socialite**

Definition: "Socialites desire to help through being active in charity work, and they rely on their close friends and family to assist them" (p. 56)

Description: Serve on many boards, attend countless benefit galas

Type: **Repayer**

Definition: "Acutely aware of how others have helped them and feel a specific and particular obligation to repay" (p. 82)

Description: Personal affiliation with organization prior to donating, gracious givers

Type: **Dynast**

Definition: "Socialized into the world of philanthropy" (p. 95)

Description: Wealthy and/or generous parents, overseers of family trusts

Type: **Altruist**

Definition: "Donor who gives out of generosity and empathy to urgent causes and who modestly 'wishes to remain anonymous'" (p. 16)

Description: Often give selflessly to social or other worthwhile causes in order to grow spiritually or because it is a moral imperative

---

with other fundraising methods. They state, "Fund raisers have found the framework a useful heuristic to supplement their experience" (Prince & File, 1994, p. 14). When used to determine general categories into which donors should be placed for purposes of fundraising appeals, this framework is useful. As Prince and File note, it does not provide a comprehensive picture of why an individual chooses to give.

We start a discussion of the concepts behind Prince and File's categories by looking at the *Devout.* This concept is fairly clear. Donors are motivated by a devotion to God. Giving can be to either religious or nonreligious causes, but motivated by faith. Altruism, the basic motivation of those in the category *Altruist*, was discussed earlier in this chapter.

A third reason that the wealthy give is the desire to give back. Prince and File (1994) describe these givers as *Repayers.* Many give back to schools that they have attended, attributing their success in part to the result of a solid education. Some give back to the neighborhood where they grew up, stating the importance of remembering where they have come from. Some give back to hospitals after benefiting from their services.

The notion of giving back also lends itself to a feeling of duty. That is, as an elite member of society, you must give back; it is your duty to do so. Many elite feel that they have a responsibility to provide for others. It was and still is an expectation. Hasbro chairman Alan Hassenfeld discusses this feeling of duty. He "inherited the rich family philanthropic tradition that made his company a model for corporate social responsibility" (The new face of philanthropy, 2004, ¶ 1). As a third-generation elite raised in a luxurious lifestyle, when asked what motivates him to give, he said, "I'm a have [as opposed to have-not]. I've lived in a certain way, but I've also been to visit refugee camps. When you look in the face of poverty, it's impossible to turn away" (¶ 6). So serious and personal is this motivation, elite givers have said, "if not us then who?" Certainly Andrew Carnegie agreed: "To consider all surplus revenues which come to him simply as trust funds, which he is called upon to administer, and strictly bound as a matter of duty to administer in the manner which, in his judgment, is best calculated to produce the most beneficial results for the community" (Carnegie, 1889, p. 8). The elite take very seriously the responsibility that their wealth has provided them with a means to help others, and so to be worthy of their wealth, they adopt their duty to give back.

When the public thinks of traditional elite giving, they are most likely thinking about the people Prince and File (1994) call *Dynasts.* They are from moneyed families, philanthropy is a tradition, and giving is expected.

Carnegie and other elites acknowledge their role in this tradition and seek to carry forth the family legacy while being able to help make positive change.

Prince and File (1994) define *Communitarians* as people who give to reinforce their business ties. However, most wealthy givers believe that positive change is best made in the form of gifts to institutions that provide the most benefit for the largest number of people. In this way, the donors want the entire community to benefit. Donors in this category consider helping the community a part of good business. A healthy community will consist of people able to purchase products and work in the factories that produce the products.

Prince and File (1994) identify *Investors* as giving based on financial reasons, but the applications are more broadly based. Investors "are the segment most likely to support umbrella nonprofits such as community foundations" (p. 15). People in this category will also have more interest in charitable trusts and other giving arrangements that combine the gift with an investment component.

Another type of philanthropist associated with the traditional elite giver is that of the *Socialite,* who gives to attend social events "to help make a better world and have a good time doing it" (Prince & File, 1994, p. 15). This category is truly directed to those in the social elite. These events are the norm to members of the elite. That one receives pleasure from attending them is a true benefit rather than a pleasant coincidence. Among the elite, Socialites are most often women who attend the various special events (Kelly, 1998). Events are notoriously time consuming and usually costly for the organization. They are also a way for new elite to "break into" the exclusive circles. Many see events as networking opportunities in addition to a method of testing whether they "fit in" or not.

Megagifts: Who Gives Them, Who Gets Them

Panas's 1984 book *Megagifts: Who Gives Them, Who Gets Them* is a "treatise on motivation" (p. 207). He wanted to capture the heart of the motivations of large donors. To do this, he compiled a list of 22 motivational giving factors and sent it out to over 1,000 fundraising professionals. He asked these professionals to rank the factors in order of importance. He also sent this list of factors to the 30 major givers in his study and asked them to rank the factors by importance. The divergence in answers between the two groups was fascinating. Both groups identified the most important factor as "belief in the mission of the institution" (p. 231). However, fundraisers thought "interest in the program" to which they are donating was the second most important factor, while donors placed "financial stability" and "regard for leadership" in a tie at the second-place position. Even where fundraisers and donors agreed, fundraisers still underestimated the value. On a scale of one to ten, the average score that "belief in the mission" received from fundraisers was 7.9, whereas the average score it received from donors was 9.6.

These findings suggest that fundraisers need to stop assuming that they know the wants and needs of donors when they approach them for gifts. Many fundraisers will be tempted to simply use the average donor responses found in the Panas's study and adjust their fundraising appeals accordingly. While this is helpful in understanding motivations on a general basis, fundraisers should not assume that this list of averages is accurate for every major donor. The list of 22 motivational factors in Panas's survey illustrates that individuals have many different reasons for choosing to give.

Why the Wealthy Give

In 1995 Francie Ostrower published *Why the Wealthy Give*. This book contains the results of 99 interviews Ostrower conducted with wealthy donors in the New York City metropolitan area. Ostrower was interested in exploring the constantly changing dynamics between nonprofits and the elite in New York. She says, "I argue that in the face of considerable change within nonprofit organizations, the elite, and the urban environment, elite philanthropy in New York City has survived by adapting and rejuvenating itself through the assimilation of new people" (p. 26). Ostrower found that the elite feel no responsibility to give in places where the government is failing. Elite donors give to causes with which they feel a connection. Many donors distinguished charity from philanthropy. These donors believe that "certain large-scale problems must be attended to by the government" (p. 120). This perspective allows wealthy donors to contribute to civic improvements such as museums and libraries, while placing the responsibility for social issues such as homelessness and disease on governmental programs. Ostrower was not trying to come up with a single common reason why wealthy people donated time and money. Instead, she listened to the elite talk about philanthropy and found that certain demographic characteristics affected the amounts and locations of their gifts.

Three key demographic determinates that she found to significantly influence gift choices were religion, gender, and education. Ostrower's study

(1995) included a disproportionately high number of Jewish participants: 59.1%. Although this number is too high to be representative of the rest of the United States, Ostrower's findings regarding the difference in giving habits among Jewish, Protestant, and Catholic participants are significant. Ostrower (1995) highlights three facts:

- Catholics gave the greatest percentage to schools at the pre-college level. This was due to their commitment to support Catholic primary and secondary schools, where they often sent their children to school.
- Protestants gave the greatest percentage to the church they attended, compared with the other two religions. In spite of this, Protestants were the least likely group to feel that their religious beliefs influenced their philanthropic efforts.
- Jewish donors gave the greatest percentage to social service agencies, although a majority of this amount can be attributed to donations to a well-known Jewish-affiliated fund that acts as a blanket organization to distribute funds to other nonprofits, much in the same way United Way does.

Gender affected the types of organizations to which elite donors contributed. In Ostrower's sample, female participants were more than twice as likely to contribute to social service organizations as male participants were (1995, p. 72). Instead of focusing on the social status of their donations, women in her study gave to causes "that are related to the life, concerns, and priorities of these women as women" (pp. 72–73).

Finally, donors directed money toward their alma maters. "Virtually everyone had contributed some money to an educational cause, with 92 percent having donated to universities or colleges alone" (Ostrower, 1995, p. 87). Such high levels of donations can be attributed to donors' thankfulness for their educational experience and in recognizing that school significantly shaped them as individuals (Ostrower, 1995).

Donors certainly develop close ties to specific cultural institutions as well, but they placed these within the context of a larger desire to be associated with the cultural field (or a subfield, such as music). Their comments imply that had they not formed a relationship with the particular cultural institutions that they did, they would have formed one with other cultural institutions (Ostrower, 1995, p. 93).

Schervish and Havens's Identification Theory states that individuals give to causes with which they strongly identify. Based on this, it is reasonable to conclude that social causes such as homelessness or inner-city after-school programs are the least likely causes to receive contributions from elite donors. "In reality, relatively few of all the donations made in the United States go to poor recipients" (Ostrower, 1995, p. 5).

Ostrower describes a subgroup of elite givers as the "social elite": "The social elite is an elite of status. It is characterized by solidarity within the group, social exclusivity, and a distinctive cultural identity. . . . In the United States, the social elite has consisted primarily of white Anglo-Saxon Protestants. Accordingly, it is the group sometimes called the 'Protestant Establishment.' . . . We can thus see how people can be wealthy or members of the elite, without necessarily being members of this particular group within the elite" (1995, p. 12). It is true that the "social elite" as described have greatly influenced the practices of giving; however, the larger elite membership is responsible for perpetuating the practices.

Other Motivations

Elites also give because an organization's mission matches values that they already share. Elites contribute to organizations in order to carry out missions and programs that have an established importance to them. Most elites want recognition and the exclusivity that expensive events allow them and others who are like them to attend. Those more established in their "social station" are more interested in the difference that their contributions can make.

Now that donors are giving, what are they giving to? As mentioned before, Carnegie had distinct ideas of what organizations elites should contribute to. With the increasing globalization of the world and new elites' preferences for measurable results, trends toward providing benefits to individuals directly (college scholarships versus building libraries) will continue to add to and augment the giving preferences of the elite.

But there are other reasons why individuals give away assets, according to Elly Bohme, director of Search & Prosper, a Cambridge, U.K.-based search consultancy. "'Altruism can be a factor,' Bohme says, 'but more important is peer pressure, or a strong belief in an issue, or fear of a particular illness or phenomenon.' Cultural background, religion and upbringing will also affect a person's decision to give and which charity to give to" (Davis, 2003, p. 7).

Motivations will vary for each elite giver, especially with the influx of new elite givers and how they are motivated. Honing in on the particular motivators of elite givers will help fundraisers better understand how to motivate them for further giving and what the necessary tools are for stewardship.

Philanthropy and the Next Generation

According to Carol Nowka, "77 percent of those who inherit money lose it within three years. This suggests that whatever is passed on from this generation to the next might be wasted" (cited in Opiela, 2000, p. 75). Preparing for the transfer of wealth is not only financial, but mental and emotional as well. Elites are planning now what their strategies are for when they pass their fortune, whether it is old money or new money, to the next generation. In many cases, the prospect of inheritances that spoil children (or worse) is a risk that wealthy parents are unwilling to take. "Why should men leave great fortunes to their children? . . . Observation teaches that, generally speaking, it is not well for the children that they should be so burdened. . . . There are instances of millionaires' sons unspoiled by wealth, who, being rich still perform great services to the community. Such are the very salt of the earth, as valuable as, unfortunately they are rare" (Carnegie, 1889, p. 5).

Some believe the easy way out is to give it all away. Others believe in leaving inheritances to children with restrictions so they can control their disbursement beyond the grave. However, most parents feel some obligation to ensure the safety of their child if they can in their absence. According to Warren Buffet, the key is to find a balance between giving heirs "enough that they can do everything and not so much that they can do nothing" (cited in Opiela, 2000, p. 78). Therefore, the great majority of elites will leave their estate or at least some portion of it to their heirs. "Mr. Schervish and Mr. Havens put the size of the transfer [of wealth] likely to occur in the United States between 1998 and 2052 as somewhere between $41 trillion and $136 trillion" (Doing well and doing good, 2004, ¶ 35) "with perhaps $6 trillion to $25 trillion winding up in charity coffers" (Roha, 2000, p. 121). There remains an ongoing debate whether or not this transfer will occur at these extraordinarily high projected levels, yet it is clear that elite bequests will always be a part of the philanthropic landscape and will represent large amounts of money to charitable causes.

In addition to having frank discussions and instilling values, savvy elite givers are using new ways to manage their wealth and teach their children the responsibility of having money. One way to ensure that values are part of the financial education that heirs receive is to establish a family foundation and encourage heirs to have a hand in the giving priorities and disbursements of foundation grants (Roha, 2000). New elites might have the most difficulty in passing on wealth to heirs. The problem is in understanding how to treat wealth and what role philanthropy plays in a next-generation elite's life.

How Elite Donors Differ from Regular Donors

Wealthy donors are a significant donor base in nonprofit organizations. Let us clarify what makes the super rich different from other individual donors.

- *Where the Money Goes.* Elite donors are most likely to give to cultural and educational institutions. A position on the board of directors at a cultural institution often translates into invitations to the best parties in town and associations with key players in the business world. Wealthy donors increase their chances of serving on these elite boards by donating large amounts of money to the organization's cause. The super rich generally feel indebted to the university they attended. This gratitude for helping them get "where they are today" generally translates into hefty donations to one's alma mater.
- *How They View Their Wealth.* In his book *Gospels of Wealth*, Schervish discovers that all 130 of his rich interviewees exhibit an attitude of "power and responsibility" toward their wealth (Schervish, 1994, p. 267). He uses the term *hyperagency* to describe the attitudes he witnessed: "Hyperagency means being able to construct a self and a world that transcend the established institutional limits and, in fact, create the limits for others" (Schervish, 1994, p. 8). The wealthy know that they have power in almost every daily interaction: as bosses, as consumers, as customers, and as donors. The knowledge of this power allows them to act freely in accordance with what they feel to be right.
- *How They View Philanthropy.* Schervish's statements sound remarkably similar to a century-old perspective on wealth. Even today, Andrew Carnegie's "The Gospel of Wealth" reflects the feelings of the rich toward philanthropy. Carnegie is a supporter of philanthropy and feels strongly that the rich should give away the majority of their fortunes. He has a very clear idea of what type of organization will benefit the masses: "The best means of benefiting the community is to place within its reach the ladders upon which the aspiring can rise" (Carnegie, 1889, p. 10). This statement

agrees with Ostrower's findings that the rich feel that it is their responsibility not to provide necessities such as food and clothing to the poor but instead to invest in the community as a whole through civic organizations (Ostrower, 1995).

The Importance of Elite Giving

80/20 Rule

✳ It is true that most people are philanthropic. However, the fact is that most of the money that fuels the philanthropy engine comes from the very wealthy. Understanding the motivations of elite giving helps nonprofits tailor-fit stewardship and cultivation events in addition to developing target messages that will resonate with this level of philanthropist. History indicates that even though the ways this sector of donor perpetuates itself may change, whether it is inheritances or "new wealth," there are fundamental principles that still hold. The elite give because it is their tradition and their responsibility to do so, especially in repayment for the luxurious life they lead. However, research has shown that the new elite, even those from old moneyed families, are taking an avid interest in determining which nonprofits to support, at what levels, and how to establish the criteria for measuring successes and failures.

In some ways, the nonprofit sector helps perpetuate elite giving because of its dependence on elite generosity to achieve its missions. However, without the sector there would be no organized forum for elite givers to flex their philanthropic muscles free of overt references to their own vanities. Though some argue there is great egoism in the way elites choose to contribute and the recognition they receive, the fact that people are being helped and issues are being brought into the national and international spotlight are perhaps the greatest benefits of elite giving.

REFERENCES

Bremner, R. H. (1990). Foreword. In J. Van Til (Ed.), *Critical issues in American philanthropy: Strengthening theory and practice* (pp. xiii–xiv). San Francisco, CA: Jossey-Bass.

Carnegie, A. (1889). The gospel of wealth. *North American Review, 148*, 653–664.

Chernow, R. (1998). Blessed barons. *Time, 152*(23), 74–75.

Davis, P. (2003). The golden science of philanthropy. *Financial Times (London), 1* [FT Money—Personal Finance], p. 7.

Doing well and doing good. (2004, July 31). *The Economist, 372*(8386), 57–59.

Independent Sector. (2001, November). *Giving and volunteering in the United States: Key findings 2001.* Retrieved June 21, 2005, from http://www.independentsector.org/programs/research/gv01main.html

Is success a sin? (2001, September). *Harvard Business Review, 7*(8), 63–69.

Jeavons, T. H. (1991). A historical and moral analysis of religious fund raising. In D. F. Burlingame & L. J. Hulse (Eds.), *Taking fundraising seriously: Advancing the profession and practice of raising money* (pp. 53–72). San Francisco, CA: Jossey-Bass.

Kafka, P., & Pappas, B. (1999). A century of wealth. *Forbes, 164*(9), 112–116.

Kass, A. A. (Ed.). (2002). *The perfect gift: The philanthropic imagination in poetry and prose.* Bloomington: Indiana University Press.

Kelly, K. S. (1998). *Effective fund-raising management.* Mahwah, NJ: Lawrence Erlbaum Associates.

Lenzer, R. A., & Ebeling A. (2000). A wealth of names. *Forbes, 165*(1), 70–71.

Merriam-Webster. (2003). *Merriam-Webster's Collegiate Dictionary* (11th ed.). Springfield, MA: Merriam-Webster. Available at http://www.m-w.com/

Mixer, J. R. (1993). *Principles of professional fundraising: Useful foundations for successful practice.* San Francisco, CA: Jossey-Bass.

The new face of philanthropy. (2004, August 3). *Business Week Online.* Retrieved March 5, 2008, from http://www.businessweek.com/bwdaily/dnflash/aug2004/nf2004084_0667_db008.htm?chan=search

Odendahl, T. J. (1990). *Charity begins at home: Generosity and self-interest among the philanthropic elite.* New York: Basic Books.

Opiela, N. (2000, August). Passing it on: Will older Americans show their children the money? *Journal of Financial Planning, 13*(8), 74–82.

Ostrower, F. (1995). *Why the wealthy give: The culture of elite philanthropy.* Princeton, NJ: Princeton University Press.

Panas, J. (1984). *Megagifts: Who gives them, who gets them.* Chicago: Pluribus Press.

Prince, R. A., & File, K. M. (1994). *The seven faces of philanthropy.* San Francisco, CA: Jossey-Bass.

Roha, R. (2000). Charity gets personal. *Kiplinger's Personal Finance, 54*(9), 116–121.

Schervish, P. G. (1997). Inclination, obligation, and association: What we know and what we need to learn about donor motivation. In D. F. Burlingame (Ed.), *Critical issues in fundraising.* New York: John Wiley & Sons.

Schervish, P. G., Coutsoukis, P. E., & Lewis, E. (1994). *Gospels of wealth: How the rich portray their lives.* Westport, CT: Praeger.

Schervish, P. G., & Havens, J. J. (2001). The methods and metrics of the Boston area diary study. *Nonprofit and Voluntary Sector Quarterly, 30*(3), 527–551.

Schervish, P. G., & Havens, J. J. (2002). The Boston Area Diary Study and the moral citizenship of care. *Voluntas, 13*(1), 47–72.

Streisand, B. (2001). The new philanthropy. *U.S. News & World Report, 130*(23), 40–42.

Wason, S. D. (2004). *Webster's new world grant writing handbook.* Hoboken, NJ: Wiley.

Yu, C. (1999). The new philanthropists. *Alberta Report/Newsmagazine, 26*(5), 45.

chapter three

Corporate and Foundation Fundraising

We move from a discussion of individual motivations for giving to the area of non-individual giving and fundraising—through corporations and foundations. Giving by organizations can at the same time be both more and less complicated than individual giving. An organization consists of multiple people, each bringing a unique mindset into the giving mix. Understanding one person doesn't mean you understand all people in the organization. There may be various pockets of giving within the organization. An organization may change its focus over time with new leaders setting direction. Organizations tend to give to new projects that require tracking and stewardship by the nonprofit at a level well beyond a simple listing in the annual report and sending a timely thank-you letter. Corporate and foundation fundraising can be a challenge.

In contrast, non-individual giving and associated fundraising can be simple in many ways. Organizations publish guidelines (which are mostly followed by the grant-making organizations) to assist the fundraiser in the process of grant seeking. Organizations' staffs are available to answer phone calls and e-mails as a part of their professional tasks. They may not agree to fund a nonprofit's project, but they will usually communicate in a professional way. Fundraisers can be more blunt about the grants requested, since the entire purpose of the giving department within an organization is to invest resources in the non-profit sector. There should be little "beating around the bush" when it comes to discussing grant amount and purpose. Therefore, seeking grants from foundations and corporations can be both simple and complex. Welcome to the paradoxical world of non-individual giving.

HISTORICAL REVIEW

At the turn of the nineteenth century, corporate and independent foundation philanthropy was tied to the personal works and policies of great industrialists through their corporate institutions and private foundations. Those who owned the companies had accumulated wealth that also established independent or private foundations. As benefactors, they determined their philanthropic attention that was characteristically focused on the social and moral condition of employees whose lives were intertwined with the commercial success of the company.

Over the past century, companies grew larger and more complex and included different structures, ownerships (private, public, multinational, etc.), and cultures. Competition, government regulations, technology, societal factors, the rise of marketing, and a global economy have compounded the complexity of doing business, as well as the complexity of corporate and foundation giving. There is no longer a simple relationship or exchange among a single corporate owner, its employees, and the local community. Rather, a multitude of factors influence corporate and foundation philanthropy in the twenty-first century, giving rise to a modern concept of philanthropy. Modern corporate and foundation philanthropy requires processes between the involved parties to be more strategic and collaborative, and the relationships more reciprocal.

CORPORATE PHILANTHROPY

Ciconte and Jacob (2005) define *corporate philanthropy* as "support from corporations and corporate foundations through gifts of cash, equipment, supplies, and other contributions" (p. 410). But this tells only part of the story. Underlying the reason that corporations provide this support is the traditionally held belief that a healthy society will translate into a healthy corporate environment. Dwight Burlingame (2003) expresses this well: "Business support of private action for the public good has been for a long time an integral part of the philosophical reason for why corporations have supported nonprofit organizations as a way to increase the quality of the environment for business. The rationale of 'the healthier the community, the more business one will be able to conduct' is often cited as a reason for corporate giving" (p. 177). Given a strong community, employees will be more content with life, will have better overall physical and mental health, and will be more prepared and better educated. Customers will be attracted to communities that are rich in services provided by nonprofits—such as museums, symphony orchestras, hospitals, universities, and churches. The company doing business in this nonprofit-rich environment will potentially benefit in many ways. There can be a self-serving element to corporate philanthropy that combines with an other-serving element when supporting the community.

Gifts from corporations and corporate foundations provide substantial support to almost every subsector within the nonprofit sector, except for religion. Education receives the most support. In 2007 some of the largest gifts were made to support school children impacted by the hurricanes Katrina and Rita, students participating in a robotics competition, college students using new buildings, teachers trained for special programs, attendees at a new museum expansion, people trying to quit smoking, and cancer patients (Giving USA Foundation, 2008, pp. 78–79).

EVOLUTION OF CORPORATE PHILANTHROPY

The origins and evolution of corporate giving provide insights that help us understand these entities. The early 1900s are considered the starting point when the modern corporation began to take form. Until this time it was accepted for the affluent to use their wealth for philanthropy, while most people felt corporations had an obligation to maximize profits for shareholders. For example, railroads supported the YMCA in their efforts to provide safe housing for railroad workers but stopped short of doing more in the communities (Wason, 2004, p. 7). Although a nonprofit provided the service, the corporation's motivation was of enlightened self-interest and protecting the shareholders' interests.

Two significant events advanced corporate philanthropy at this time. With the passage of the 1935 Revenue Act, corporate giving was first included on federal corporate income tax forms and provided incentive for regular corporate giving programs. The IRS encouraged businesses to donate to charitable, medical, and educational institutions that served the needs of their employees, known as "direct benefit" giving (Ciconte & Jacob, 2005,

p. 157). At the time corporate giving was recorded at about $30 million, which has since increased to nearly $10 billion at the beginning of the twenty-first century (Burlingame, 2003, p. 178). The second event occurred when the United States entered World War I and corporations were asked to fund the relief efforts of the Red Cross (Ciconte & Jacob, 2005, p. 157).

World War II brought a dramatic rise in philanthropy due to high income and high taxes coupled with an increasing need for support for social welfare causes in the United States and abroad. During this period, business began to be a powerful force in American philanthropy. Corporations realized that investments in human capital not only helped individuals in the community but ultimately benefited businesses. In 1953 the Supreme Court of New Jersey reinforced this direction by ruling that corporations had a larger social responsibility than that of just supporting programs that directly benefited themselves. This marked the creation of separate corporate foundations established for giving purposes (Ciconte & Jacob, 2005, p. 158).

Through the 1950s and 1960s, state and federal governments took a more active role in regulating corporate philanthropy by legally authorizing it and encouraging corporate gifts through deduction provisions in the tax laws. In the 1980s the Reagan administration encouraged greater corporate social responsibility by allowing deductions of up to 10% of their taxable income for charity (Wason, 2004, p. 8). "Cause-related marketing" made a successful debut when the American Express Company aligned itself with a charitable cause, the renovation of the Statue of Liberty (Ciconte & Jacob, 2005, p. 158).

Finally, the 1990s brought an economic boom tied into the high-tech industry, which created new wealth and produced a new breed of donor. The twenty-first century also brought new corporate donors, especially those in technology. Technology brought more than philanthropic dollars; it also began to play a fundraising role in the late 1990s by giving both corporate givers and nonprofit organizations the ability to do research online to obtain information about each other (Ciconte & Jacob, 2005, p. 161).

FOUNDATION PHILANTHROPY

The Association for Fundraising Professionals defines *foundation* as "an organization created from designated funds from which the income is distributed as grants to not-for-profit organizations or, in some cases, to people" (Levy, 1996–2003, p. 53). A foundation is an entity that is established as a nonprofit corporation or a charitable trust, with a principal purpose of making grants to unrelated organizations, institutions, or individuals for scientific, educational, cultural, religious, or other charitable purposes. This broad definition encompasses different foundation types that reflect the funders' philanthropic interests. Foundation philanthropy is usually made possible through the assets acquired and accumulated through business.

Foundation Giving Structures

The IRS defines four basic types of foundations: independent, corporate, community, and operating. *Independent foundations* are private and are created with gifts from individuals or families. They are established to contribute funds to charitable organizations and usually include the name of the founder or family within the foundation name. The broad spectrum of independent foundations varies in terms of size and administration, focus of funding, and amounts distributed. This type of foundation has experienced expansion in numbers and compounded asset growth in past years fueled by gains in the stock market, increased gifts to all foundation types, and legislated taxes (such as inheritance taxes).

Another type of private foundation is the *corporate foundation*. Instead of receiving assets from private individuals or families, corporate foundations generally receive their assets from association with a for-profit company. A corporate foundation will usually mirror the business and social interests of the funding corporation, including interests of its consumers and employees (Perry, 2003, p. 190).

Community foundations are a relatively new and rapidly growing segment of the foundation world. These are public charities with a large public donor base, which enables them to address a broad spectrum of community needs applied to a specific geographic area. Another unique feature of community foundations is that they generally receive gifts and make grants through special IRS provisions (Perry, 2003, p. 190).

Operating foundations research and promote their own programs. "The IRS mandates that they spend at least 85 percent of their income in support of their own programs" (Perry, 2003, p. 191). Unless a nonprofit is somehow directly related to the foundation, this type of foundation is usually not considered a source of general cash grants. However, in addition to their research and program influence, they have considerable impact through publications, research, and their body of knowledge made available to other nonprofits (p. 191).

Nonprofits can benefit from the four types of foundations through five common types of support: operational or unrestricted, program, capital, pilot, and challenge or matching. Since the IRS requires an annual percentage distribution amount through grants to qualified 501(c)(3) charitable organizations, it behooves a nonprofit to research and match its needs with the type and specific requirements of a foundation (Perry, 2003, pp. 191–192).

EVOLUTION OF FOUNDATIONS

As government, economic, and societal changes have influenced the behavior and evolution of corporate giving, so have they influenced the brief history of foundations. The great industrialists and philanthropists Andrew Carnegie and John D. Rockefeller sought ways to systemize their charitable giving through the structure of foundations. Understanding the stewardship responsibility that comes with wealth, they genuinely desired to address the ills of society (Wason, 2004, p. 8). Those foundations dominated the foundation arena until the 1940s when economic prosperity encouraged giving, and foundations provided tax incentives to give. These reasons, coupled with the international perspective Americans developed as a result of World War II, fueled the development of private foundations. The expansion continued until the Tax Reform Act of 1969, which established excise taxes, regulations, and standards on income earned by private foundation investments that effectively slowed the expansion of foundations. The government regulations and standards of philanthropic practice are efforts to legitimize its reason to exist. As Greenfield (2002) shares:

> Government also advocates that its citizens engage in charitable acts because these acts improve the common good. In most nations, government is responsible for a wide spectrum of public services. By contrast, whole areas of American enterprise, from the arts to education, from social welfare to health care, from religion to civic causes, are often carried out by citizens, acting alone or together. The consensus in America is that government cannot and should not be involved in many of these areas. (p. 3)

Since the mid-1980s, the number of private foundations has doubled. Unfathomable and catastrophic events such as the terrorist attacks on the United States on September 11, 2001, global epidemics, war, and tsunamis have catapulted the corporate, individual, and foundation intellect and soul into a new stratosphere of awareness and concern for others. Philanthropy has changed rapidly during this time, causing foundations and corporations to assess their giving structures, ideas of corporate social responsibility, and relationships. As they do this they also require more interaction with those they support. Accountability is now a major consideration in the development and sustaining of relationships. As our world has "shrunk" and we have become more global in our perspective, so has philanthropy. There is the desire to impact both locally and globally. An example of global philanthropy is the Bill and Melinda Gates Foundation. "We're supporting efforts to protect children and help raise global immunization rates to 90%, lower deaths from measles by 90%, and make polio the second vaccine-preventable disease the world has eradicated. We're also helping countries quickly adopt and introduce new vaccines" (Bill and Melinda Gates Foundation, 2008).

CORPORATE AND FOUNDATION GIVING: PIECES OF THE PIE

Historically, 90% of giving has come from individuals (through direct giving and bequests) and about 10% from institutions such as corporations and foundations (about 5% from each). According to the 2008 *Giving USA* report, total charitable giving reached an estimated $306.4 billion in 2007. This report showed that corporate and foundation institutions have expanded their influence in philanthropic giving. In Chapter 1, Figure 1-1 depicts 2007 contributions by source. Note that corporate contributions totaled 5.1% and foundations totaled 12.6% of $306.4 billion total contributions (Giving USA Foundation, 2008, p. 10). **Tables 3-1** and **3-2** provide Foundation Center statistics of top U.S. corporate foundation contributors in terms of total assets

Table 3-1 Ten Largest Corporate Foundations by Asset Size

Rank	Name/(State)	Assets	As of Fiscal Year End Date
1.	Alcoa Foundation (PA)	$593,947,740	12/31/06
2.	The Wells Fargo Foundation (CA)	551,651,158	12/31/06
3.	Fidelity Foundation (MA)	381,506,664	12/31/06
4.	The Pfizer Foundation, Inc. (NY)	378,554,886	12/31/06
5.	The Wachovia Foundation (NC)	377,239,704	12/31/06
6.	Verizon Foundation (NJ)	343,008,317	11/30/06
7.	The Batchelor Foundation, Inc. (FL)	329,385,709	06/30/07
8.	The Goldman Sachs Foundation (NY)	289,665,104	11/30/06
9.	General Motors Foundation (MI)	222,500,120	12/31/06
10.	Freddie Mac Foundation (VA)	214,833,217	12/31/06

Source: Foundation Center (2008a).

Table 3-2 Ten Largest Corporate Foundations by Total Giving

Rank	Name/(State)	Total Giving	As of Fiscal Year End Date
1.	Aventis Pharmaceuticals Health Care Foundation (NJ)	$221,676,217	12/31/06
2.	The Bank of America Charitable Foundation, Inc. (NC)	144,833,778	12/31/06
3.	Wal-Mart Foundation	128,043,643	1/31/07
4.	GE Foundation (CT)	88,252,767	12/31/06
5.	JPMorgan Chase Foundation (NY)	79,895,591	12/31/06
6.	Citi Foundation (NY)	73,881,690	12/31/06
7.	The Wachovia Foundation (NC)	64,418,266	12/31/06
8.	The Wells Fargo Foundation (CA)	64,359,430	12/31/06
9.	ExxonMobil Foundation (TX)	62,495,330	12/31/06
10.	Verizon Foundation (NJ)	59,847,733	12/31/06

Source: Foundation Center (2008b).

Table 3-3 Top Ten U.S. Foundations by Asset Size

Rank	Name/(State)	Total Giving	As of Fiscal Year End Date
1.	Bill & Melinda Gates Foundation (WA)	$38,921,022,000	12/31/07
2.	The Ford Foundation (NY)	13,798,807,066	09/30/07
3.	J. Paul Getty Trust (CA)	10,133,371,844	06/30/06
4.	The Robert Wood Johnson Foundation (NJ)	10,094,684,000	12/31/06
5.	The William and Flora Hewlett Foundation (CA)	9,284,917,000	12/31/07
6.	W. K. Kellogg Foundation (MI)	8,402,996,155	08/31/07
7.	Lilly Endowment Inc. (IN)	7,734,860,156	12/31/07
8.	The David and Lucile Packard Foundation (CA)	6,350,664,410	12/31/06
9.	John D. and Catherine T. MacArthur Foundation (IL)	6,178,196,933	12/31/06
10.	The Andrew W. Mellon Foundation (NY)	6,130,849,701	12/31/06

Source: Foundation Center (2008c).

Table 3-4 Top Ten U.S. Foundations by Total Giving

Rank	Name/(State)	Total Giving	As of Fiscal Year End Date
1.	Bill & Melinda Gates Foundation (WA)	$2,011,675,000	12/31/07
2.	The Ford Foundation (NY)	583,915,463	09/30/07
3.	The William and Flora Hewlett Foundation (CA)	421,400,000	12/31/07
4.	The Bristol-Myers Squibb Patient Assistance Foundation, Inc. (NJ)	416,632,202	12/31/06
5.	The Robert Wood Johnson Foundation (NJ)	367,570,000	12/31/06
6.	Lilly Endowment Inc. (IN)	341,863,979	12/31/07
7.	Janssen Ortho Patient Assistance Foundation, Inc. (NJ)	339,648,095	12/31/06
8.	GlaxoSmithKline Patient Access Programs Foundation (NC)	324,284,214	12/31/06
9.	W. K. Kellogg Foundation (MI)	302,844,012	08/31/07
10.	The Annenberg Foundation (PA)	279,744,155	06/30/07

Source: Foundation Center (2008d).

and annual giving, and **Tables 3-3** and **3-4** provide Foundation Center statistics of top U.S. private foundation contributors in terms of total assets and annual giving.

MOTIVATIONS FOR CORPORATE AND FOUNDATION PHILANTHROPY

Corporate Motivations

Researchers indicate a myriad of reasons why corporations give to the nonprofit sector. These reasons range from altruism to self-interest, and it is difficult to know where one ends and the other begins (Nauffts, 1994, p. 124). According to Greenfield (2002) some of the most common reasons for corporate giving include:

- *Good corporate citizenship:* The company wants to create a positive image in the community in which it operates by making charitable gifts to local nonprofits that provide community service.

- *Enlightened self-interest:* It is in the company's interest to support the work of local charities like colleges and hospitals that help keep the workforce healthy and educated.
- *Individual leadership initiatives:* Those with clout in the business community are able to pursue an interest in selected nonprofits in their community.
- *Civic participation:* The company gives to nonprofits in the communities where it operates and its employees live.
- *Quid pro quo interests:* The company seeks a tangible return for its investment (p. 279).
- Nauffts adds more reasons that include giving back to the community, increasing brand loyalty, and obtaining tax benefits (1994, p. 124).

Benefits for Nonprofits in Accepting Grants from Corporations

Just as there are many reasons why corporations align themselves with nonprofits, there are many benefits for nonprofit organizations to seek funding from corporations. Some of these motivations are:

- Increased revenue
- Flexible use of funds: usually unrestricted
- Minimal paperwork required, sometimes only a one- or two-page letter
- Connection to a corporation's network (employees, suppliers, contacts)
- Opportunity to enhance funding appropriations; may encourage other corporations to donate when they see support from a well-known corporation
- Help corporations to give back, be socially responsible

    It is essential for a nonprofit organization to determine, or at least think about, why a corporation would want to give to its cause. Knowing a corporation's potential motivation provides a strategy or angle on how to approach it, as well as anticipate possible conflicts.

Foundation Motivations

Foundations are organized with the specific purpose "to make grants to unrelated organizations or individuals for scientific, cultural, religious, or other charitable purposes" (Wason, 2004, p. 10). Their existence is predicated on giving money away to society. Most foundations have been established through money designated by families or individuals to carry out the original donor's wishes. Their mission can be broad (allowing flexibility in application and

response of funds) or specific. It may change over time. In any case, what moti- ✳
vates the institution and to whom, where, and when they give depends on the
personality and interests of the original donor, institution, and trustees.

Benefits for Nonprofits in Accepting Grants from Foundations

Just as there are many reasons why nonprofits accept grants from corporations, there are many benefits for nonprofit organizations to seek funding from
foundations. Some of these motivations include:

- Increased revenue
- Help in expanding into new programmatic areas
- Clear and organized directions for paperwork required
- Knowing decision dates for grants
- Connection to the foundation's network (other nonprofits, government
  officials)
- Signaling high-quality programs; may encourage other foundations to
  donate when they see support from a well-known foundation

As with corporations, it is essential for a nonprofit organization to determine why a foundation would want to give to its cause as a part of the grantseeking process.

CORPORATE GIVING STRUCTURES

Corporate giving structures vary from very informal decision-making
processes to bureaucratic company-sponsored foundations. For example, it
may take a simple letter to a neighborhood bank to obtain funding versus a
lengthy online grant proposal to a major corporation whose decisions will be
made in several months. Most companies sustain a corporate giving structure that is either a company-sponsored foundation, a direct corporate giving
process, or a "hybrid giving" structure that offers both direct corporate giving and a foundation (Sheldon, 2000).

Corporate Foundation Giving

Corporate foundations are 501(c)(3) nonprofit organizations regulated and
mandated by the IRS to donate at least 5% of their assets annually. Instead
of making a gift directly to a charitable organization, the corporation makes

a corporate tax-deductible gift to its corporate foundation. This way, if profits are down one year, the corporate contributions program can be supported by disbursing some of the assets that have built up in the foundation (Bauer, 1999). If profits are way up one year, the corporation can move extra funds to the foundation. The result is a fairly steady stream of revenue to the charitable organizations that are supported by the corporation.

Direct Corporate Giving

Support to the nonprofit community can also come via direct corporate giving that is not linked to a corporate foundation. Direct corporate giving is a method that allows corporations to donate much more freely than corporate foundations (e.g., without the 5% minimum restriction mentioned above). In 1997 direct corporate giving accounted for over 75% of total corporate giving in the United States (Sheldon, 2000, pp. 6–7).

Corporations have various budgets that they can tap to provide direct support to nonprofits, such as funds from marketing, public relations, research and development, advertising, and senior management discretionary dollars. Direct support can take the form of a grant, sponsorship, gift-in-kind, volunteers, cause-related marketing or joint ventures, and licensing arrangements. Each form will be examined in the following section.

Grants

A nonprofit applying for a grant goes through an application process that can be either a simple request letter or a competitive grant application. The more extensive the process is, the greater the likelihood that it involves a corporate foundation or a corporation's well-structured philanthropic program (Sheldon, 2000). The key for fundraisers is to be very clear about the details of the application process, to be in as close contact as possible with the staff at the company, and to be sensitive to the motivations and needs of the corporation.

Sponsorships

Sponsorships are another common source of corporate funding for nonprofits. Sponsorship funding is easily accessible because it requires minimal, if any, paperwork and can be considered a business-related expense for the company.

According to Chicago-based IEG, a firm that studies the sponsorship industry, most charities are not charging their corporate partners enough fees for marketing and sponsorship arrangements (Association of Fundraising Professionals, 2004). The *IEG Strategic SR Philanthropy Study* surveyed 145 nonprofit managers about their marketing and sponsorship deals. According to the Association of Fundraising Professionals (2004):

> The study found that although 9 out of 10 respondents said they offer marketing benefits in their grant proposals and 76 percent offer their donors rights to promote their partnership, only 23 percent of respondents request a servicing fee. The reason? Seventy-two percent of those surveyed said they were unsure of what to charge. In addition, 45 percent were uncertain about what benefits companies wanted, while 44 percent cited a lack of understanding among charity employees on benefits of partnering with for-profit organizations.

IEG recommended that charities add 15% to 25% to the fee they already charge companies in marketing promotions to offset the costs. This fee may seem high to some nonprofits that fear alienating their donors. However, IEG insisted that return on the donor's "investment" increases with its philanthropic partnerships (Association of Fundraising Professionals, 2004).

Gift-In-Kind

Corporations can further help nonprofits by providing in-kind support, which is a non-cash contribution. Special tax incentives are available to companies that contribute their own products. In addition, corporations have the opportunity to donate other items and services, including use of office space for meetings, office furniture and equipment, use of the company's staff as advisers and/or board members, and affordable loans.

Corporate Volunteerism

The U.S. Department of Labor's Bureau of Labor Statistics (2008) reported that from September 2006 through September 2007, 26.2% of the U.S. population was active in volunteering, with each volunteer giving an average of

52 hours during that year. The Bureau of Labor Statistics' report indicated that 60.8 million people volunteered at least once during this one-year time period. Furthermore, Independent Sector (IS) estimated that in 2007 the dollar value of volunteer time was $19.51 per hour. It is important to know the estimated value of volunteer time because the dollar amount provides a uniform way for volunteer managers, nonprofit executives, government agencies, and others to account for the value of time contributed by volunteers (Independent Sector, 2008).

Independent Sector identifies the following motivations, which are seen as benefits for the nonprofit organization:

- Impact on mission
- Enhanced visibility of the cause or the nonprofit's message
- Access to new audiences
- Expertise in marketing, strategy development, and other corporate experience

Benefits for the company include:

- Brand differentiation
- Enhanced employee recruitment and retention
- Building new and deeper community networks
- Fostering talent and teaching new skills to employees
- Improved relations with regional and federal governments
- Enhanced credibility and education information
- Access to knowledge and experience to aid in research and development (Independent Sector, 2004a, pp. 3–4)

Herman highlights additional benefits to volunteer utilization for nonprofit organizations: delivery of services at reduced cost, better contact with the community, and better assistance to clients. He also notes some possible disadvantages of using corporate volunteers: lack of control and reliability of volunteers, time demands for volunteer supervision, potential negative impact on paid jobs, and difficulties in recruiting enough qualified volunteers (Herman & Associates, 1994, p. 513).

Brian O'Connell (as cited in Shannon, 1991) agrees that corporations should promote corporate volunteerism because, in addition to goodwill, it provides employees the opportunity to do and see things differently, more creatively.

Sheryl Wiley Solomon, an executive at Ralston Purina Corporation (as cited in Shannon, 1991) gives her advice for establishing a volunteer program. "The task does require a staff person develop the program, publicize it to employees, and implement it on an ongoing basis. It also requires some money" (p. 311), especially to sponsor special events and to pay for promotional material. Purina's volunteer program is an example of a "clearinghouse model which provides employees with information about volunteer opportunities available in the community and refers them to appropriate nonprofit agencies" (p. 311). The goal is to match the volunteer interest of employees with community needs.

Herman (1994) recommends that a nonprofit organization integrate the volunteer program within its policies and throughout the organization. Herman also recommends having a volunteer coordinator on staff, but he adds that it is also important to develop job descriptions for volunteers and provide flexible hours. Most important, the nonprofit organization must have a sincere appreciation for its volunteers.

Cause-Related Marketing

Cause-related marketing is a relatively modern and popular corporate source of funding. It is an agreement between a corporation and a nonprofit in which the nonprofit agrees to support the corporation's initiative, and in turn the corporation compensates the nonprofit (Ciconte & Jacob, 2005). Cause-related marketing offers the opportunity for nonprofits to receive funding and for corporations to obtain benefits such as development of brand loyalty and increased employee morale. Cause-related marketing is considered to have begun in 1983 when American Express donated a penny toward the restoration of the Statue of Liberty every time someone used their charge card. The Statue of Liberty benefited from the relationship by receiving funds for its restoration, while American Express benefited from the relationship by increasing its number of new cardholders and increasing card usage.

A more recent example of a joint venture between a nonprofit and a corporation is the Starbucks collaboration with the international relief organization CARE. Starbucks put up banners in its stores commemorating the 50th anniversary of CARE and highlighted its programs in the very countries where Starbucks buys coffee. Customers were encouraged to buy canisters of coffee from those countries, with proceeds from the sale of the special coffee going to CARE (Austin, 2003). If structured properly, such relationships provide a "win-win" situation for both nonprofit and corporation.

Independent Sector (2004a) indicates that "generally an underlying premise of most corporate-nonprofit partnerships is the goal of strengthening the organization's and company's brand identity" (p. 1). Ciconte and Jacob explain that people develop strong emotional attachments or loyalty to certain nonprofit organizations, especially those that provide services that they have used at some point in their lives. A corporation that aligns with nonprofits benefits from these relationships. As a result, the corporation's sales increase and it is able to share a portion of its incremental income with the nonprofit with which it has a formal alliance. It is a win-win situation for all, because the nonprofit organization and the profit-making corporation benefit from the partnership and the consumer gains a sense of "doing good" by purchasing the product and thus helping the nonprofit organization (Ciconte & Jacob, 2005, p. 175).

Overton and Frey (2002) advise nonprofit boards that enter into joint ventures to "make sure that the joint venture is not structured or operated in a manner that would constitute an undue benefit to its for-profit partner and other for-profit entities" (p. 97). They emphasize that a nonprofit must "take care to structure the joint venture, and the nonprofit's role therein, in a manner that minimized the risk that the nonprofit's participation might put the organization's tax-exemption in jeopardy or generate unexpected UBI [unrelated business income]" (p. 97).

Nonprofits need to be cautious when arranging a cause-related marketing initiative with a corporation since they are usually the weaker financial partner and are subjecting their name to possible negative public reaction. The nonprofit representatives should make sure that (1) the mission of the nonprofit is aligned with the public brand of the corporation, (2) the financial arrangement is fair, and (3) the donors to the nonprofit will not confuse their annual donation to the nonprofit with purchasing a product from the company. When the nonprofit considers these three factors as a part of the decision-making process, the arrangement will most likely benefit both parties.

Licensing Arrangements

Licensing is the legal term used for the binding agreement of "one party to allow a second party to use its name, logo, characters, or products" (Herman, 1994, p. 385). In a corporate-nonprofit partnership, the corporation typically pays the nonprofit a royalty for licensing rights based on sales. Herman (1994) notes, "When licensing arrangements are well targeted, both the licenser and licensee benefit financially, as well as in increased publicity" (p. 386). Herman (1994, p. 386) gives the following examples of successful licensing agreements:

- The Sierra Club licenses the rights to its name and photographs to companies that manufacture greeting cards and calendars.
- The Metropolitan Museum of Art earns substantial income by licensing artistic design from its collections to textile companies.
- The Children's Television Workshop (CTW), the nonprofit organization that originated the television show *Sesame Street*, partners with many toy, video, book, record, and clothing manufacturers, including Hasbro, Playskool, Western Publishing, and J. C. Penney. In 1991 CTW grossed $22 million from its agreements.

CORPORATE AND FOUNDATION PARTNERSHIP CONCERNS

In today's environment of accountability, corporations, foundations, and nonprofits need to make sure each potential partnership is a good idea. The Campaign for Tobacco-Free Kids offers an evaluation model for proposed partnerships that includes guidelines to consider when evaluating a potential relationship. The evaluation model includes a six-step analysis of the proposed partnership (see **Exhibit 3-1**).

A good question for each party to ask itself is: would we be comfortable if the details of this relationship appeared on the front page of a major newspaper? The Campaign for Tobacco-Free Kids recommends discussing these other key questions:

Exhibit 3-1 Model Guidelines for Nonprofits Evaluating Proposed Relationships with Other Organizations

1. Nature of the proposed partner
2. Goals of the proposed partner
3. Potential conflicts of interest due to the subject area of the proposed relationship
4. Role of the proposed partner
5. Potential consequences of the relationship
6. Evaluation process

Source: Campaign for Tobacco-Free Kids (March, 2000). www.tobaccofreekids.com

- Does the proposed activity and/or the proposed relationship promote the mission and values of our organization?
- Will the relationship promote or enhance activities or organizations whose goals are inconsistent with the mission and values of our organization?
- Will the relationship maintain our organization's reputation for objectivity, independence, integrity, credibility, social responsibility, and accountability? (www.tobaccofreekids.com)

Overton and Frey (2002) propose some critical questions on joint ventures, especially those that may have fiscal and legal consequences, as follows:

- Does the nonprofit appoint a majority of the joint venture's governing body?
- Does the for-profit partner (or partners) have a veto power over significant corporate actions?
- Will a for-profit entity (whether a partner, a partner's affiliate, or an unrelated third party) manage the operations of the joint venture? If so, what is the term of the management contract? How are the management fees determined?
- Do the governing documents of the joint venture explicitly provide that the joint venture will be operated consistently with the charitable purpose of the tax-exempt partner?
- Does the tax-exempt partner have the ability to require the joint venture to put charitable purposes ahead of economic objectives?
- Will the compensation paid to the joint venture's officers and vendors (especially the for-profit partner or any affiliate) be reasonable in light of the services and/or goods provided?
- Will the joint venture use space financed by tax-exempt bonds? If so, have the implications of such "bad use" on the tax exemption of the bonds been considered? (p. 98)

Other ethical issues and conflicts of interest to consider are:

- Use of corporate philanthropy only to increase profits
- Corporate desire to buy silence and/or influence outcome
- Undisclosed information (keeping in mind the Sarbanes-Oxley Act)

Finally, it is important that the evaluation of the relationship itself is not shortchanged. This evaluation is truly a critical step, because such analysis will demonstrate if the partnership is a successful one, if it is consistent with policies and missions, and if it is ethical and legal.

TRENDS IN CORPORATE AND FOUNDATION PHILANTHROPY

Sheldon (2000) points to two interesting trends in corporate philanthropy. He describes one as proactive corporate philanthropy and the other as judicially related. Sheldon indicates that proactive corporate philanthropy, unlike the traditional "reactive" corporate philanthropy, is a more dynamic, strategic approach. We can see this in major corporations that include this as part of their triple bottom line (financial, society, and environment). Additionally, the same strategic philanthropy is mirrored in corporate foundations.

> In the reactive model, company executives basically responded with gifts of cash only after being solicited by a nonprofit. In the proactive model, company officials often re-identify causes and organizations with which they wish to be associated and work with these agencies to provide a mix of support options that could include, for example, a loaned executive, sponsorship dollars from the public relations budget, and below market-rate loans for capital improvements. (p. 12)

Again, many foundations apply the same type of reasoning to how they approach their causes.

Another phenomenon that Sheldon identifies is "the growing interest of the U.S. judicial system to include court ordered corporate gifts to the nonprofit sector as part of an overall civil or criminal awards settlement" (2000, p. 98). In such cases, the court orders a corporation bound to a legal settlement to give part of the cash settlement to the benefit of one or more nonprofit organizations.

We already discussed Austin's (2000) community wealth partnerships, which are trends that include licensing arrangements, cause-related marketing programs, and joint ventures. **Exhibit 3-2** provides additional facts on the growing trends of community wealth partnerships.

Another engaging trend is Austin's (2000) community wealth enterprise. In a community wealth enterprise, the nonprofit organization operates more like a business than a typical nonprofit service provider. The nonprofits "provide products or services but do not necessarily involve a corporate partner" (p. 46). See **Exhibit 3-3** for an example.

Exhibit 3-2 Growing Trends of Cause-Related Marketing, Sponsorships, and Other Partnerships

- An all-time high of **84% of Americans** say they are likely to switch brands, when price and quality are equal, to help support a cause. *Source: 2002 Cone Corporation Citizenship Study, The Role of Cause Branding (2002).*
- **More than 7 out of 10 Americans (75%)** say a company's commitment to causes is important when they decide which products and services to recommend to others. *Source: 2002 Cone Corporate Citizenship Study, The Role of Cause Branding (2002).*
- Among shareholders that rated a company's philanthropy favorably, **78%** say they will continue to invest in the company. *Source: National Philanthropy Benchmark Study, Council on Foundations & Walker Information (2002).*
- Employees whose companies support social issues are **40% more likely** to say they are proud of their company's values, and nearly **25% more likely** to be loyal to their employers than those whose companies do not have such programs. *Source: 2002 Cone Corporate Citizenship Study, The Role of Cause Branding (2002).*
- In 2001 corporate charitable contributions equaled **$9.05 billion**, which represents **1.3% of corporate pre-tax profits**, one of the highest shares of profits in recent years. (These figures do not include corporate sponsorships, volunteer time, and donations of facilities or services—which do not qualify as gifts under the tax code.) *Source: Giving USA Annual Report for 2001, AAFRC Trust for Philanthropy (2002).*
- **92% of Americans today** have a more positive image of companies and products that support causes, significantly higher than figures preceding September 2001 (81% in March 2001, 83% in 1999, and 85% in 1993). *Source: Cone Corporate Citizenship Study, The Role of Cause Branding (2002).*

Source: Copyright 2004 Independent Sector. All Rights Reserved. www.independentsector.org/mission_market/facts_figures.htm

Exhibit 3-3 Community Wealth Enterprise

The Enterprising Kitchen (TEK), based in Chicago, is a 501(c)(3) nonprofit organization that enables women to maximize their individual potential. TEK is considered a social enterprise, because it operates a light manufacturing company that produces specialty soap products and enables women to participate in an intensive, individually oriented workforce development program. The women-participants are employed 25 hours per week in all aspects of the soap making business. The revenues generated through product sales help sustain the workforce development program and enable participants to benefit from a wide range of onsite resources and activities.

Source: Enterprising Kitchen (n.d.).

Philanthropy continues to change rapidly, producing variations within the four IRS-designated foundation structure models as well as new models. New types of donors are emerging that are changing the focus of giving (such as attention to women's issues and creation of venture philanthropy funds). This rapid change necessitates vastly different thinking from the traditional foundation and puts a burden on the leadership of foundations and nonprofits to communicate effectively with all parties in an established or growing relationship as well as plan strategically for the future. Foundations need the flexibility to change with the trends.

Giving does not occur in a vacuum. Many factors influence current giving trends. Although the 1990s were a period of economic prosperity, the beginning of the twenty-first century presented an end to that as well as increased concern with financial soundness of foundations and corporate philanthropies. World events such as the 9/11 terrorist attacks, the war in Iraq, and the world threat of terrorism have deeply impacted the philanthropic climate and have catalyzed change within the philanthropic world (Wason, 2004, p. 26). The stock market recovered nicely from these challenges in 2006 and 2007, although the economic crisis of 2008 threatens economic growth.

Stock market values and levels of personal income, both of which have seen volatility since 2000, are good predictors of philanthropic giving. During each economic downturn, foundations tend to react by cutting administrative services along with the number and size of grants. This is countercyclical to the needs of people, which can cause frustration for nonprofit leaders. Just when support is most needed in the community, the economic problems drive foundations to reduce their support. However, over the past few years foundations have tried to manage smarter and more efficiently. It is yet to be seen if this will be the case following the current economic downturn. Wason (2004) writes: "In an article for the *Chronicle of Philanthropy*, Mark R. Kramer, founder of the Center for Effective Philanthropy, postulates that economic downturns will result in a restructuring of the foundation world similar to the 'reengineering' of corporate America after the economic decline in the 1980s" (p. 28). He predicts three shifts:

- *Increased focus:* Instead of supporting several types of programs with a myriad of small grants, funders will give larger grants to fewer organizations in fewer focal areas to cut down on time spent reviewing grants.

- *More responsibility to staff:* Instead of having staff write memos and make recommendations for board approval, big foundations may encourage staff to make decisions themselves.
- *Different rules for repeat grantees:* Those who have received grants in the past may be required to fill out less paperwork, submitting only a brief letter or concept paper rather than lengthy applications that take longer to review (Wason, 2004, p. 28).

Foundations, nonprofits, and for-profits have agreed to move toward greater transparency because of the recent attention paid to scandals. Shareholders and stakeholders alike are demanding more accountability. The Sarbanes-Oxley and Charitable Giving acts of 2002 affect all charitable giving. These acts impact foundations' administrative costs since a move toward greater transparency requires more administrative attention. Fundraisers should understand and then compensate for the increased administrative burdens for foundations by being even more careful about following specific grant requirements. Nonprofits should not submit requests to foundations that are clearly outside the scope of funding interest.

Another factor impacting foundation giving is the expansion of interest into global affairs, particularly as U.S. businesses move operations abroad, expanding their communities to include other countries. Demographics such as race, ethnicity, sex, and age continue to rapidly change the appearance and attitudes of the donors and constituents. The bottom line is that the future means *change* and will require constant learning and flexibility from foundations and nonprofit organizations.

In review, corporate giving continues to be a key source of funding for nonprofit organizations in many creative ways. Corporations and nonprofit organizations are motivated to partner in order to increase revenue; connect to each other's networks of employees, suppliers, and contacts; and help each other achieve their own missions. Corporate philanthropy is becoming more proactive. In addition to cash contributions, companies provide various support options, such as corporate volunteers, in-kind contributions, and special lending programs.

Foundations are private entities, and because of periods of economic prosperity, they have expanded in numbers, growth, and impact. Although mostly private, foundations are accountable to growing federal legislation requiring smarter and more efficient use of funds. Although there are many large, traditional foundations, there are also many new ones that reflect a change in donor interests and application of funds. As corporate philanthropy has responded to local and global changes, so has the face of foundation philanthropy. Foundation philanthropy has become more focused and proactive in interactively forming and participating in partnerships with nonprofits to address the challenges of local and global societies.

REFERENCES

Association of Fundraising Professionals. (2004, September 7). Charities not charging enough for marketing, sponsorship deals. Retrieved November 16, 2008, from http://www.afpnet.org/ka/ka-3.cfm?content_item_id=17968&folder_id=2345

Austin, J. E. (2000). The collaboration challenge. San Francisco, CA: Jossey-Bass.

Austin, J. E. (2003). Marketing's role in cross-sector collaboration. In W. Wymer & S. Samu (Eds.), *Nonprofit and business sector collaboration: Cause-related marketing, sponsorships, and other corporate-nonprofit dealings* (p. 31). New York: Hawthorne Press.

Bauer, D. G. (1999). The "how to" grants manual: Successful grantseeking techniques for obtaining public and private grants (4th ed.). Phoenix, AZ: American Council on Education; Oryx Press.

Bill and Melinda Gates Foundation. (2008). Our Approach: Vaccine-Preventable Diseases. Retrieved November 16, 2008, from http://www.gatesfoundation.org/topics/Pages/vaccine-preventable-diseases.aspx

Bureau of Labor Statistics. (2008). Giving and volunteering in the United States, 2007. Washington DC: U.S. Department of Labor. Retrieved August 14, 2008, from http://www.independentsector.org/programs/research/gvresources.html

Burlingame, D. F. (2003). Corporate giving and fund raising. In E. R. Tempel (Ed.), *Hank Rosso's achieving excellence in fund raising* (pp. 177–187). San Francisco, CA: Jossey-Bass.

Campaign for Tobacco-Free Kids. (2000, March). *Model guidelines for nonprofits, evaluating proposed relationships with other organizations.* Retrieved August 22, 2005, from http://www.tobaccofreekids.org/research/factsheets/pdf/0151.pdf

Ciconte, B. K., & Jacob, J. G. (2005). Fundraising basics: A complete guide (2nd ed.). Gaithersburg, MD: Aspen.

Enterprising Kitchen. (n.d.) Who we are. Retrieved August 22, 2005, from http://www.theenterprisingkitchen.org/aboutus.html

Foundation Center. (2008a). Top funders: 50 largest corporate foundations by asset size. Retrieved August 12, 2008, from http://foundationcenter.org/findfunders/topfunders/top50assets.html

Foundation Center. (2008b). Top funders: 50 largest corporate foundations by total giving. Retrieved August 12, 2008, from http://foundationcenter.org/findfunders/topfunders/top50giving.html

Foundation Center. (2008c). Top funders: Top 100 U.S. foundations by asset size. Retrieved August 12, 2008, from http://foundationcenter.org/findfunders/topfunders/top100assets.html

Foundation Center. (2008d). Top funders: Top 100 U.S. foundations by total giving. Retrieved August 12, 2008, from http://foundationcenter.org/findfunders/topfunders/top100giving.html

Giving USA Foundation (2008). *Giving USA 2008.* Glenview, IL: Giving USA Foundation.

Greenfield, J. M. (2002). Fundraising fundamentals: A guide to annual giving for professionals and volunteers (2nd ed.). New York: John Wiley & Sons.

Herman, R. D., & Associates. (1994). The Jossey-Bass handbook on nonprofit leadership and management. New York: John Wiley & Sons.

Independent Sector. (2004a). Mission and market: Motivations for partnering. Retrieved August 22, 2005, from www.independentsector.org/mission_market/motivations.htm

Independent Sector. (2004b). Value of volunteer time. Retrieved August 22, 2005, from http://www.independentsector.org/programs/research/volunteer_time.html

Independent Sector. (2004c). Mission and market: Facts & figures on corporate philanthropy and cause-related marketing. Retrieved November 17, 2008, from www.independentsector .org/mission_market/facts_figures.htm

Independent Sector. (2008). Value of volunteer time. Retrieved August 2008, from http://www.independentsector.org/programs/research/volunteer_time.html

Levy, B. R. (Ed.), (1996–2003). *The AFP fundraising dictionary online.* Retrieved February 6, 2007, from the Association of Fundraising Professionals Web site, http://www.afpnet.org/content_documents/AFP_Dictionary_A-Z_final_6-9-03.pdf

Nauffts, M. F. (Ed.), (1994). *Foundation fundamentals: A guide for grantseekers* (5th ed.). New York: Foundation Center.

Overton, G. W., & Frey, J. C. (Eds). (2002). Guidebook for directors of nonprofit corporations (2nd ed.). Chicago: American Bar Association.

Perry, G. (2003). Foundation fund raising. In E. R. Tempel (Ed.), *Hank Rosso's achieving excellence in fund raising* (pp. 188–199). San Francisco, CA: Jossey-Bass.

Shannon, J. P. (Ed.), (1991). The corporate contributions handbook: Devoting private means to public needs. San Francisco, CA: Jossey-Bass.

Sheldon, K. S. (2000). *Successful corporate fund raising: Effective strategies for today's nonprofits.* New York: John Wiley & Sons.

Wason, S. D. (2004). *Webster's new world grant writing handbook.* Hoboken, NJ: Wiley.

chapter four

History of Fundraising

Fundraisers tend to think of their profession as relatively new. And in many senses, it is new. However, the concept of giving gifts to support the public good has been a part of civilization from the start of recorded history. Humans are by nature social creatures. People feel the need to give and provide aid to each other. Beyond giving, we do see glimpses of how the early pioneers in the fundraising profession were able to work with philanthropists and the general public to achieve great results. In fact, various aspects of fundraising were practiced over the past 2,000 years. What is remarkable in what we find is the extent of similarity in technique over the years and the continuing concern by donors and the public for ethical behavior among fundraisers.

Although the study of the history of fundraising might provide a better understanding of various techniques used in years past and how to apply them in a modern context, more appropriate is to look at the overall trends in fundraising as the profession developed. We see a movement from occasional and sporadic philanthropy to regular and purposeful philanthropy. We see part-time consultants working on a specific project to full-time fundraising staff numbering in the hundreds in many organizations. We see a changing framework of understanding from a "sales" orientation, where high emotions and pressure raise the gifts—through a "product" orientation, where information about the cause and clear communication raise the gifts—to a "marketing" orientation, where careful attention to the needs of the donor and looking for matches of interest to the organization raise the gifts. Overall, we see the growth in the size of the fundraising endeavor and the sophistication and professionalization of the industry.

EARLY PHILANTHROPY

The world's first philanthropist is generally considered to be the mythical Prometheus who loved mortals so much that he gave them the gift of fire against the will of the gods. The gods sentenced him to eternal suffering (Prometheus, 2008). The world's history is full of examples of human compassion, philanthropy, kindness, and charity.

The earliest recorded bequest in history is Plato's donation of all his land on which the Academy was founded sometime around 350 B.C. Shortly thereafter, Ptolemy I created an endowment for the world's first library in Alexandria, circa 280 B.C. These gifts benefited society while raising the social status of the donor (Weidman, 2003, p. 2).

Women also played a central role in philanthropy in ancient Greece. A woman by the name of Euxenia "not only built a temple in which she served as a priestess, but the temple also served as a hostelry for visitors and strangers to rest" (Constantelos, 2003, p. 14). Another woman by the name of Menodora, from Pisidia, is honored because she donated 300,000 dinarii to aid orphaned children (Constantelos, 2003, p. 15).

BIBLICAL GIVING

Fundraising was a part of life in both the Jewish and early Christian societies more than 2,000 years ago. The apostle Paul, while not exclusively a fundraiser, did direct Christians in their giving. Paul developed a systematic way for donating money, an idea on which much of fundraising rests in the current time: "Now about the collection for God's people: Do what I told the Galatian churches to do. On the first day of every week, each one of you should set aside a sum of money in keeping with his income, saving it up, so that when I come no collections will have to be made. Then, when I arrive, I will give letters of introduction to the men you approve and send them with your gift to Jerusalem" (1 Corinthians 16:1–4).

OTHER EARLY RELIGIOUS GIVING

Documents prove that as early as the sixth century A.D., Buddhist temples in Japan were involved in coordinating *kanjin*, which were essentially fundraising campaigns for orphanages, elderly homes, and general social services. Kukai is a Buddhist monk from the ninth century who could be called "the founder of Japan's private nonprofit, or third sector" (Japan: History of the third sector, 2005, p. 2). He is known for his public works, including an irrigation pond, education facilities, and hospitals (p. 2). Many monks were actively involved in raising money for those in need as well as for restorations of the temples. In some instances, records indicate that the higher-end donors were given a higher rank or social standing in gratitude for their gifts (Gifts and debts, 2000). "Traditionally, Buddhist monasteries functioned as centers for intellectual, cultural, recreational and community life. Buddhist temples were health centres for traditional medicine and treatment, refuge for patients with deadly disease, and hostels providing food and lodging to the travellers. People were inspired to donate to appease the monks and earn 'merit'" (Thailand: History of philanthropy, 2005).

The same method existed in the Hindu religion and is known as the Pania fund, which was collected in Hindu temples.

VIETNAMESE ORGANIZED GIVING

Vietnam has been a place of warfare and famine for centuries. The Vietnamese people have had to unite and support one another in order to survive. These groups that were created in times of need actually became philanthropic organizations called *phuongs*. The people promised to help each other in all kinds of ways: sharing finances, creating products, and supporting people in need (Vietnam: History of philanthropy, 2005, p. 2).

There were also several forms of mutual financial supporting organisations called ho. People in one ho used to contribute money or rice and receive, in their turn, the total amount contributed by all members of the ho. The primary purpose of a ho was to help its members accumulate a large quantity of rice or sum of money for special family events, for example, house building or repairing, children's wedding, birthday celebration of old parents or parents' death anniversary, etc. The members of a ho used to support each other in the utilisation of the specific fund received from the group fund. Thus one person's house building or repairing activity, or social events used to be supported by volunteer labours of the others in the ho and outside the hos. (Vietnam: History of philanthropy, 2005, p. 4)

One of the first instances of tax breaks for giving was introduced by King Le Thanh Tong (1460–1497). He reduced the rice paddy tax for wealthy families who contributed to their local community fund. Because the people were supported by the government, they created compassion funds in the late fifteenth century that still exist today (Vietnam: History of philanthropy, 2005, p. 5).

MIDDLE AGES FUNDRAISING

Mullin (2007, pp. 12–13) describes a strikingly familiar list of techniques used in Europe in the 1300s to raise funds for building cathedrals and other charitable projects:

- Indulgences (purchase of salvation)
- Collection boxes
- Matching funds
- High-society/major patron fundraising for noblemen and noblewomen, kings and queens, and wealthy merchants
- Endowment through income-earning assets
- Sponsored bell-ringing

The fundraisers in the Middle Ages were conspicuously successful and hence became regulated. "The 1215 Lateran Council decreed that quaestores eleemosynarii, as they were called, could only operate under licence from their bishop or from the Pope, a formula already guaranteed to stir strife where papal demands for funds were unwelcome" (Mullin, 2007, p. 14).

GIVING IN THE NEW WORLD

Robert Bremner (1960) observes that the earliest recorded acts of philanthropy on the American continent can be credited to the native inhabitants of the Bahama Islands, who warmly greeted the ships of Christopher Columbus when they first landed in the New World in 1492. Philanthropy does not consist only of large amounts of money given by the wealthy. Columbus wrote that the natives not only gave away whatever was asked of them but also were "ingenuous and free" (p. 5) in bestowing their property on the European explorers. Indeed, they gave each gift "with as much love as if their hearts went with it" (p. 5).

When the Pilgrims arrived in North America in December 1620, history records that the fledgling colony would have died had it not been for the aid of a Patuxet Indian named Squanto, who served as guide to the white settlers. The starving English settlers regarded him as "a special instrument sent of God" (Bremner, 1960, p. 6) to prevent their death. Though Squanto's giving did not consist of money, Governor William Bradford recorded with gratitude that Squanto taught the settlers "how to set their corn, where to take fish, and to procure other commodities, and was also their pilot to bring them to unknown places for their profit, and never left them till he died" (p. 6).

FUNDRAISING IN THE UNITED STATES

The United States was founded on independence with a great understanding of social responsibility. Americans, from early colonial days to the present, have always been involved in philanthropy. The first recorded instance of fundraising in the colonies was in 1643, when Harvard College conducted the first fundraising drive. Three pastors from America went to England to cultivate donors and raised £500. Tradition has it that one remained in England, one was hanged as a criminal there, and one returned to America with the funds. They used a somewhat emotionally charged pamphlet to convey the need for support: "After God had carried us safe to New England and we had built our houses, provided necessaries for our livelihood, reared convenient places for God's worship, and settled the civil government; one of the next things we longed for and looked after was to advance learning and perpetuate it to posterity, dreading to leave an illiterate ministry to the churches when our present ministers shall lie in the dust" (New England's First Fruits, 1643, as cited in Riss, 2001, p. 13).

Benjamin Franklin: A Fundraising Strategist

Benjamin Franklin was the states' first well-known philanthropist and fundraiser. On top of being a tireless inventor, publisher, and statesman, he raised money for relief agencies, libraries, fire departments, and schools. He believed in preventing poverty before it started rather than curing it afterward. Franklin wrote, "I am for doing good to the poor, but I differ in opinion about the means. I think the best way of doing good to the poor is, not making them easy in poverty, but leading or driving them out of it" (Bremner, 1960, p. 17).

According to legend, he created a system for raising donations. Franklin suggested making three lists of names: the first, people you know will give; then second, people you think may give; and the third, people you doubt will give. The fundraiser then asks the first group to give and then shows their names to the second group, who should theoretically feel compelled to give after seeing what their peers gave. After their donations have been collected, the fundraiser shows the combined list to the third group—who might just surprise the fundraiser and actually give to the cause!

Benjamin Franklin left a bequest in 1790 of almost $4,000 to be split between the people of the Commonwealth of Pennsylvania (76%) and the City of Philadelphia (24%). He left it on the condition that it could not be touched for 200 years. In 1998 his bequest was worth $2.3 million, and it was decided that Philadelphia would keep its money in a permanent endowment for the city, and the commonwealth's money would be shared between the Franklin Institute and several community foundations (Klein, 2006, pp. 13–14).

Williams College: Building an Alumni Association

The first society of alumni in the world was founded at Williams College in 1821 in an effort to support the school financially after its president, Zephaniah Swift Moore, and many faculty left to form another college, which is now Amherst College (Williams College, 2008). In 1850 Williams built the first alumni hall entirely from alumni funds (Alumni Association, n.d.). Alumni funds continue to be an integral part of fundraising strategies at colleges and universities today.

The American Civil War: Philanthropy Through War Bonds

Armies of volunteers on both sides of the conflict during the Civil War gathered contributions for the soldiers. Jay Cooke, an American financier, began to sell bonds during this time. He worked with the secretary of the treasury to secure loans from large northern cities and sold bonds door to door to support the union. His bonds reached a total of $830 million, allowing the union soldiers to be supplied and paid. Cooke was a devout Christian and gave 10% of his income for religious purposes, including the building of several Episcopal churches and a school for girls (Jay Cooke, 2005).

John Morton Greene and Sophia Smith: Counsel in Philanthropy

John Morton Greene, a reverend and trustee of Smith College, could be called one of the first planned giving officers in the United States. Sophia Smith came to him in 1861 when she realized she would be inheriting great wealth. She entrusted him with a personal journal and asked him what she should do with her money. He provided her with four possible plans:

- An academy in Hartfield
- A deaf-mute institution
- A scientific school connected to Amherst College
- A college for women

On February 12, 1868, Sophia Smith asked John Morton Greene to change her will and asked him to draw up plans for a women's college. This was the beginning of Smith College (John M. Greene, 1997).

Andrew Carnegie

Andrew Carnegie is the famous Scottish American industrialist, as well as a great philanthropist. Carnegie was the son of a master weaver born in a small town in Scotland. The Carnegies immigrated to Pittsburgh, Pennsylvania, because Carnegie's father's employment became obsolete upon the development of the power loom. It was here Andrew Carnegie finagled his first big break, as secretary and telegrapher to the powerful Pennsylvania railroad industrialist Tom Scott. At the age of 23, Carnegie headed the Pennsy's Pittsburgh division, while adding to his own fortune through investments made in oil and iron bridges. Ten years later, his business acumen further intensified. Though it was progress that forced the Carnegies out of their native Scotland, Andrew Carnegie built his fortune on progress and the way it would revolutionize the steel industry. He concentrated on bringing the most up-to-date technologies to America from abroad, ever in pursuit of efficiency. It paid off. In 1901 the 66-year-old Carnegie sold his empire to J. P. Morgan and spent the rest of his life giving away the fortune that he had amassed (Chernow, 1998).

In line with his famous essay "The Gospel of Wealth," Carnegie spent much of his wealth during his lifetime on philanthropic interests. He opened what were known as "Carnegie libraries" across the United States, creating at least one in every state, with the exceptions of Alaska and Delaware. What made these 3,000 libraries different is that he only partially funded them. His requirement was that the local government had to assist financially and maintain the libraries. He felt that if people were somewhat invested financially they would take better care of the libraries.

Andrew Carnegie used the same acumen for business as he did for his philanthropic pursuits. He reasoned that because of his wealth, he would be the best one to dictate what the common people needed and how to give it to them. It was imperative to him that these decisions were made when he was alive so he could oversee the administration of his wealth. Though he expounded the virtues of living modestly, the sheer volume of his benevolence could be categorized as conspicuous consumption. After all, Carnegie's name remains on countless buildings, plaques, and educational programs. Some examples of his philanthropy are:

- He gave $2 million in 1901 to start the Carnegie Institute of Technology in Pittsburgh (now Carnegie Mellon University).
- In 1902 he gave another $2 million to start the Carnegie Institute in Washington, DC.
- He was a large benefactor of the Tuskegee Institute, which educated African Americans.
- He funded 7,000 church organs (Andrew Carnegie, 2006).

Julius Rosenwald Fund

In "The Gospel of Wealth," one of Carnegie's arguments for giving away money while a donor was still alive was that one could be sure it was used as intended. In keeping with this tradition, in 1917 Julius Rosenwald created a foundation and planned on closing its operations no later than 25 years after his death. The foundation closed in 1948, 16 years after his death. Rosenwald wrote "Principles of Public Giving" in 1929, in which he promoted the idea of exhausting a foundation's funds within a generation so "no bureaucracy is likely to develop around them" (Wooster, 2006, ¶ 31). He gave primarily to promote the education of African Americans but was also a major contributor to the Museum of Science and Industry in Chicago and to various Jewish causes (Wooster, 2006, p. 11).

John D. Rockefeller

John Davison Rockefeller, the great American capitalist, is best known for Standard Oil, the largest oil refining business in the United States, and was the richest man in the United States, until he began to give it away to philanthropic causes. He is one of the first benefactors of scientific medical research. He founded the University of Chicago in 1892, the Rockefeller University in

1901, the General Education Board in 1902, and the Rockefeller Foundation in 1913 (John D. Rockefeller, 2006). The Rockefeller Foundation Web site states, "Mr. Rockefeller's contributions to the Foundation's endowment totaled about $240 million. In today's dollars, this would amount to about $2.8 billion. Our endowment, even after distributing the modern equivalent of $13 billion, is actually more than 10 percent higher, in current dollars, than what Mr. Rockefeller contributed" (Responding to the challenges, 2006, ¶ 4).

Rockefeller was also known as "the man who gave away shiny new dimes." According to legend, he handed out about $10,000 worth of dimes before his death (John D. Rockefeller, 2006).

YMCA School, Ward and Pierce: Whirlwind Campaign

Both Frank Pierce and Charles Sumner Ward worked their respective ways up through the Young Men's Christian Association, better known as the YMCA. In 1902 Pierce worked for two years to raise funds for a new building in Washington, DC. He had raised $270,000 (including $50,000 from Rockefeller), but he needed $80,000 more. So in 1905 Ward and Pierce worked together in what became known as the "YMCA school" of fundraising. They were the first fundraisers to hire a publicist as well as to pay for advertising through corporate donations. They also limited the whirlwind campaign to 27 days and incorporated the use of the "campaign clock." They fostered competitions among solicitation teams and used emotional high pressure to make sure the solicitations were made in a timely manner. This method was so successful that they became famous in the fundraising circle. Their fame spread from coast to coast and eventually overseas. In 1907 Pierce worked in Australia and Ward worked in England, and they returned in 1913 to raise $4 million for the New York YMCA (Wooster, 2000, ¶ 4–6). The fundraising campaign is an example of the "sales" orientation in fundraising.

Bishop William Lawrence

Bishop William Lawrence was the pastor of St. John's Memorial Church at Harvard, and in 1904 he became the head of the Harvard alumni association. At graduation that year, he announced that Harvard needed to raise $2.5 million for professors' salaries, and he was subsequently asked to head the campaign. He created many successful fundraising techniques that differed greatly from those of the YMCA school. He decided only a letter was necessary and used a more informational, rather than emotional, technique of raising money. In a 1923 *Atlantic Monthly* article he wrote, "If you dominate or dragoon a man by your personality, you may get his money once, but not the next time" (Wooster, 2000, ¶ 7). He raised $2.4 million within the year, and for the first time, it became clear that alumni would donate for all the school's needs, not just for buildings. In 1914 Lawrence raised $2 million to rebuild Wellesley College after it burned to the ground, and in 1916–1917, he ran the drive for the Episcopalian Church's pension fund. He used the *New York Times* to publicize the concern for senior citizens' welfare, asking the paper to mention his fundraising campaign. By the end of the drive, Lawrence had raised $9 million for the fund, the largest amount raised up until that time (Wooster, 2000, ¶ 7–11). Bishop Lawrence's technique of using facts and information to raise money is an example of the "product" orientation in fundraising.

World War I Campaigns

Ivy Lee, John D. Rockefeller's publicist, who some suspect may have been behind the "man with the shiny new dimes" plan, became even more well known after teaming up with Ward for a $114 million three-month drive for the American Red Cross. People all across the nation joined in: U.S. Steel gave $8 million, the Rockefeller Foundation gave $5 million, and a woman from Ohio gave a hen and 12 eggs that were auctioned off for $2,000 (Wooster, 2000, ¶ 12).

During this time, Secretary of State Newton D. Baker asked charities to aid the war effort by joining together. These organizations became known as the United War Work Campaign, and it was effective at raising funds (Wooster, 2000, ¶ 13).

The Beginnings of Corporate Philanthropy

Corporate philanthropy began with contributions made by railroad companies to the YMCA to provide housing for their workers as they traveled across the country. Corporate philanthropy developed during World War I. "The pressure to give and the participation of big businessmen in the fund drives of World War I led to the first major acts of corporate giving" (Cutlip, 1965, p. 151). There was initially a considerable amount of backlash against corporate philanthropy, spurring regulations that stated that corporate contributions could be deductible only when made to organizations that benefited that company's employees. Franklin D. Roosevelt said that allowing tax deductions on any corporate giving would sanction the "purchase of goodwill by corporations" (p. 327). Despite the criticism, there were gaps in philanthropy that could be filled with corporate gifts. Until the Great Depression, these regulations would guide the world of corporate philanthropy.

The End of World War I and Its Effects on Philanthropy

World War I encouraged a culture of philanthropy in the United States. The nation was ready to give, but after the war was won, the people had lost the cause to which they were accustomed to giving. War chests across the country quickly turned into community chests and raised millions of dollars. In 1918 the group that would call themselves the Association of Community Chests in 1933 came together "(1) to provide service to local chests, councils and funds, (2) to organize and direct a national public relations program . . . (3) to provide national leadership in the field of health and welfare" (Cutlip, 1965, p. 223).

At the war's end, John Price Jones entered the philanthropy business. Jones established a firm that married fundraising and the art of public relations. He took a very businesslike approach to fundraising and spent countless hours keeping records and doing paperwork. He was a star in his field, and his counsel was sought on nearly all of the major fundraising campaigns of his time. The Price firm handled campaigns for Harvard, Johns Hopkins, a controversial cathedral project in the 1920s, community chest drives, the United Service Organizations for National Defense (USO), and countless other causes (Cutlip, 1965, pp. 245, 284, 307, 317). Jones's emphasis on understanding donors and developing communication messages geared toward their needs is an example of the "marketing" orientation in fundraising.

Jones also set a precedent that fundraising firms still follow today, when he moved from collecting a certain percentage of the dollars raised to charging a set fee for services regardless of funds raised (Cutlip, 1965, p. 164). When Jones sold his firm in 1955, he "had directed money appeals netting $836,380,351, of which $746,625,351 was given to philanthropy" (p. 170). The increase in philanthropic options and appeals created the need for a body to check the validity of the many requests for funding. During the war this concern was met by the National Investigation Bureau of War Charities. In 1919 the bureau changed its name to the National Information Bureau (NIB). The NIB was funded by membership dues and donations. The bureau, although started with the best of intentions, struggled to fulfill its purpose when an unmanageable amount of new appeals were made (p. 224).

Philanthropy's Fight Against the Great Depression

Up until the stock market crash of 1929, philanthropy had been growing rapidly. As more and more men and women lost their jobs, the need for health and human service agencies increased dramatically, but the lack of income created a major challenge for fundraisers. In fiscal year 1929, the American Red Cross received $4,554,000. Two years later, after the Great Depression began to run its course on the economics of the nation, the ARC would bring in less than half of that amount (Cutlip, 1965, p. 383).

In 1935, during a desperate time of need, tax reforms were passed that would change the face of corporate philanthropy. The legislation stated that a corporation could deduct 5% of its net income (Cutlip, 1965, p. 325). These reforms freed corporations to give to any cause, without having to prove that the donation directly supported their own employees. The effects of this tax reform would become exceptional during the economic boom after World War II.

FDR's Fight Against Polio: Creative Fundraising

President Roosevelt became famous for his New Deal plans, which helped restore the nation's economy. Roosevelt is also recognized for helping end the fight against polio. Roosevelt had been stricken with polio as a child and was committed to funding paralysis research and treatment. The Roosevelt campaigns were innovative, led by Carly Byior and Henry Daugherty. The first major campaign was a series of presidential birthday balls across the nation with the slogan "Dance so that a child can walk." In the first year there were 6,000 events in 3,600 communities (Cutlip, 1965, p. 366). The balls were highly publicized, and during later years they were attended by Hollywood stars. The events also introduced the concept of sponsored advertising.

As the popularity of the birthday balls began to wane, Byior and Daugherty retired from the project, and two new fundraisers took over, Basil O'Connor and Keith Morgan. O'Connor and Morgan knew that the birthday ball needed to be replaced by a new idea. In an effort to remove the president from the center of the campaign, Roosevelt established the National Foundation for Infantile Paralysis. As O'Connor and Morgan and their publicists brainstormed new ideas, Eddie Cantor suggested the March of Dimes concept (Cutlip, 1965, p. 385). The March of Dimes campaign requested that the households across the nation send in their dimes to support the National Foundation for Infant Paralysis. In the first year of the campaign, 1938, $268,000 in dimes was sent to the White House (Cutlip, 1965, p. 386).

Out of the Depression into World War II

In World War II, campaign fundraisers were well equipped with the lessons of World War I and the Great Depression. Community chests turned back into war chests, and the American Red Cross was organized to provide for the needs of wartime. In 1940 the YMCA, the YWCA, the National Catholic Community Service, the Salvation Army, and the Jewish Welfare Board established the United Service Organizations for National Defense (USO). The USO followed in the tradition of reducing appeals, reducing volunteer energy, and streamlining the fundraising process. Many campaigns were also launched to raise funds to alleviate the needs of the other countries involved in the war.

World War II also brought the benefits of a wartime economy. This led to more and more individuals and corporations taking full advantage of the tax deductions, which meant increased philanthropy. "Suddenly, millions of Americans were paying income tax, and they had a motivation to shelter some of their wealth from the Internal Revenue Service by making donations to charity. By 1945, the last year of World War II, charitable contributions reported in income-tax returns were five times as large as they were in 1939" (Billitteri, 2000, ¶ 25).

The Growth and Abuse of Foundations

"In the 1940s and '50s, thousands of private foundations were established by wealthy individuals, ostensibly to contribute money to charitable causes. . . . While some foundations rose to distinction, many were little more than abusive tax shelters" (Billitteri, 2000, ¶ 36). There were also complaints that the individuals and families behind these foundations wielded too much power (¶ 41). One of the most infamous foundation scandals was the National Kids' Day Foundation, headed up by Abraham Koolish. The foundation's mission was to promote the celebration of National Kids' Day. Of the nearly $4 million raised, only 7.5% was used to fulfill the mission of the foundation. Eighty-two percent went to fundraisers. The foundation raised its dollars mailing out unsolicited items and asking for donations in return. The foundation was also found guilty of using celebrity names without permission to grow its publicity. The foundation had to face a committee of the New York legislature called the Tompkins Committee (created in 1953) and was eventually forced to shut down (Cutlip, 1965, pp. 444–445).

The difficulty of accountability in foundations continued to plague the government and nonprofit world for the next several decades. A major breakthrough was the Tax Reform Act of 1969. The act forced foundations to redistribute a percentage of their assets each year and prevented individuals from using foundations for their own gain (Billitteri, 2005).

Creating a Fundraising Profession

The fundraising profession in the United States really grew and developed during the second half of the twentieth century. Since the 1960s, many organizations began to hire full-time fundraisers instead of hiring consultants to run campaigns. Consultants continued to be used for feasibility studies and other short-term projects. As the profession grew, several important organizations were set up to protect and advance the field and study of philanthropy, including the Association of Fundraising Professionals (AFP), the Association for Healthcare Philanthropy (AHP), Independent Sector (IS), the Association for Research on Nonprofit Organizations and Voluntary Action (ARNOVA), and the Council for the Advancement and Support of Education (CASE).

The professionalization of fundraising can be demonstrated by several key indicators. A jointly held ethical statement (Donor Bill of Rights) sets the foundation for behavior within the profession. Membership in AFP, for example, requires the participant to agree to commonly held ethical practices and principles. Members have been dismissed from the association for ethical breaches through action of an ethics committee of peers. Also, there are now graduate-level programs that concentrate on fundraising at the master's level and at least one doctoral program in philanthropy (at the Center on Philanthropy at Indiana University–Purdue University at Indianapolis). Finally, a body of theoretical and practical knowledge is developing around the topics of fundraising and philanthropy to guide the future growth and record the history of ideas and practices within this new profession.

REFERENCES

Alumni Association. (n.d.). History. Retrieved January 28, 2006, from http://www.alumnifriends .mines.edu/Alumni/history/default.htm

Andrew Carnegie. (2006). Retrieved January 29, 2006, from http://en.wikipedia.org/wiki/ Andrew_Carnegie

Billitteri, T. J. (2000, January 13). Donors big and small propelled philanthropy in the 20th century. *Chronicle of Philanthropy* [electronic version]. Retrieved September 19, 2006, from http://philanthropy.com/premium/articles/v12/i06/06002901.htm

Billitteri, T. J. (2005). Money, mission, and the payout rule: In search of a strategic approach to foundation spending. *Nonprofit Sector Research Fund Working Paper Series*. Washington, DC: The Aspen Institute.

Bremner, R. H. (1960). *American philanthropy*. Chicago: University of Chicago Press.

Chernow, R. (1998). Blessed barons. *Time, 152*(23), 74–75.

Constantelos, D. J. (2003). Women and philanthropy in the history of Hellenism. Retrieved January 28, 2006, from http://www.goarch.org/en/ourfaith/articles/article8144.asp

Cutlip, S. M. (1965). Fund raising in the United States: Its role in American philanthropy. Rahway, NJ: Quinn and Boden.

Gifts and debts: Ritual economy in pre-modern and early modern Japanese society. (2000, March 9–12). Presented at Association for Asian Studies Annual Meeting, March 9–12, San Diego, CA. Retrieved January 28, 2006, from http://www.aasianst.org/absts/2000abst/ Japan/J-49.htm

Japan: History of the third sector. (2005). Retrieved January 28, 2006, from http://www .asianphilanthropy.org/countries/japan/history_third.html

Jay Cooke. (2005). Retrieved January 28, 2006, from http://en.wikipedia.org/wiki/Jay_Cooke

John D. Rockefeller. (2008). Retrieved February 14, 2008, from Encyclopedia Britannica Online Web site, http://search.eb.com/eb/article-9063982

Five Colleges, Inc. (1997). John M. Greene. Retrieved February 9, 2008, from http://www.smith .edu/libraries/ca/sophia/greene/greene.htm

Klein, K. (2006). You should have a will. Retrieved January 28, 2006, from http://www.crossroadsfund .org/YouShouldHaveWill.html

Mullin, R. (2007). Two thousand years of disreputable history. In J. Mordaunt and R. Paton (Eds.), *Thoughtful fundraising: Concepts, issues, and perspectives* (pp. 9–18). New York: Routledge.

Prometheus. (2008). Retrieved February 14, 2008, from Encyclopedia Britannica Online: http://search.eb.com/eb/article-9061532

Responding to the challenges of the 21st century. (2006, November). Retrieved February 10, 2008, from http://www.rockfound.org/about_us/news/2006/111006responding.shtml

Riss, R. (1996). The drift from Christian culture consensus in Western culture. Retrieved January 28, 2006, from http://www.grmi.org/renewal/Richard_Riss/evidences2/01drift.html

Thailand: History of philanthropy. (2005). Retrieved April 28, 2006, from http://www .asianphilanthropy.org/countries/thailand/history_phi.html

Vietnam: History of philanthropy. (2005). Retrieved January 28, 2006, from http://www .asianphilanthropy.org/countries/vietnam/history_phi.html

Weidmann, K. T. (2003, Summer). Hail to philanthropy! [electronic version]. Retrieved January 27, 2009, from www.martsandlundy.com/pdf/counsel/2003summer.pdf

Williams College. (2008). About Williams. Retrieved October 18, 2008, from http://www .williams.edu/home/fast_facts/

Wooster, M. M. (2000, May/June). The birth of big time fundraising and the rise of national non-profits. *Philanthropy Roundtable*. Retrieved January 31, 2006, from www.philanthropyroundtable.org/magazines/2000-05/wooster.htm

Wooster, M. M. (2006, May 1). The greatest 20th-century donor you've never heard of. Retrieved February 17, 2008, from www.philanthropyroundtable.org/printarticle.asp?article=1219

chapter five

Theories of Fundraising

Fundraising theory has developed along many different fronts over the past several years. From among the fields of management, marketing, organizational behavior, economics, sociology, and psychology, informed practitioners and academic researchers developed the theories of fundraising. The concepts help to guide practice. In contrast, understanding practice drives further development of theory. It is a two-way street. This chapter will touch on just some of the theory that has emerged and will present a case for how the theory might best inform fundraising process and practice.

In addressing the professional and scholarly interest in developing theories of the nonprofit sector, Lohmann (1992) notes that the nonprofit sector needs a "general paradigm or theoretical model to unify and bring some conceptual order to the whole" to address the problem of defining the nonprofit sector and its various practices, including that of fundraising (p. 311). His suggestion is to unify the name of the sector under the structural term *commons* (referring to "civil society") or *common goods* as an "associated term for labeling the goals, objectives, purposes, outputs, outcomes, products, and results of the sector . . . that are uncoerced, that are associated with shared purposes and pooled resources, and that engender a sense of mutual-ity (we often say community) and fairness (or justice)" (pp. 312, 320).

Public goods are defined as goods that are available to everyone in the country and provided for via taxes, while *private goods* are available to a private individual willing to pay something in exchange for the goods. The term *common goods* describes goods available only to a particular group of individuals through the funding of individuals interested in that particular cause. This conceptual framework is known as the theory of the commons. The theory of the commons can be applied directly to fundraising. It lets the fundraisers understand that not everyone they meet is a potential donor, since not everyone is concerned about their particular cause. Not everyone is in your "commons." Sitting on the street holding a tin cup for those passing by does not usually make sense in light of the theory of the commons. People associated with a particular commons should be asked to support that commons. The exception might be those motivated by the economists' concept of a "warm glow," which will be explained later in this chapter. Such a donor would receive a good feeling from giving to any cause, not any particular cause.

SYSTEMS THEORY

Systems theory, the primary paradigm governing nonprofit management, is a theory of organizational management synthesized from multiple disciplines: management, sociology, psychology, and communication. Kelly (1998) asserts that systems theory provides a foundation for a conceptual framework for fundraising. Systems theory demonstrates that "Organizations do not exist in isolation but are part of larger social, economic, and political systems that affect and are affected by the organization's behavior. How an organization operates in relation to its environment (i.e., the larger system of which it is a part) determines its success and survival. . . . Systems theory provides the 'reason for being' of fund raisers and legitimizes the practice" (p. 325).

Organizations adopt either an open or closed system orientation, determined by the amount of interaction and adaptation an organization undergoes in response to its environments, both general and specific. The general environment is made up of larger factors, such as changes in the economy. A specific environment might be that of the pressure an organization's constituencies or stakeholders put on it, which is unique to each organization. Most specialists believe that the health and even the survival of an organization depend on its ability to change in response to changing environmental factors. An organization that adopts an open system will respond to its vari-

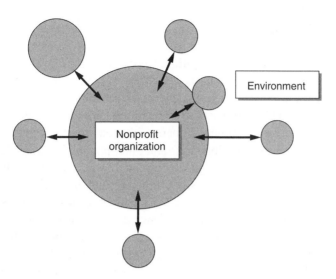

Figure 5-1. Open system

ous environments, and one that is closed would be insensitive to these factors, either deliberately or because of a lack of knowledge on the part of its management. Open systems result in the interdependence of an organization and its environment (see **Figure 5-1**). An organization is dependent on or controlled by those that provide its resources. The amount of control or its opposite, the degree of autonomy, is negotiable. Organizational effectiveness is based on how well an organization satisfies the needs and interests of those in its environment from whom it requires resources and support for operations (Kelly, 1998).

Tempel (1991) applies systems theory specifically to fundraising, asserting that "For an organization to be successful in fund raising, it must be connected to its external environment. It must understand the changing needs of that environment and its facility to respond to the organization's need for human and financial resources to remain functional. The organization must have management structures in place that interpret its mission in relation to changing external needs" (pp. 19–20).

Thus, the relative degree of open or closed system an organization adopts directly affects its fundraising ability, according to Tempel. Those that choose to be independent of external environmental factors, or adopt a closed system, usually do so because they have "strong institutional value systems that they wish to perpetuate" (1991, p. 20). Tempel notes the example of religious organizations or those organizations that are considered controversial by the public, who choose to operate as closed systems in order to maintain the support of their constituencies who share their beliefs and values in spite of the general public's possible disapproval. In this case, a closed system is an organizational strength.

However, a closed system is more often a liability to an organization. In the desire for stability and security, in the resistance to change, an organization might ignore environmental changes that call for organizational changes and may result in a loss of donations and other possible revenue. Tempel gives the example of higher-education institutions, "where the label 'ivory tower' describes colleges and universities that are out of touch with the world beyond the institution" (1991, p. 20). The effect of this closed system would eventually be loss of "a hospitable and supportive environment for supplies of human, fiscal, and material resources, as well as for consumption of goods and services" (p. 20). In other words, a closed system might result in loss of resources due to lack of need or desire for its products and services, as a result of insensitivity to environmental change. Thus, Tempel believes that to function effectively, organizations "must continually monitor the environment and either adapt to changes or attempt to change inhospitable elements in the environment" (pp. 20–21). Failure to do so risks the ability to attract support or even to offer services and goods that are desired or needed.

Successful fundraising depends on an open system to enable an organization to keep current with change and with need, and thus to continue to draw support. As Tempel also notes, however, an organization should not drift away from its mission in order to meet donor demands. Doing so might result in changing institutional values to the extent that future operation is jeopardized. Instead, an organization should remain "in harmony" with its mission and values but include its constituents and potential donors in its affairs, in the "life and spirit of the organization" (1991, p. 21), in order to respond to changing environmental needs. In sum, Tempel believes:

> Fund raising is an effective test of organizational viability. As such, fund raising can become the catalyst for organizational renewal and commitment. To be successful in fund raising, the organization must be viewed by potential supporters as responsive in its delivery of quality services. These services must be provided in an effective and efficient manner to constituents. Potential supporters must understand and accept the value systems that affect these services. An organization that lacks internal meaning has no basis for stimulating philanthropy. (p. 22)

Tempel believes that it is possible to maintain organizational values, even under pressure from external sources, while simultaneously being able to adapt to changing environmental conditions. Fundraisers contribute to the success of this open system because they work so closely with environmental sources. They have a finger on the pulse of environmental changes, and they are in an excellent position to respond to these changes effectively.

Systems theory provides a great backdrop or grounding to many of the theories of fundraising that will be discussed in this text. The interdependencies of external and internal components of the system within a fundraising context are handled by professional fundraisers. Their role is to make sure the donor and organization are held together in a mutually beneficial way and to realize that every gift received comes with a relationship that needs to be monitored and nourished. The relationship mentioned here can also be thought of as an exchange between donor and recipient organization. This theory of social exchange builds on the concept of system theory.

SOCIAL EXCHANGE THEORY

Social exchange theory adapted to the world of fundraising builds on the basic idea of systems theory by concentrating on the donor and the organization as two components of a subsystem. The donor provides financial support to the organization, but the organization is not just the quiet and nonresponsive recipient. The organization provides nonfinancial, yet important, rewards to the donor. A warm feeling in the heart, prestige among peers, increased self-esteem, recognition plaques, and other satisfactions are provided by the organization to complete the exchange. When the social exchange gets into an ongoing pattern, it represents the relationship fundraising that was discussed in Chapter 1. Mixer (1993) extends the definition of social exchange theory within the context of fundraising in the following way:

> The process of giving involves a circumstance in which individual prospects and donors have needs and desires that can be defined as internal motivations and that can be activated or channeled by external influences. The circumstance also includes recipients— individuals or organizations—with desires and needs that can be met in part by gifts. The transactions between the givers and the recipients are triggered by an argument or case for support, and result in what Blau (1968) calls *social exchange*. (p. 9)

Social exchange theory aligns with two principal concepts, discussed below.

Grants Economics

According to economist Kenneth Boulding (1973), financial transactions are most familiar to us as two-way transfers, where money is exchanged in return for goods or services. Boulding considers all two-way transfers as an exchange (p. 1). A one-way transfer or grant, however, is a "change in ownership of economic goods from a donor to a recipient" (p. 1). Boulding believes this one-way transfer to be "a significant element in social life" and one "whose importance has been growing rapidly" (p. 1).

Boulding places this grant transfer on a spectrum, one end being an internal transfer within an organization within the organizing framework of a budget, and the other end the gift, or "grant made out of benevolence" (1973, p. 4) from donor to recipient. In the case of such a grant, Boulding says: "There is no discernible organization that unites the donor and the recipients, there is certainly no hierarchical relationship by which the donor can give conditional grants. However, even though there is no organization of clear structure, there must be something of a sense of community, even if the community is as vague as the common humanity that unites the donor and the recipients" (p. 4).

At the opposite extreme of the gift is the tribute or "grant made out of fear and under threat" (Boulding, 1973, p. 4). In other words, there are two motivations for grants, and most grants are made through a mixture of these two motivations (e.g., not being made solely for benevolent reasons nor strictly for malevolent ones—or what Boulding refers to as love and fear). Boulding goes on to argue that the integrative or gift element in grants economics determines "its patterns and structure": "It is to the subtle dynamics of the integrative system—that set of social relations involving status, identity, community, legitimacy, loyalty, love, and trust—that we have to look at if we are to understand the growth and structure of the grants economy" (p. 5).

In more and more instances, it is for these integrative, intangible rewards that donors give to nonprofit organizations and to which recipient organizations must appeal in order to maintain continued support. These are the most powerful internal motivations for donors, the intangible social rewards they seek in exchange for their continued support.

A useful contribution to understanding the grants economy model for purposes of fundraising comes from Brown, Horvath, and Neuberger (1998), who developed a comprehensive classification scheme for all types of grant and exchange transactions. The authors note that grants economics "accepts many different types of motivations: benevolence (altruism) and malevolence, love and fear—as well as self-interest" (p. 20).

Under this new field of study, the term *explicit grant* has become generally recognized as a major type of grant that is a unilateral transfer of material values, as contrasted with the bilateral, reciprocal transfer of material values generally characteristic of the exchange economy (Brown, Horvath, & Neuberger, 1998, p. 20). They define *implicit grants* to be "the difference between existing relative prices and some norm or benchmark, due to differential taxes, subsidies, price fixing, as well as monopoly power" (p. 20). To distinguish a grant from an exchange transaction, they adopt the criterion from Kenneth Boulding's 1981 *Preface to Grants Economics: The Economy of Love and Fear* that "if there is no decrease in the net worth of either party, the transaction is exchange; if there is, it contains some grant element, and is an explicit or implicit grant" (Brown et al., p. 20).

Brown et al. note some intrinsic difficulties with grants economics in comparison to an exchange economy. Whereas there is consumer sovereignty in the market system of an exchange economy, it is not clear who is sovereign in a grants economy—the donor, recipient, or some third party (Brown, Horvath, & Neuberger, 1998, p. 20). Also, pricing is the efficient means of shaping decisions in the exchange economy. The grants economy lacks such an automatic feedback of information to allocate goods and resources. This disadvantage can create the "ignorance trap," in which divergence between the objectives of grants and their actual consequences can go on for a long while and even cause harm. Citing Boulding's *Preface to Grants Economics: The Economy of Love and Fear*, Brown, Horvath, and Neuberger note another potential weakness of the grants economy, the "dependency trap," in which grants designed to serve a temporary need create such a successful adaptation that the need becomes permanent (p. 21). Extending the discussion further within a fundraising context, exchanges can be considered to be on a continuum between those that are exclusively economic in nature and those that are exclusively gift in nature.

Reciprocity

Taking a similar approach, but from a sociological perspective, Blau (1964) explains the concept of social exchange through the lens of reciprocity. Blau (p. 88) cites Homans's (1961) definition of processes of social behavior "as an exchange of activity, tangible or intangible, and more or less rewarding or costly, between at least two persons" (p. 13). Blau distinguishes social from economic exchange through "the unspecified obligations incurred in it and the trust both required for and promoted by it" (Blau, p. 8). Social exchange incorporates the elements of both trust and reciprocity. Blau summarizes his theory:

> The concept of social exchange directs attention to the emergent properties in interpersonal relations and social interaction. A person for whom another has done a service is expected to express his gratitude and return a service when the occasion arises. Failure to express his appreciation and to reciprocate tends to stamp him as an ungrateful man who does not deserve to be helped. If he properly reciprocates, the social rewards the other receives serve as inducements to extend further assistance, and the resulting mutual exchange of services creates a bond between the two. (p. 4)

Blau maintains that although behavior is reinforced by rewards, this psychological process (sharing similarities with behaviorism) is not enough to explain social exchange. Rather, social relations are interdependent, a "joint product of the actions of both individuals" (Blau, 1964, p. 4), and trigger not only relations between individuals but also between groups, "both differentiation of power and peer group ties; conflicts between opposing forces as well as cooperation; both intimate attachments and connections between distant members of a community without direct social contacts" (p. 4). Thus, according to Blau, social exchange has two possible goals or functions: to "establish bonds of friendship and to establish superordination over others" (p. 89). Very often an exchange does both. The process is simple: an individual who "supplies rewarding services to another obligates him" (p. 89). In order to "discharge this obligation" the second person must return the favor or service. The benefits of this reciprocal exchange can be either extrinsic or intrinsic to the association itself, personal or social. If both parties value the rewards gained, they will want to continue the exchange in a relationship based firmly on reciprocity.

Blau points out that social exchange is based on voluntary actions only—it cannot be coerced (in this he differs a bit from Boulding's position that a "gift" or "tribute" is often made out of "fear"). Compliance with certain forms of power must be considered voluntary. For example, Blau notes, "conformity to social pressures tends to entail indirect exchanges" (1964, p. 92). This type of indirect exchange would include charitable donations, which are "exchanged for social approval" from peers (p. 92). In an indirect exchange, the benefits may be diffused and the rewards intangible. The group norm of reciprocity also governs group social exchange "which makes failure to discharge obligations subject to group sanctions" (p. 92). Blau distinguishes his idea of social exchange from Boulding's economic perspective by noting how social exchange differs from economic exchange: "The basic and most crucial distinction is that social exchange entails *unspecified* obligations" (p. 93), unlike in an economic exchange, where money is exchanged for a commodity that has an exact price. Furthermore, there is no formal contract or time limit—it is an exchange based on trust. It "involves the principle that one person does another a favor, and while there is a general expectation of some future return, its exact nature is definitely *not* stipulated in advance" (p. 93). The parties in the transaction do not specify any return or obligation in advance, so there is no quid pro quo exchange, nor are specified time limitations placed upon it. In other words, obligations and their returns are not specified and are left to the discretion of the individuals. Thus, it is an exchange based on trust that others will discharge their obligations sometime in the future, so it requires a trust in social relations.

According to Blau, there are three forms of benefits that result from and generate social exchange. The first, extrinsic benefits, are "detachable from the source that supplies them" (1964, p. 95). These include such things as advice, invitations, assistance, or compliance. The second, intrinsic benefits, can be considered internal motivations like social acceptance and personal attraction. Finally, "rewards that individuals may mutually supply for each other" (p. 100) may include such things as general respect and prestige for an individual that then leads to "compliance with his requests that bestows superior power on him" (p. 100).

The strongest motivating factor, however, is the norm of reciprocity. Lack of reciprocity reinforces social disapproval and "disinclination to do favors . . . as a punitive reaction against a violator of a moral standard" (Blau, 1964, p. 97). An internalized norm of reciprocity also works to make someone feel guilty for failure to discharge obligations, and thus places pressure on someone to do so. Again, trust is key in any social exchange: "Social bonds are fortified by remaining obligated to others as well as by trusting them to discharge their obligations for considerable periods" (p. 99). These bonds form the primary motivation for selfless gestures. As Blau points out, "In the narrow circle of intimates whose approval is highly salient for modern man, the main function of his wealth is that it enables him to be generous in dispensing rewards that help win their approval and sustain their affection" (p. 107). Finally, as applied to fundraising, making generous donations confers high status on the donor and benefits the recipient organization and the community at the same time. "The benefits a modern community derives from charitable and philanthropic donations correspondingly help to sustain the high status of those who make them" (p. 109). These benefactors gain power and status through their gifts because others become obligated to them and dependent on them, thus "subject to their power" (p. 112).

Application to Fundraising

Applying the social exchange theory to fundraising, Mixer (1993) explains that a charitable organization will present its needs and services to a prospect and request funds (see **Figure 5-2**). In return, the prospect recognizes the need favorably with a donation. The recipient organization then must provide "some form of satisfaction" (p. 10) to the donor in order to continue receiving donations. This satisfaction comes in the form of psychological and social recompense. "An enhanced degree of self-esteem, a feeling of achievement, a new status, and a sense of belonging are among the most powerful rewards donors can receive. Giving satisfies donors' fundamental human needs and desires" (p. 11). Additionally, Mixer explains Blau's concept of timing: although a reciprocal reward is not formally acknowledged, "the expectation, however, is that it will be reasonably prompt" (p. 11). This punctuality is a necessity in order to maintain the relationship; donors need to feel their donations are appreciated. Further, as Mixer notes, the relationship of the donor to the recipient organization is strongest when the donor is personally tied to the cause. Any donor with a personal interest in or tie to an organization's mission will be far more likely to sustain this reciprocal relationship. In order to maintain the relationship of exchange, the element of trust must also be present: "Donors trust organizations to be faithful to their stated purposes, and anticipate some report on accomplishments. Likewise, organizations presume that donors, once having made a commitment, will have a continuing concern for the agencies and their work and will continue giving. A mutual interest and trust underlies the relationship" (p. 12). If an organization is fully accountable to its constituencies and to the public trust, it will continue to benefit from donations made in good faith, based on a sense of trust in the organization's integrity.

Social exchange theory, as an element of the larger systems theory, governs the profession and practice of fundraising because it is based on the principles of interpersonal social relations. Successful development profes-

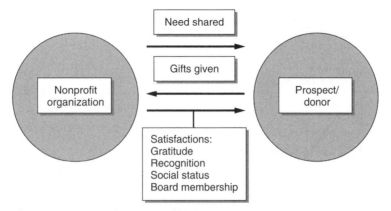

Figure 5-2. Social exchange theory in fundraising. *Source:* Adapted from Mixer (1993, p. 11). Reprinted with permission of John Wiley & Sons, Inc.

sionals know that raising money for an organization is based upon maintaining and, even more, nurturing these interpersonal social relationships. Social exchange depends on an organization's ability to serve its various publics or "commons" by engendering a sense of community in all its constituencies and environments.

Social exchange and the concept of reciprocity can be used in both a manipulative and nonmanipulative way by fundraisers. Cialdini (2003) points out the example of the short-term strategy of the Hare Krishna Society as their members would hand out flowers to people and expect a donation to reciprocate for the action. Eventually people caught on to this manipulation and the society went bankrupt in the United States. Cialdini states:

The good news is that it is not necessary to use the rule in such a manipulative way. Nonprofit leaders can tap the reciprocity rule by uncovering and pointing out the services, benefits, and advantages that having their organization in the community has already provided to potential contributors. To corporate contributors, they can point to the benefits their organization has been providing to the community by making it a better place for the company to be located—making it easier for them to retain good employees and to attract new ones. To individual donors, development directors can point to the services and resources their organization has been providing all along—perhaps the social safety net they have been providing. The savvy nonprofit leader taps the reciprocity rule by describing future support as payback for what their organization has already given. (p. 20)

SOCIAL INTERACTIONS MODEL

Another perspective on social exchange emerged when the innovative economist Gary Becker published the article "A Theory of Social Interactions" in 1974. Becker attempted to integrate sociological and anthropological phenomena into one behavioral theory, including family relationships and the caring for children, criminal behavior, efforts to achieve status in society, and charitable giving. His approach was to take the existing standard body of economic theory about consumer behavior—consumers maximize their utility (satisfaction) by the optimal acquisition of goods and services as constrained by monetary income and the prevailing set of prices—and adding a new variable to the utility function, social income (Becker, 1974, p. 1067). Social income represents the sum of the individual's monetary income plus the value of his or her social environment as reflected in characteristics of other people that affect the individual, which constitute the "social interactions." The individual "spends" his or her social income to obtain such characteristics of others as the love of one's own children, friendships, reputation and esteem, and a reduction in envying others. Even in its pure mathematical form—that is, before empirical estimation, Becker's model predicts that the more a person's social income is determined by his or her social environment, "the more his welfare is determined by the attitudes and behavior of others rather than by his own income" (p. 1070). As an extension, Becker's model predicts that the more the individual's "social income was determined by his social environment, the greater would be the percentage change in his contributions to the characteristics of others as his own income changed" (p. 1072).

After analyzing family interrelations, Becker applied his model to considerations of charity or philanthropy, defined as making "contributions of time or goods to unrelated persons or to organizations" (1974, p. 1083). Becker simplified the motivation for charitable behavior to the "desire to improve the general well-being of recipients," though noting that his theory could also explain charitable motivations based on the "desire to avoid the scorn of others or to receive social acclaim" (p. 1083).

Calling the charitable person and all of the recipients of his charity a synthetic "family," Becker states some of the implications of the model (1974):

> No member's well-being would be affected by a redistribution of income among them, as long as *i* [the donor] continued to give to all of them. For he would simply redistribute his giving until everyone losing income was fully compensated and everyone gaining was fully "taxed." . . . Each member of a synthetic "family" is at least partially "insured" against catastrophes because all other members, in effect, would increase their giving to him until at least part of his loss were replaced. Therefore, charity is a form of self-insurance that is a substitute for market insurance and government transfers. (pp. 1083–1084)

The concept of self-insurance can be applied to donors who give to the local hospital, for example. Even though they don't need the services of the hospital at the moment, they and others in the community often give to the hospital so that it will be available when needed by them and loved ones—extended to the "synthetic family" represented by the community around the hospital.

WARM-GLOW GIVING

Recognizing that "social pressure, guilt, sympathy, or simply a desire for a 'warm glow' may play an important role," Andreoni (1990) specifies a consumer utility function that includes as variables the private goods the individual consumes, x; the total amount of spending on the public good, G; and the individual's gift to the public good, g, as well (p. 465). He points out that the utility function $U = U(x, G)$ is the *purely altruistic* case, since the individual does not care about his or her own gift to the public good. "Happiness" comes from the individual's private consumption and the total public goods available to everyone. The level of the person's own giving to the public good (g) is not in the formula at all. Conversely, he calls $U = U(x, g)$ the *purely egoistic* model, since the individual is motivated to give only by warm glow—the happiness gained from having given an amount to the public good (g). Thus, Andreoni terms $U = U(x, G, g)$ the *impurely altruistic* case (p. 465). Here the model shows that happiness is determined by a combination of the overall provision of public goods (G), the donor's personal level of giving to the public good (g), and the personal private goods purchased by the person (*x*). The terms used in the warm-glow theory (altruistic and egoistic) are not exactly what are used in common speech. The key is understanding the basic motivations: is someone made happy when others are helped, or is someone made happy just knowing that he or she is giving support to a good cause? The egoistic person doesn't care how many are being helped, or how they are being helped, or where they are being helped. He or she just wants to feel good about giving something. The altruist wants to help as many people as possible, not because he or she wants a good feeling, but because he or she wants to help people.

There are public policy implications as well. Suppose one attempted to increase total giving to support a public good by reallocating funds among the population. An income transfer between any two people (dollar for dollar) will increase public giving if and only if the income gainer is more altruistic than the income loser. "Hence, when we take a dollar from someone with low altruism, he is unwilling to reduce *g*, while when we give the dollar to one with high altruism, he is very willing to reduce *g*. The net effect is an increase in total giving" (p. 468).

Andreoni next modifies his impure altruism model so that government subsidizes private giving at a rate *s*, funded by lump sum taxes *t* (1990, p. 468). For the optimal tax treatment of charity, subsidies are categorically superior to direct grants (p. 470). Putting it simply, Andreoni says,

> Individuals are not indifferent between allocations that offer the same mix of public and private goods. Moreover, people are not indifferent between paying for the public good voluntarily (through private donations) or involuntarily (through taxes). Given the choice, people are assumed to prefer to give directly, that is, they prefer the bundle with the most warm glow. . . . Because public giving is an imperfect substitute for private giving, people prefer to make donations directly rather than indirectly. Hence, subsidizing altruistic behavior is more efficient because of the egoistic motive for giving. (pp. 470–471)

As fundraisers, the warm-glow theory provides support for the notion that many potential donors gain a satisfaction from the very act of donating to a public good, regardless of the particular cause. Some people indeed will get a "utility" from dropping a dime in the cup, without really knowing much about the particular cause. This theory does conflict with the theory of the commons to some extent. The wise fundraiser can make use of both ideas.

Certainly the application of the theory of the commons to target prospects is a reasonable approach for the most part, but many donors (the egoistic ones, using Andreoni's term) will gain the warm glow wherever they give. If you are proposing two projects to a prospect, in many cases he or she will get a good feeling from giving to either project—for certain people, charitable giving is charitable giving.

PRESTIGE AND SIGNALING

Building on the work of Becker and Andreoni, Harbaugh (1998) developed a model to incorporate two separate types of benefits one might receive from making charitable donations, the "intrinsic effect" and the "prestige effect" (p. 277). Intrinsic effects reflect how people care about the public good their donations underwrite. Harbaugh notes, however, that significant anonymous (major) gifts are a rarity. In contrast, evidence of the value of recognition in giving is everywhere, in the naming of university buildings, endowed chairs, and the fact that many large gifts are made under a legal contract stipulating how the charity will provide public recognition.

Harbaugh postulates a donor utility function $U = U(x, p, d)$, where x is the private good, p is prestige, and d is the intrinsic benefit, assumed to be equal to the actual amount donated (1998, p. 278). Maximizing the donor's utility subject to a budget constraint, he solved for a utility contour map, which he could use to graphically analyze the effect of the various reporting plans of a charity on prestige and donations. Considering three different plans, Harbaugh found that when no reports are made, the donation is the least, since there is no prestige benefit. In the second case, reporting the exact amount of the gift, the dollar amount increases to the highest utility value where the value of the prestige equals the value of the donation ($p = d$). In the third plan, the charity reports gifts by category, with a minimum lower amount required to gain classification in that category. "Under this plan, the optimal donation depends on preferences and the bracket. . . . A person's optimal donation may be either greater or less than what it would have been under exact reporting" (p. 278).

Harbaugh went on to formulate an econometric model and tested it using income and donations data on donors to the alumni fund of a prestigious law school (1998, pp. 278–280). Overall, the results confirmed his theory, and the model was a good predictor of the number and amount of gifts in each reported bracket. The equation tended to overestimate the number of donations in the lower brackets and underestimate the higher brackets.

Fundraisers utilizing Harbaugh's theory will continue to use the categorical approach to listing donors. His theory predicts that overall giving will increase as donors' need for prestige causes them to give donations, over time, that move the donor to the next highest listing category.

Glazer and Konrad (1996) likewise modified the traditional utility function of the consumer to include more than goods. They include the consumer's income status, which they define as the perception by others of the individual's income net of donations (p. 1021). Such perception is based on observable donations to a charity. As evidence of the desire for status (as opposed to the warm-glow model), they note that relatively few donations are anonymous. Also, when donors' names are made public by dollar amount categories, most gifts tend to be for the minimum qualifying amount. Thus, individuals use giving to signal relative wealth (when the charity publicizes such gifts), perhaps because they prefer to socialize with people of the same or higher social status. Indeed, giving may be superior to the conspicuous consumption of luxury goods, since the target audience may well not notice such acts of extravagant consumption when undertaken in private. Additionally, people may assume that the individual's flashy diamond ring is really cubic zirconium or that an expensive car is really leased.

Glazer and Konrad (1996) go on to explain: "For signaling wealth, people will make donations only when income in the community is heterogeneous. If, for example, everyone at a university has the same income after graduation, then none will make any donations as alumni" (p. 1023). They suggest that a university could increase future donations from rich alumni by increasing the heterogeneity of its student body, say by giving scholarships (p. 1023). Likewise, clubs may elicit donations from members wishing to signal their wealth by lowering fees to poorer members, thereby increasing the heterogeneity of the membership.

Vesterlund (2003) explores the issue of signaling and prestige from an economic perspective. Organizations that announce leadership gifts (for example, in a capital campaign) help to reveal the quality of the organization and influence other prospects to contribute to the fundraising effort. This theoretical work supports the common practice in fundraising of soliciting leadership gifts first before appealing to the rest of the nonprofit organization's constituency.

Duncan's (2004) "impact philanthropy" economic theory presents the idea that certain donors (impact philanthropists) want to personally "make a difference." Such a donor may be motivated to be either the first donor or the last donor in a campaign, as long as it made an impact on the campaign. This contrasts to the idea of "warm glow," where donors are motivated to give by the good feelings they receive from making a gift, not by other donors or the particular cause.

Varian (1994) predicts that contributions will be largest when donors are uninformed of the contributions made by others. This is sometimes referred to as a classic public goods model, where donors will "free ride" off the gifts of others if given the opportunity. List and Lucking-Reiley (2002) expect that as the leadership portion of a campaign (the "seed proportion," using their terminology) nears 100%, the response from donors eventually becomes lower as the amount of seed money increases. This theory assumes that the last group of potential donors are "free riding" on the earlier donors' gifts.

COORIENTATION MODEL

Based on a psychological view of communication, Theodore Newcomb (1953) developed the coorientation model to help understand the relationship between two individuals and some object of communication. The object of communication could be an actual physical object, an event, an ideology, an attitude, a behavior, or some opportunity. Each individual has a perception of the object of communication. One person could really like the object. For example, the person could be very excited about a movie he or she had seen. The other person would also have a perception of that movie. The second person, however, might strongly dislike the movie, even as the first person strongly liked the movie. If there is a relationship between the two individuals, their mixed perceptions will cause a tension and demand increased communication. Either their relationship will suffer or they will tend to be willing to moderate their perception of the object of communication. In our movie example, if the two people are best friends, they will talk and each will feel the pressure to agree with their friend about the movie. In order to maintain a strong friendship, they will take time to increase communication and may end up convincing each other to change their minds about their evaluation of the movie. Conversely, if the friends continue to hold opposite views of the object of communication, their friendship will weaken and the level of communication will decrease in order for equilibrium to occur.

The coorientation model is useful in fundraising since it helps define relationships among the fundraiser, donor, and fundraising opportunity. If the fundraiser (A) and the donor (B) have positive relationships, and the

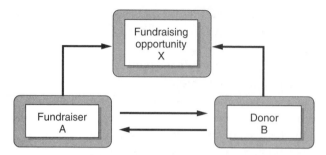

Figure 5-3. Coorientation model applied to fundraising

fundraiser has a positive feeling about the fundraising opportunity (X), then the theory predicts that the system must balance. Either B will also move to a positive feeling about the fundraising opportunity, or B will move to a negative feeling about the fundraiser. This theory supports the importance of maintaining and building a strong relationship between the fundraiser and the donor as fundraising opportunities develop. **Figure 5-3** illustrates this particular application.

PERSUASION THEORY

Cialdini (2003) provides us with a theory of persuasion that takes the form of several rules for dealing with potential donors. The first rule, reciprocity, was discussed earlier in this chapter. The second is the rule of scarcity. Cialdini states:

> While scarcity is commonly thought of as consuming products or services in limited supply, development directors can also take advantage of the scarcity rule by uncovering and describing their organization's uncommon or unique features that cannot be found elsewhere. If an organization is the only one in a given country, or even a given city, providing a needed service, development officers can and should let potential donors know this. Giving to such an organization may make donors feel special and privy to something few are part of. And directors should stress how a particular fundraising campaign will facilitate that uniqueness. (p. 22)

This rule can be applied, for example, with matching gifts, where there is a deadline for participation or a level of gift that can be applied to the match. Or in a capital campaign the leadership gifts for naming a facility are available only in limited quantities. Only one donor gets to put his or her name on the building in most cases.

The third rule is credibility. People who have credibility are more persuasive. Cialdini reports research that shows credibility as consisting of two features: knowledge and trustworthiness. He states: "A credible expert is first of all knowledgeable, but also can be trusted to provide information in a way that is honest and not self-serving. Both factors are important, but of the two, it is usually more difficult to establish trustworthiness. Even acknowledged experts will not be persuasive unless they are also viewed as trustworthy" (Caildini, 2003, p. 24). An organization can be more credible if it confronts the negative aspects of an issue up front. Make clear what the difficulties are in a transparent manner and then follow up with the strengths of the funding proposal.

Finally, the rule of consistency helps persuade. Once a person makes a stand on an issue and declares his or her intention, the person feels compelled to be consistent with the declaration. "Research indicates that a person's sense of commitment deepens even further if the commitment is made voluntarily and publicly, and if it is written. Donors, for example, are much more likely to fulfill pledges that are uncoerced, public, and put in ink" (Cialdini, 2003, p. 25). This concept extends to the idea of establishing fundraising committees for soliciting gifts. Once a person agrees to be on a committee, he or she tends to take on the roles associated with the committee, including soliciting others for donations to the fundraising opportunity. When the members of the committee divide up the list of prospects and "take on assignments" in a public way during the meeting, they tend to keep their commitments.

MARKETING EXCHANGE

Many marketing concepts from the for-profit setting are useful to fundraisers, as mentioned in Chapter 1. The concept of exchange is fundamental to marketing and can be more clearly understood for use by fundraising professionals following the discussion of social exchange earlier in this chapter. Instead of thinking of exchanges as either being totally economic or totally social, fundraisers need to understand that there is a continuum from a sales transaction to a gift transaction. Activities such as special event dinners and

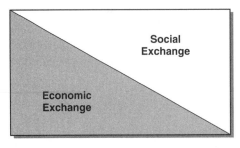

| Sale (museum shop; candy sale) | Mixed motive (carnival; fundraising dinner; corporate sponsorship) | Gift (cash, in-kind, corporate, and foundation grants) |

Figure 5-4. Exchanges

corporate sponsorships that include advertising are really combinations of sales and gifts. Fundraisers should work toward having the donor develop as strong a gift exchange relationship as possible to prevent confusion with a "sales customer" relationship. **Figure 5-4** provides a way to conceptualize this idea.

LIFETIME VALUE

Lifetime value is "essentially a measure of how much a donor will be worth to an organization over the duration of the relationship" (Sargeant & Jay, 2004, p. 161). Since fundraising is a relationship business, it is crucial to consider longer-term results rather than to concentrate only on the particular gift that might be generated by a single mailing, phone call, or visit. Lifetime value is a bit tricky to calculate, but it consists of the sum of a donor's net annual contribution (including discounting the value of future contributions) over the number of years of the expected relationship. A historical analysis provides the baseline for projecting into the future. The more years that are projected, the more difficult it is to determine a reasonable estimate. Extending the concept to planned gifts (e.g., charitable remainder trusts) and bequests is not suggested unless the organization has an ability to predict these gifts accurately (Sargeant & Jay, 2004). Lifetime value analysis can be used to assist with several key management decisions: "establishing acquisition budgets, choosing media for initial donor acquisition, determining development strategies, and investing in the reactivation of lapsed donors" (p. 168).

REFERENCES

Andreoni, A. (1990). Impure altruism and donations to public goods: A theory of warm-glow giving. *Economic Journal, 100*, 464–477.

Becker, G. (1974). A theory of social interactions. *Journal of Political Economy, 82*, 1063–1093.

Blau, P. M. (1964). *Exchange and power in social life*. New York: John Wiley & Sons.

Blau, P. M. (1968). Social exchange. In D. L. Sills (Ed.), *International Encyclopedia of the Social Sciences*. New York: Macmillan.

Boulding, K. E. (1973). *The economy of love and fear: A preface to grants economics*. Belmont, CA: Wadsworth.

Boulding, K. E. (1981). *Preface to grants economics: The economy of love and fear*. New York: Praeger.

Brown, A. A., Horvath, J., & Neuberger, E. (1998). The economics of grants and exchange: The transactions matrix. *American Economist, 42*(2), 19–33.

Brown, A. A., & Neuberger, E. (1986). Grants and exchange from a comparative systems perspective. *American Economist, 30*(2), 14–21.

Cialdini, R. B. (2003). The power of persuasion: Putting the science of influence to work in fundraising. *Stanford Social Innovation Review, 1*(2), 8–27.

Duncan, B. (2004). A theory of impact philanthropy. *Journal of Public Economics, 88*, 2159–2180.

Glazer, A., & Konrad, K. (1996, September). A signaling explanation for charity. *American Economic Review, 86*(4), 1019–1028.

Harbaugh, W. (1998). The prestige motive for making charitable transfers. *American Economic Review, 88*, 277–282.

Homans, G. C. (1961). *Social Behavior*. New York: Harcourt, Brace and World.

Kelly, K. S. (1998). *Effective fund-raising management*. Mahwah, NJ: Lawrence Erlbaum Associates.

List, J. A., & Lucking-Reiley, D. (2002). The effects of seed money and refunds on charitable giving: Experimental evidence from a university capital campaign. *Journal of Political Economy, 110*(1), 215–233.

Lohmann, R. A. (1992). The commons: A multidisciplinary approach to nonprofit organization, voluntary action, and philanthropy. *Nonprofit and Voluntary Sector Quarterly, 21*(3), 309–324.

Mixer, J. R. (1993). *Principles of professional fundraising: Useful foundations for successful practice*. San Francisco, CA: Jossey-Bass.

Newcomb, T. M. (1953). An approach to the study of communicative acts. *Psychological Review, 60*(6), 393–404.

Sargeant, A., & Jay, E. (2004). *Building donor loyalty*. San Francisco, CA: Jossey-Bass.

Tempel, E. R. (1991). Assessing organizational strengths and vulnerabilities. In H. A. Rosso & Associates, *Achieving excellence in fundraising: A comprehensive guide to principles, strategies and methods* (pp. 19–27). San Francisco, CA: Jossey-Bass.

Varian, H. R. (1994). Sequential provision of public goods. *Journal of Public Economics, 53*, 165–186.

Vesterlund, L. (2003). The informational value of sequential fundraising, *Journal of Public Economics, 87*, 627–657.

chapter *six*

Government Regulation of Fundraising and Charitable Giving

Fundraising involves building relationships between donors and nonprofit organizations, and government regulation provides some of the basic ground rules that form the legal context of those relationships. The federal government, state governments, and even some local municipal governments have set up regulations that provide for the creation and categorization of nonprofit organizations, the solicitation of the public, and rules for handling charitable gifts. Understanding these basic regulations is critical for understanding the fundraising process. Understanding donors' tax consequences when making charitable gifts is important in developing gift proposals that meet donors' needs.

Keep in mind that the legal context changes often and occasionally quite dramatically. The Pension Protection Act of 2006, for example, now requires donors to document charitable gifts under $250 using a canceled check or a receipt from the organization. It also sets up new rules for supporting organizations (defined later in this chapter). Future changes may involve rollover legislation for individual retirement accounts (IRAs), allowing certain people to convert their IRAs directly to charitable gifts. This was a feature of the Pension Protection Act of 2006, but it expired after a trial period. Rules regulating the estate tax will also certainly change. The current legislation is set to expire in 2010 and come leaping back the following year with a $1 million exemption and a 55% tax rate. Of course, tax law is subject to change and is continually evolving. Refer to the IRS Web site (http://www.irs.gov/) to verify specific information found in this chapter. Keeping up to date on IRS rules for both donors and nonprofits is essential for fundraisers as they work with donors to achieve their philanthropic goals.

FEDERAL, STATE, AND LOCAL REGULATION OF FUNDRAISING

State and local regulation of fundraising involves requiring nonprofit organizations to register before starting to solicit gifts. Registering usually involves a fee. National organizations that solicit donations across the United States are required to register in each state where they intend to solicit gifts. Certain organizations, such as churches and those with very small fundraising programs, are exempt from this regulation. For-profit companies that solicit gifts or individual fundraising consultants are typically required to register in the state where they are working. Professional fundraisers are consultants who work with a charity on fundraising but do not solicit gifts directly. Paid solicitors are outside people hired to solicit gifts. In addition, paid solicitors are often required to post a bond, since they usually handle the gifts and divide the funds received between themselves and the charity.

Although each state may have different requirements for regulation of fundraising, over the years the states have developed a set of statutes that results in somewhat similar treatment of fundraising across the nation. According to the Online Compendium of Federal and State Regulations for U.S. Nonprofit Organizations (1999),

The Model Charitable Solicitations Act is a comprehensive set of statutes offered for adoption by states to regulate charitable solicitations conducted within their jurisdictions. It was developed by the National Association of Attorneys General (NAAG), the National Association of State Charity Officials (NASCO), and a Private Sector Advisory Group (composed of representatives from the nonprofit sector who were not directly affiliated with the two sponsoring organizations). It was completed in 1986 and there have been no updates. Unfortunately, the original Model Charitable Solicitations Act included several serious flaws. Two of its provisions have been struck down by the U.S. Supreme Court as unconstitutional, specifically, the requirements that professional solicitors register with the state and that certain financial details of service contracts be disclosed as part of any professional solicitation. . . . Consequently, most of the states that adopted the model act have modified their requirements for professional solicitor registration and solicitation disclosures to accommodate the Supreme Court decisions. (p. 7)

There is not a consensus among the states of what is the appropriate amount of nonprofit organizational disclosure or reporting. "Along with annual state filings, nonprofits may be required to file audited financial statements once they exceed an asset or revenue threshold" (Keating & Frumkin, 2003, p. 8). As of 2003, out of 50 states, 21 required audited financial statements along with Internal Revenue Service (IRS) Form 990, 14 required only Form 990, 2 required either Form 990 or audited financial statements, and 13 required no charitable financial reporting at all (p. 8).

States are beginning to get more involved in standardizing regulation forms. The Unified Registration Statement (URS) represents a joint effort by the National Association of State Charities Officials and the National Association of Attorneys General that provides standardized, simplified, and efficient compliance of nonprofits under states' solicitation laws. As of 2003, 32 states plus the District of Columbia have agreed to accept the URS in place of their unique state forms (Keating & Frumkin, 2003, p. 8).

Specific regulations for each particular state and certain local communities are not included in this book. The IRS provides links to state information (http://www.irs.gov/charities/article/0,,id=129028,00.html). You can also look up the particular regulations for your state and local communities directly. For example, Georgia's Web site is at http://www.sos.ga.gov/securities/. The rest of this chapter will focus on federal laws and regulations that involve tax-exempt status, fundraising, and charitable giving.

NONPROFIT ORGANIZATIONS

The term "nonprofit organization" can be confusing, since such an organization is allowed by law to make profits. What defines an organization as nonprofit is a regulation—commonly referred to as the "nondistribution constraint"—that prevents it from distributing the profit to board members, ✸ the chief executive officer, the executive director, or other stakeholders of the organization. This concept is also referred to as "private inurement." Compare this with the for-profit world, where shareholders have the legal right to take profits from the companies they have invested in and use them for their own personal gain via dividends and other means. Fundraisers who take a percentage of a gift as compensation not only may be breaking the ethical standards of the industry, but if the dollar amount involved is big enough, they may be breaking the law as well and risking IRS sanctions.

Setting up a nonprofit organization involves working within the legal context of the state where the organization plans to operate. The document of creation is typically referred to as the articles of incorporation. In the articles, the organization describes its name, officers, board of directors, purpose, and so on. States may include a requirement for other documents such as the bylaws, minutes, and conflict of interest statements (if not within the bylaws). Once established through its home state regulations, the nonprofit may look to the federal government for recognition of tax-exempt status.

Tax-Exempt Organizations

The term *tax-exempt organization* generally refers to nonprofit organizations that are exempt or excused from paying federal income tax under Section 501(c) of the U.S. Internal Revenue Code. There are 27 types of 501(c) tax-exempt organizations, including charities, labor organizations, business leagues, chambers of commerce, real estate boards, fraternal societies, cemetery associations, and veterans' organizations. "What these disparate types of organizations have in common is that they are tax exempt" (Berry, 2005, p. 569). Most nonprofit organizations are tax exempt. Other federal tax exemptions may include excise and employment taxes, and state or local exemptions may include income, sales, use, excise, and property taxes. Several types of tax-exempt organizations are eligible for preferential postal rates. If an organization is exempt under federal law, it is not automatically exempt from state and local taxes. For example, in 2002 the State of New Hampshire denied Pilgrim Pines, a tax-exempt nonprofit Bible camp, a local property tax exemption even though the camp was exempt from federal taxes. In most cases, however, states and local communities will recognize the tax-exempt standing at the federal level.

Charitable Organizations

The term *charitable organization*, as defined by the Internal Revenue Code (IRC), is a tax-exempt nonprofit organization to which gifts are deductible to the donor for income, gift, or estate tax purposes. "It is tax deductibility, not tax exemption, that is the crown jewel because tax deductibility is a significant incentive to donors, and many institutions will only donate to a 501(c)(3)"

(Berry, 2005, p. 569). Fundraisers work mainly for charitable organizations, since donors can deduct some or all of their gifts to these organizations. Although people frequently use the terms *nonprofit*, *tax exempt*, and *chari-* ✳ *table* interchangeably, they are distinct. Charities are subsets of tax-exempt organizations, which are subsets of nonprofit organizations.

To qualify as a charitable organization under IRC Section 501(c)(3), an organization must typically be a corporation, community chest, fund, or foundation. Unincorporated associations may also be eligible in certain situations. Additionally, the organization must operate exclusively for one or more of the following purposes: charitable, religious, educational, scientific, literary, testing for public safety, to foster national or international amateur sports competition (but only if no part of its activities involve providing athletic facilities or equipment), or for the prevention of cruelty to children or animals (IRS, 2008b, p. 19). In addition to the prohibition against private inurement of earnings, the organization must not operate for the benefit of private interests nor participate in political campaigns or substantial lobbying activities.

Private Foundations and Public Charities

Charities are further categorized by whether or not they are private foundations or public charities. Once an organization receives recognition as a charitable tax-exempt organization, the appropriate classification as either a private foundation or a public charity must be determined. The IRS assumes that all Section 501(c)(3) organizations are private foundations unless the organization notifies the IRS within a specified time frame and the IRS recognizes the organization's claim. The organization must fall into one of the categories expressly excluded from the definition of a private foundation to qualify as a public charity. In general, public charities have broad public support or actively support an organization with broad public support (2008b, p. 27). "Since there is no tax advantage to being a private foundation, most charitable organizations strive to rebut this presumption, principally to avoid the private foundation rules, to facilitate maximum charitable contribution deductions, and to escape the more burdensome federal reporting obligations of private foundations" (Hopkins, 2000, p. 111). Supporting organizations, set up to provide exclusive support to a public charity, are themselves public charities but are subject to special IRS rules. An example of these organizations is the University of Illinois Foundation. Although it has the word "foundation" in its title, it is a public charity, not a private foundation. However, its purpose is to support the University of Illinois—hence it is a supporting organization.

Public Charitable Organizations

Although there are fairly complex technical rules for determining status as a public charity, most charitable organizations are public charities. A local nonprofit hospital, a nonprofit university or college, a nonprofit theater, a nonprofit museum, and a nonprofit health clinic are all public charities. Fundraisers typically would work for such organizations. These organizations ask the public to contribute to support in a broad-based way. No one person controls the organization or funds the organization. Fundraisers working with major donors who are planning to make an extremely large "transformational" gift to their organization may want to seek counsel to ensure that the very large gift will not "tip" the organization into the status of a private foundation.

Private Foundations

A *private foundation* is a nonprofit, tax-exempt, charitable organization that does not meet the standards for public charities. A single source usually funds

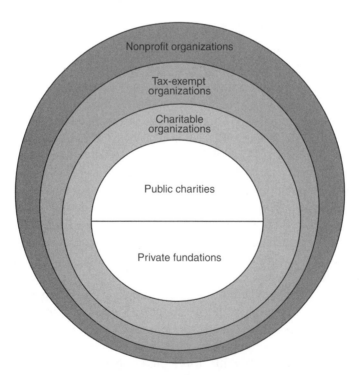

Figure 6-1. Types of nonprofit organizations.

the organization; the organization does not run its own charitable programs; and it uses the income stream from its invested assets for its operations. One distinct characteristic of private foundations is that Section 829 of Public Law 97-34 requires annual distribution of their minimum investment return, statutorily defined as 5%, to other charitable organizations (IRS, 1999). In addition, an excise tax exists on the net investment income of most domestic private foundations. Other rules for private foundations include restrictions on self-dealings between substantial contributors and other disqualified persons, limits on private business holdings, as well as provisions that prioritize the organization's exempt purposes (2008b, p. 27). **Figure 6-1** provides a visual representation of the different types of organizations.

FEDERAL TAX LAW FOR CHARITABLE CONTRIBUTIONS

Disguised as a simple subject, charitable contributions and their deductibility can involve extensive tax and legal regulations. The determination of the availability and amount of a charitable contribution deduction can become quite complex. Deductibility is not limited to gifts to 501(c)(3) organizations. Contributions to government organizations and certain non-charities (e.g., veterans' organizations, fraternal associations, or cemeteries) are also deductible if designated for specific purposes. In addition, both the charitable organization and donor must possess an awareness of their responsibility in recordkeeping. Sometimes the burden lies with the donor to maintain and request documentation for charitable donations, and sometimes the burden lies with the charitable organization to supply such documentation.

Since only approximately one-fourth of all tax filers in the United States even take the charitable deduction, an organization's obligations to provide documentation can seem burdensome for staff. Regardless of legality or amount of effort required, a charitable organization should go beyond what is legally required of it by supplying written documentation that complies with IRS requirements for contributions of any amount. Quality recordkeeping and timeliness in providing donor documentation help to ensure that all aspects of a donor's experiences in contributing remain positive and overall relationships with the organization remain strong.

Charitable Contribution Deductions

According to Hopkins (2000), there are three federal tax deductions: one for income tax, one for estate tax, and one for gift tax. Some counties, cities, and states have charitable deductions as well. The most often used deduction, however, is the federal income tax deduction. IRC Section 170(a)(1) establishes the general rule allowing the federal tax deduction of a charitable contribution made within the taxable year (Charitable, 2007).

In general, to qualify as a charitable contribution under IRC Section 170, a contribution to a charitable organization must be a gift. A gift to a charitable organization involves a transfer with charitable intent of money or property without receipt of adequate consideration (IRS, 2004). Courts use an objective test of the contribution to determine what a charitable contribution is and whether a contested payment was in fact quid pro quo. A *quid pro quo* contribution means that the donor made the payment partly as a contribution and partly in consideration for goods or services received. The U.S. Supreme Court has adopted this objective test, holding that: "The *sine qua non* of a charitable contribution is a transfer of money or property without adequate consideration. The taxpayer, therefore, must at a minimum demonstrate, that he purposely contributed money or property in excess of the value of any benefit he received in return" (*U.S. v. American Bar Endowment*, 477 U.S. 105 (1986), 106 S. Ct. 2426, 58 AFTR2d 86-5190, 86-1 USTC, ¶ 9482, as cited in Arthur Andersen Private Client Services, 1999, pp. 14, 22).

In reaching the decision noted above, the Supreme Court recognized the "dual character" transfer. In other words, if the size of the payment is out of proportion with the benefit received, the transfer may be deductible as a charitable contribution only to the extent that the fair market value exceeds the benefit. Additionally, the transfer may be deductible only if the donor intended the excess amount as a gift.

Income Tax Deductions

As noted earlier, most U.S. taxpayers do not take the charitable gift deduction in calculating their annual tax obligations. Instead, they use the standard deduction, which already contains within it an allowance for some estimated amount of charitable giving. When itemizing and deducting cash gifts to public charities, up to 50% of adjusted gross income may be deducted, while for gifts of appreciated securities, only up to 30% of adjusted gross income may be deducted. If the gifts are to private foundations, the percentages change to 30% and 20%, respectively. In both cases, the deductions may be spread over five additional years, if necessary. There are many other complex rules that tend to be based on a donor's specific circumstance. Fundraisers will not always know the specifics; however, it is helpful to keep in mind three important concepts: (1) donors of very large gifts may not be able to use the entire income tax deduction in a single year, (2) there are huge tax savings from donating appreciated securities and property, and (3) donors should always be advised to consult their accountants regarding specific tax consequences of any major gift.

Estate Tax Deductions

Other than the marital deduction (unlimited estate value may be transferred to a spouse upon his or her death) and the base credit ($2 million deduction equivalent in 2008), the charitable deduction remains essentially the only "game in town" for shielding very large estates from federal estate tax. Estates over that limit are taxed at 45%. As mentioned previously, these numbers will be changing over the coming years. The expectation is for new laws enacted eventually to stabilize the estate tax deduction level. Currently (and expected into the future once Congress takes care of the 2010 dilemma mentioned earlier), donors with very large estates and without a living spouse will be forced either to give to charity or to give to the government upon their death. Understanding this dilemma will help fundraisers as they work with wealthy prospects. Beyond this simple conceptualization of estate tax deduction options lies a very complicated set of rules and regulations regarding estate planning. There are also planned giving instruments used in estate planning, such as Charitable Remainder Unitrusts, Pooled Income Funds, and Charitable Lead Trusts, whose definitions and use can be very complex. Donors should be encouraged to work with their accountants and attorneys as they work their way through the options available to them.

Written Disclosure

As mentioned above, the IRS does not consider a payment to a charitable organization where the payor receives something of equivalent value in return as a gift for charitable deduction purposes. When the payor receives value in return for his or her contribution, it is only deductible as a charitable gift to the extent that the amount transferred exceeds the value received by the donor. The charitable organization must provide *written disclosure* to

Exhibit 6-1 Example of a Quid Pro Quo Contribution

A donor gives a charitable organization $100 in exchange for a concert ticket with a fair market value of $40. In this example, the donor's tax deduction may not exceed $60. Because the donor's payment (quid pro quo contribution) exceeds $75, the charitable organization must furnish a disclosure statement to the donor, even though the deductible amount does not exceed $75.

Source: IRS (2008a, p. 11).

a donor who receives goods or services in exchange for a single payment in excess of $75 (IRS, 2008a, p. 11). See **Exhibit 6-1** for an example.

The required written disclosure that a charitable organization must provide should include two items. First, it must inform the donor that the deductible amount is limited to the excess of the amount paid over the value of the goods or services provided. Second, the written disclosure should provide the donor with a good-faith estimate of the value of the goods and services (Disclosure, 2007). The organization must provide the written disclosure with either the solicitation or receipt of the quid pro quo contribution. In addition to the written requirement, the charitable organization must issue the statement in a manner that is likely to come to the attention of the donor. A penalty of $10 per contribution and a maximum of $5,000 for the event or mailing is imposed for not meeting the written disclosure requirement.

A written disclosure statement is not required in two cases. The first case is where the donative element does not exist in the transaction. For example, in a museum gift shop an individual might purchase an art poster. Such a transaction constitutes a sale and not a receipt of quid pro quo contribution. The second case is where the goods or services provided meet the token exception, membership benefits exception, or the intangible religious benefits exception described below (IRS, 2008a, p. 12).

The token exception involves goods or services that have an insubstantial fair market value. The payment must occur in the context of a fundraising campaign in which a charitable organization informs the donor of the amount of the contribution that is deductible, and

- The fair market value of the benefits cannot exceed the lesser of 2% of the payment or $91 (2008 value, then adjusted for inflation), or
- The payment is at least $45.50 (2008 value, then adjusted for inflation) and the organization provides only token items that bear its name or logo. Token items include mugs, calendars, and posters that fall within the limit

Exhibit 6-2 Example of a Membership Benefits Exception

If a charitable organization offers a $75 annual membership that allows free admission to all of its weekly events, plus a $20 poster, a written acknowledgment need only mention the $20 value of the poster, since the free admission would be considered insubstantial and, therefore, would be disregarded.

Source: IRS (2008a, p. 7).

for "low-cost articles" defined at $9.10 (2008 value, then adjusted for inflation) (IRS, 2008a, p. 5).

The annual membership benefits exception involves an annual payment of $75 with receipt of annual recurring rights or privileges. Such rights or privileges might involve free or discounted admission to the organization's facilities or events, purchase discounts at the organization's gift shop, free or discounted parking, and free or discounted admission to member-only events where a per-person cost is within the "low-cost articles" limits (IRS, 2008a, p. 6). See **Exhibit 6-2** for an example of a membership benefits exception.

The intangible religious benefits exception involves receipt of benefits not usually sold in commercial transactions. Usually, charitable organizations operated exclusively for religious purposes provide such benefits. Examples include admission to religious services as well as de minimis tangible benefits such as the wine used during such services (IRS, 2008a, p. 7).

Written Acknowledgment

A donor is responsible for maintaining adequate records for cash contributions of less than $250. Cash contributions include those paid by cash, check, electronic funds transfer, credit card, or payroll deduction. A donor can use a canceled check or bank record. A receipt from the charitable organization that includes the name of the organization as well as date and amount of the contribution also functions as an adequate record (IRS, 2007a, pp. 17–18).

A donor must obtain a receipt from the charitable organization for a non-cash contribution of less than $250. The receipt must include the name of the organization, date and location of the charitable contribution, as well as a reasonably detailed description of the property. A donor does not need a receipt if it is impractical to obtain one—for example, at an unattended drop site. A donor must also keep written records for each item donated, including the name and address of the charitable organization, date and location of the contribution, a detailed description of the property, cost or other basis of the property, amount claimed as a deduction, and terms of any conditions attached to the donated property (IRS, 2007a, p. 18).

For any single cash contribution of $250 or more, the donor must obtain a contemporaneous, *written acknowledgment* of the gift from the charitable organization. The written acknowledgment must include all of the following: name of organization, amount of cash contribution, description of noncash contribution, statement of whether goods or services were provided, as well as a description and good-faith estimate of the value of goods or services provided. The responsibility to obtain a written acknowledgment rests with the donor; however, charitable organizations can help the donor by providing a timely written document (IRS, 2008a, p. 3).

The definition of contemporaneous involves receipt by the donor of the acknowledgment by the earlier of the date on which the donor files his or her tax return for the year of the contribution or the due date of the return, including extensions. Written acknowledgment can involve either a paper or an electronic copy of the information. In addition, charitable organizations can provide separate acknowledgments for each gift over $250 or an annual summary for several single contributions over $250. Charitable organizations do not need to aggregate separate contributions of less than $250 even though such contributions may summarize to more than $250. For example, a donor does not need to obtain a written acknowledgment of weekly offerings to his or her church even though the annual contribution may sum to more than $250 (IRS, 2008a, pp. 4–5).

A donor who makes a single contribution of more than $250 by payroll deduction may use documentation other than a written acknowledgment. Instead, a donor may substantiate a contribution with both a pay stub or Form W-2 and a pledge card that includes a statement indicating that the organization does not provide goods or services for contributions received by payroll deduction. For purposes of the written acknowledgment threshold, a donor must treat each payroll deduction over $250 as a separate contribution (IRS, 2008a, p. 8).

If a donor renders services to a charitable organization and has out-of-pocket expenses related to those services, the donor may deduct such expenses with the proper written acknowledgment. For example, a donor acts as a guest speaker at a charitable organization's annual convention and pays for his or her plane ticket to the convention without reimbursement. In such a case, the donor must maintain adequate records of the expenditure and obtain a written acknowledgment that includes all of the items required above for written acknowledgments (IRS, 2008a, p. 9).

A donor must obtain an acknowledgment of a noncash contribution of at least $250 but not more than $500. The acknowledgment must contain all of the information required for noncash contributions of less than $250 in addition to including a description of the property, whether goods or services were received, as well as a good-faith estimate of such goods or services. The charitable organization must issue the acknowledgment in writing before the earlier of the date on which the donor files his or her tax return for the year of the contribution or the due date of the return, including extensions. The donor must also keep a written record of each item donated as with noncash contributions of less than $250 (IRS, 2007a, p. 19).

For noncash contributions over $500 but not more than $5,000, a donor must obtain an acknowledgment and written records described above plus records of how the donor got the property, the approximate date the property was received by the donor or the date the property was substantially completed if created, produced, or manufactured by or for the donor, and the cost or other basis of the property (IRS, 2007a, p. 19).

Appraisal Requirements

Donors must provide an additional requirement if the contributed property has a value in excess of $5,000. In general, such contributions require a *qualified appraisal* of the property prepared and signed by a qualified appraiser. The donor must attach the qualified appraisal to Form 8283 of his or her tax return. The qualified appraisal must include detailed information about the appraiser, including qualification, name, address, and taxpayer identification. The qualified appraisal must also include a description of the property and its condition, date of the contribution, terms of any agreement relating to subsequent disposition or use of the property, the appraised fair market value of the property, method for evaluating the property, and a statement that the appraisal was prepared for income tax purposes. A few exceptions to the need for a qualified appraisal exist, including stock publicly traded, stock not publicly traded valued at $10,000 or less, a vehicle, qualified intellectual property, and inventory. Form 8283 is still required for such contributions exempt from the qualified appraisal (IRS, 2007c, pp. 8–10). Special rules were developed for donations of vehicles as a part of the Pension Protection Act of 2006. Only the gross proceeds from the sale of a vehicle can be deducted instead of the fair market value, unless the organization either plans to use the car internally or plans to give the car to a needy individual, or if the value of the deduction is under $500.

✕ Disposition of Contributed Property

[handwritten marginal note: PARTICULAR RETURN]

A charitable organization must file Form 8282 with the IRS if, within three years, it sells, exchanges, consumes, or otherwise disposes of property donated as a charitable contribution and has a value in excess of $500. A charitable organization must file Form 8282 within 125 days after the date of disposition. Information required on the form includes the organization's name, address, and employer identification number. The organization must also make its best effort to provide a description of the property, date received, date original donee received the property, date items were disposed, and amount received in disposal (IRS, 2007d, p. 3).

International Charitable Giving Under U.S. Tax Law

"As economic and cultural globalization advance, charitable giving also increasingly takes on an international complexion because more and more families are establishing personal and financial ties with countries and even continents beyond the borders of their ancestry and original heritage" (Galligan, 2004, p. 151). This section will discuss the general tax rules in connection with international charitable giving and will present the issue of U.S. income tax deductibility for international charitable giving. It is worth mentioning that U.S. deductibility for international giving under transfer tax, as well as special rules applicable to foreign charitable trusts and the U.S. tax treatment of foreign public charities and foreign private foundations, are also relevant aspects of the tax law governing international charitable giving.

"The United States does not permit individuals to claim an income tax deduction for direct contributions to foreign charities" (Galligan, 2004, p. 153). According to Section 170(c)(2):

> When a contribution is made to or for the use of a charitable corporation, trust or community chest, fund or foundation, the donee must have been created or organized in the United States or in any of its possessions or under the laws of the United States, its possessions, the states or the District of Columbia, if the gift is to qualify for the income tax charitable deduction. Thus, the donee must be

> a domestic organization. . . . A domestic organization cannot, however, act as a mere conduit for funds that flow to a foreign organization for ultimate use abroad; in such case, the foreign organization is considered the actual donee and contributions are not allowed as charitable deductions to the donors. (Arthur Andersen Private Client Services, 1999, pp. 20–21)

The IRS has ruled favorably, however, to allow a charitable contribution deduction in the following scenarios:

- A domestic charity conducts various domestic programs. From time to time this domestic charity also makes grants to foreign charities for purposes the domestic charity reviews and approves. Grants are paid from *general* funds of the domestic charity and *no special funds* are raised by solicitation from the public for purposes of the foreign charity. Contributions to this type of domestic charity, the IRS says, are deductible.
- A domestic charity, which conducts charitable activities in a foreign country, forms a *subsidiary* to facilitate its operations there. The foreign charitable subsidiary is completely controlled by the domestic charity. This domestic charity solicits funds to support its activities abroad. Following the formation of the foreign subsidiary, the domestic charity will transmit funds it raises for its foreign activities directly to the subsidiary. Contributions to this domestic charity for its foreign activities, the IRS says, are deductible. (Galligan, 2004, p. 154)

Furthermore, in some cases a contribution by a U.S. citizen or U.S. permanent resident to a foreign donee "may qualify for deduction under the terms of a treaty between the United States and a foreign government" (Arthur Andersen Private Client Services, 1999, p. 20). This is the case of treaty exceptions provided under the U.S.-Canada Income Tax Treaty, the U.S.-Mexico Income Tax Treaty, and the U.S.-Israel Income Tax Treaty (Galligan, 2004, p. 155). All these treaties provide exceptions to the prohibition on deductibility of contributions to foreign charities, including those located in Canada, Mexico, and Israel.

FEDERAL REPORTING REQUIREMENTS: IRS FORM 990

Tax-exempt organizations are obligated to report to the federal government using Form 990 and to allow public access to the form. Form 990 is not a tax return. Although it functions as an informational return in which a tax is never paid, the IRS will apply penalties for failure to file or late filing of a return in the Form 990 series. We will address general aspects of Form 990 and especially its fundraising contents and implications.

> The Form 990 serves multiple purposes. First, it enables the IRS to ascertain that organizations that have been granted tax-exempt status are undertaking those activities for which that status was granted. . . . Second, the Form 990 is a public document that can be obtained by any interested party including the press, potential donors, and the organization's competitors. Additionally, many states require organizations to file the Form 990 as part of the annual charitable registration process (some states even require a Form 990 for organizations that are under the IRS $25,000 filing threshold). (Sorrells & Lang, 2001, p. 5)

The purpose of Form 990 is also to determine whether an organization meets the public support test and other disclosure requirements. Generally, "a charitable organization or other tax-exempt organization must provide a copy [of their Form 990] without charge . . . of all or any part of any return required to be made available for public inspection to any individual who makes a request for the copy" (Hopkins, 2002, p. 262). The organization can charge a minimal copy fee or mailing fee for sending the copy to the person requesting it. Under certain circumstances, the organization can post the document on the Internet. "A tax-exempt organization is not required to comply with requests for copies of the returns by posting them on a World Wide Web Page that the organization has established and maintains" (Hopkins, p. 263).

Form 990 is also supposed to fulfill a function as a tool of accountability to donors and the public. However, this function is not always properly fulfilled. See **Exhibit 6-3** for an excerpt of a study performed by the U.S. General Accounting Office (GAO) dated April 30, 2002.

A study conducted by Krishnan, Yetman, and Yetman (2005) found that "nonprofits do misstate the information on their IRS 990. . . . Many nonprofits that report zero fundraising expenses do in fact incur fundraising expenses" (p. 32). They also found that "nonprofits overstate the amount of program expenses on their IRS 990s" (p. 32). Board members or employees of nonprofits who believe their organization's Form 990 is misrepresenting

Exhibit 6-3 Tax-Exempt Organizations: Improvements Possible in Public, IRS, and State Oversight of Charities

Form 990 disclosures may not give an accurate or complete picture regarding charity spending data, and the public is cautioned that it cannot depend upon this instrument exclusively in order to determine a charity's spending efficiency. The GAO cites two problems with Form 990 expense data:

1. There is no evidence available to substantiate the accuracy of the reported expense data. Because grantmakers use the Form 990 in order to make their funding decisions, the study suggests that grantseekers have an "incentive" to report the best possible use of their funding. . . .
2. Charities exercise too much discretion in how they categorize expenses. This study cites IRS discoveries that charities misreport the actual cost of fundraising, or "net" the cost of the service provided by a professional fundraiser by subtracting that service fee from the actual amount raised and only reporting that amount as the direct public contribution. Also, the study claims that professional fundraising fees have been misreported as "other" expenses. The study acknowledges that the IRS does not know the extent of this misreporting.

Source: Independent Sector (n.d., p. 1).

the facts "can confront the folks who they believe are behind the malfeasance. They can share their suspicion with state and federal regulators and, perhaps most likely of all, they can go to the media" (Swords, 2004, Section 2, ¶ 6). Nonprofit governance requires boards with many independent members who are attentive to "the possibility of malfeasance and who read and know how to read the Form 990" (Section 2, ¶ 8). Fundraisers have an obligation that goes beyond loyalty to the mission of the organization and extends to donor relationships. Staff working with donors will want to make sure their Form 990 information describes reality for donors. Nothing in the document should hinder the development of strong relationships with the donor and the organization.

Filing Categories

Most tax-exempt organizations must file a return in the Form 990 series. Unless an exception exists, most charitable organizations, or 501(c)(3) organizations, must file a Form 990 along with Schedule A and Schedule B. Organizations with gross receipts less than $100,000 during the year and total assets less than $250,000 at the end of the year may file a Form 990-EZ, which is a shorter return (IRS, 2007b, pp. 6–8). To determine *annual gross receipts* an organization should include the "total amount it received from all sources during its annual accounting period, without subtracting any costs or expenses" (IRS, 2007e, p. 4). All private foundations and most nonexempt charitable trusts must file Form 990-PF. Exceptions to the requirement of filing a return in the series of Form 990 include:

1. Churches and certain church-affiliated organizations,
2. Certain organizations affiliated with governmental units,
3. Organizations (other than private foundations) with annual gross receipts typically less than $25,000, and
4. Organizations covered by a group return (IRS, 2007b, p. 7).

In 2007 a new form, 990-N, was developed by the IRS that must be completed by most small, non-church, tax-exempt organizations that are not required to complete the 990 or 990-EZ. It is an electronic notice returned via e-mail each year (IRS, 2007e, p. 1).

General Reporting Content

The information required on the Form 990 is extensive and includes the following financial and nonfinancial data:

- Statement of revenues, expenses, and changes in net assets or fund balances
- Statement of functional expenses (program services, management and general, as well as fundraising)
- Statement of program service accomplishments (including measurement such as number of clients served or publications issued as well as other achievements not measurable) and program service expenses
- Balance sheets
- Reconciliation of revenue per audited financial statements with revenue per return
- Reconciliation of expenses per audited financial statements with expenses per return
- List of current officers, directors, trustees, and key employees
- List of former officers, directors, trustees, and key employees that received compensation or other benefits
- Other information, including many probing questions added to the form in 2007
- Analysis of income-producing activities

- Information regarding taxable subsidiaries
- Information regarding transfers associated with personal benefit contracts
- Information regarding transfers to and from controlled entities
- Schedule A for 501(c)(3) organizations, which includes information on highest-paid individuals and prior years' condensed revenues and expenses
- Schedule B, which includes information on contributors that donate an aggregate amount in excess of $5,000 during the year

Revenues from Fundraising

The first item in Part I of the Form 990 requires an organization to report all amounts received as contributions, gifts, grants, and other similar amounts. The instructions state that amounts included in this line involve "voluntary contributions; that is, payments, or the part of any payment, for which the payer (donor) does not receive full retail value (fair market value) from the recipient (donee) organization" (IRS, 2007e, p. 25). For the purposes of this line on Form 990, donated services such as free office space are not considered contributions and should not be included. The total of contributions, gifts, grants, and other similar amounts must be broken down into the following separate categories: contributions to donor-advised funds, direct public support, indirect public support, and government contributions or grants. In addition, organizations must attach Schedule B, which requires a listing of contributors who, during the year, gave the organization, directly or indirectly, money or property worth at least $5,000. Schedule B does not need to be made available to the public, to protect the confidentiality of the donor. Special fundraising events and activities produce revenue that the organization must report on a separate line. However, such events and activities might also involve contributions. See **Exhibit 6-4** for an example.

Exhibit 6-4 IRS 990 Example

An organization announces that anyone who contributes at least $40 to the organization can choose to receive a book worth $16 retail value. A person who gives $40, and who chooses the book, is really purchasing the book for $16 and also making a contribution of $24. The contribution of $24, which is the difference between the buyer's payment and the $16 retail value of the book, would be reported on line 1b and again on line 9a (within the parentheses). The revenue received ($16 retail value of the book) would be reported in the right-hand column on line 9a.

Source: IRS (2007e, p. 26).

Fundraising Expenses

Part II of Form 990 requires an organization to prepare a statement of functional expenses by program services, management and general, as well as fundraising. *Fundraising expenses* include "the total expenses incurred in soliciting contributions, gifts, grants, etc." (IRS, 2007e, p. 32). Organizations must report all expenses and even allocate overhead costs such as the publication of fundraising campaigns, distribution of fundraising manuals, and organization of special events that generate contributions (IRS, 2007e, p. 32). This requirement "may reveal some indirect fundraising costs that, when combined with direct fundraising expenses, result in the reporting of considerably higher total outlays of fundraising" (Hopkins, 2002, pp. 259–260). Organizations are under pressure by the public to allocate as few dollars to fundraising as possible. The public thinks of program services expenses and even management and general expenses as more appropriate expense categories. Fundraisers should be looking closely at the accounting for their department's expenses and work with management to provide accurate information.

CURRENT REGULATORY ENVIRONMENT

The revamp of the Form 990 in 2007 is symbolic of an increased level of accountability requested by government and by the public. According to Vincent Carrodeguas, "What we're seeing now are huge evolutionary changes in the nonprofit industry. . . . Donors are now saying, 'No more [operating nonprofits like] mom-and-pop shops.' They want to see where the money is going" (as cited in Spinelli, 2005, ¶ 2). This sentiment sums up the position of certain donors, the federal government, the state regulators, and the plethora of watchdog organizations that have grown up around the current nonprofit segment of the economy. The BBB Wise Giving Alliance, the National Charities Information Bureau (NCIB), the National Center for Charitable Statistics, and Guidestar are all involved in gathering, evaluating, or disseminating financial data from charitable organizations.

In October 2004, in response to the Senate Finance Committee hearings, Independent Sector (IS) created a "Panel on the Nonprofit Sector" that included government officials as well as board members and volunteers from the charitable community to focus on the nonprofit sector's governance, transparency, and ethical standards. In June 2005 IS issued a report to Congress on its recommendations, which include changes in federal reporting and regulations.

More and more donors are holding charitable board members accountable for their management of the financial affairs of the organization. Consequently, a thorough understanding of the basic IRS regulations for fundraising and charitable giving is a necessary first step to good governance. Professionals working in the development office have a special obligation to donors in seeing that the organizations are accountable and transparent as they work to achieve their missions.

REFERENCES

Arthur Andersen Private Client Services. (1999). *Tax economics of charitable giving.* Private Client Services (13th ed.). Chicago: Arthur Andersen & Co.

Berry, J. M. (2005). Nonprofits and civic engagement. *Public Administration Review, 65*(5), 568–578.

Charitable, etc., contributions and gifts. 26 U.S.C. § 170 (2007).

Disclosure related to quid pro quo contributions. 26 U.S.C. § 6115 (2007).

Galligan, M. W. (2004, May 13). International charitable giving and planning under U.S. tax law. *Tax Management Estates Gifts and Trust Journal, 29*(3). Retrieved May 16, 2008, from http://www.phillipsnizer.com/pdf/Article-MGIntlLawCharUSTax5-13-04.pdf

Hopkins, B. R. (2000). *The tax law of charitable giving.* New York: John Wiley & Sons.

Hopkins, B. R. (2002). *The law of fundraising.* New York: John Wiley & Sons.

Independent Sector. (n.d.). *GAO study of tax-exempt organizations.* Retrieved December 29, 2004, from http://www.independentsector.org/programs/gr/GAOrpt.html

Internal Revenue Service. (1999, April 1). Taxes on foundation failure to distribute income. In *Internal revenue manual* (Part 7, Chapter 27. Section 16). Retrieved October 12, 2006, from http://www.irs.gov/irm/part7/ch12s13.html

Internal Revenue Service. (2004, January 20). Charitable contributions of patents and other intellectual property. In *Internal revenue bulletin: 2004-3.* Retrieved October 12, 2006, from http://www.irs.gov/irb/2004-03_IRB/ar10.html

Internal Revenue Service. (2007a). Charitable contributions [Publication 526]. Retrieved October 19, 2008, from http://www.irs.gov/pub/irs-pdf/p526.pdf

Internal Revenue Service. (2007b, June). Compliance guide for 501(c)(3) public charities [Publication 4221-PC]. Retrieved November 30, 2008, from http://www.irs.gov/pub/irs-pdf/p4221pc.pdf

Internal Revenue Service. (2007c, April). Determining the value of donated property [Publication 561]. Retrieved October 19, 2008, from http://www.irs.gov/pub/irs-pdf/p561.pdf

Internal Revenue Service. (2007d, January). Donee information return (sale, exchange, or other disposition of donated property). Form 8282. Retrieved October 19, 2008, from http://www.irs.gov/pub/irs-pdf/f8282.pdf

Internal Revenue Service. (2007e). Instructions for form 990 and 990-EZ. Retrieved October 19, 2008, from http://www.irs.gov/pub/irs-pdf/i990-ez.pdf

Internal Revenue Service. (2008a, March). Charitable contributions: Substantiation and disclosure requirements [Publication 1771]. Retrieved October 19, 2008, from http://www.irs.gov/pub/irs-pdf/p1771.pdf

Internal Revenue Service. (2008b, June). Tax-exempt status for your organization [Publication 557]. Retrieved October 19, 2008, from http://www.irs.gov/pub/irs-pdf/p557.pdf

Keating, E. K., & Frumkin, P. (2003, January/February). Reengineering nonprofit financial accountability: Toward a more reliable foundation for regulation. *Public Administration Review, 63*(1), 3–15. Retrieved May 19, 2008, from WilsonSelectPlus database.

Krishnan, R., Yetman, M., & Yetman, R. J. (2005, September 8). Expense misreporting in non-profit organizations: An agency based analysis. Retrieved May 19, 2008, from http://papers.ssrn .com/sol3/papers.cfm?abstract_id=590963

Online Compendium of Federal and State Regulations for U.S. Nonprofit Organizations. (1999, March 15). The legal basis for NPO regulation. Retrieved October 10, 2004, from http://www.muridae.com/nporegulation/main.html

Sorrells, M., & Lang, A. S. (2001). *The IRS form 990: A window into nonprofits.* Washington, DC: National Center for Nonprofit Boards.

Spinelli, L. (2005, September 26). Consulting to nonprofits: Nonprofits adopt for-profit efficiency, accountability. *Accounting Today.* Retrieved October 16, 2005, from http://www.webcpa .com/article.cfm?articleid=14609

Swords, P. (2004, June 15). *Working a form 990.* Nonprofit Coordinating Committee. Retrieved October 16, 2004, from http://www.npccny.org/Form_990/Working_a_990.htm

chapter seven

The Fundraising Process

If the first misconception of the public's understanding of fundraising is the idea that raising money always involves the sale of cookies, cakes, and candy, the second is that fundraising is simply asking for money for a good cause. If you were to ask the average person on the street what phrase comes to mind when you say the word *fundraising*, more often than not you would hear something along the lines of, "It's when one person (or group) asks another person (or group) to give them money for a specific cause." From the perspective of the professional fundraiser, however, the term *fundraising* takes on a much deeper meaning. While the public views fundraising primarily in terms of "the ask," those behind the scenes know that fundraising is a much more involved process. While it would indeed be nice to think that fundraising revolves strictly around the solicitation itself, it is only a small part of the process. The complete fundraising process contains several functions: Research, Planning, Cultivation, Solicitation, Stewardship, and Evaluation. ✳ From the initial stages of prospect research to the final stages of evaluating the overall success of the effort, the fundraising process takes time, patience, and the motivation to succeed.

This chapter will cover each of these areas sequentially, although they may in practice overlap and come into play at different times. A full-functioning development office should be doing all of these functions simultaneously, but to varying degrees. Even in the case of a specific donor, there might be, for example, cultivation for a new gift, stewardship of a previous gift, and planning for a solicitation of a new gift all within the same time frame.

RESEARCH FOR FUNDRAISING

Broom and Dozier define research as "the controlled, objective, and systematic gathering of information for the purposes of describing and understanding" (1990, p. 4). But does this definition of research serve the fundraising world? As we have seen above, raising funds for an organization requires much more than simply asking for money. If fundraisers are to get their prospects fully involved in giving, they must know all relevant information about the prospect and the environment in which they are raising money. Research is a necessary function for fundraising. Fundraisers need to research prospective donors, including individuals, foundations, and corporations as well as their own organizations and other organizations with a similar mission. Prospect research includes collecting the prospect's contact information, giving history, and information about the prospect's connections to other sources of support. Serious fundraisers gather information about foundations and publicly traded companies, read market and trend journals, and track economic trends.

Research Throughout the Fundraising Process

In 1998 the Association of Professional Researchers for Advancement (APRA) determined that research is essential across every stage of the development process, including planning, cultivation, solicitation, stewardship, and evaluation. Their statement provides a definition of the role of researchers within the development department. "Researchers are the development officers on the front line of information management, uniquely positioned—and qualified—to gather, interpret, analyze, disseminate and direct data critical to securing support for non-profit organizations" (APRA, 1998, ¶ 1). From the initial identification of a donor prospect to the follow-up note after the donation, professional researchers' involvement in the fundraising process can be the "glue" that holds the puzzle pieces together.

Prospect Research

Throughout his years working in a fundraising capacity, Thomas Broce developed a set of "cardinal principles" designed to assist development professionals in achieving their solicitation goals. The importance of prospect research is illustrated by the seventh of Broce's nine cardinal principles: "prospect research must be thorough and realistic" (Broce, 1986, p. 23). Broce goes on to discuss the topic of prospect research further, stating the one question that he believes all fundraisers should ask themselves prior to implementing a fundraising program: "Who is going to give us the money" (p. 24)? The question, if answered properly, can transform into the initial building block on which an organization's fundraising initiative can begin: prospect research.

Following the lead of some for-profit organizations, many nonprofit organizations have identified possible prospects through a variety of different research methods. These methods include surveys, focus groups, participant observation, prospect information sheets, feasibility studies, electronic screening, and rating and screening. Indeed, while there are a variety of analytical research methods currently in use and discussed below, the most effective method may be the interpersonal aspect of research—meeting the prospect face to face and through conversation find out about their philanthropic intentions and relevant background.

Surveys

Surveys, one of the most popular forms of research in the field of fundraising today, come in a variety of forms and produce a variety of results. When used correctly, surveys can provide an organization with extremely targeted information regarding a subset of requested information. Common formats for surveys are mail, telephone, in-person, and online. Before an organization invests the time and energy into implementing a survey, it should consider the costs associated with each of the formats before making a decision as to how it would like to proceed.

Universities and colleges use alumni surveys to help with developing a strong database of information for both alumni relations efforts, such as for setting up reunion programs, and specifically for fundraising, by identifying prospects for major or planned gifts. Besides basic contact information such as updated phone numbers and work/home/e-mail addresses, the surveys contain the following information that might help with identifying prospects and developing fundraising relationships: employer, business title, spouse, advanced degrees, directorships, children, household income (optional), and net worth (optional).

Focus Groups

Perhaps one of the most common research methods, focus groups are made up of individuals who, under the instruction of a facilitator, gather in a common location to discuss a predetermined topic and provide feedback to the organization. The facilitator, who has previously received training, encourages the participants to engage in an open dialogue, directing the conversation toward a specific goal while helping them clarify their ideas. Once recorded, the participants' answers and comments are transcribed and analyzed. As Kelly (1998) has observed, the analysis of the data is an in-depth process that involves "looking for consensus, patterns, and insightful comments" (p. 404). While focus groups are an important research tool for conducting prospect research, the data collected should be used in conjunction with other forms of research to ensure that the results achieved are representative of the organization's prospect base. The small number of people participat-

Exhibit 7-1 Using Focus Groups in a University Setting

In the 1980s UCLA was faced with the challenge of increasing the involvement of the UCLA Foundation volunteer trustees who were not actively engaged with the campus. While they had expressed their desire to be more involved, the institution had failed to provide them with sufficient avenues for direct participation.

Although the organization knew that there was no quick fix to the problem, they took the time to ascertain the volunteers' concerns and interests through a focus-group study. The idea of the focus group was introduced as a means of discovering how the volunteer leaders viewed their roles within the organization. Foundation trustees were asked the following questions: What do you think you should be doing for UCLA? What do you think the University should be doing for you? What aspects of our operation would you liked to see changed and why?

Across every focus group, a common thread emerged: Volunteers wanted to be asked to do more. They wanted demands made upon them. They wanted the University to request more of them than merely to be present at a board meeting once or twice a year. They asked why they were invited to meetings, but then not given anything to do. After listening to them carefully, the University decided to ask more of them in the future.

Source: Young (1997, pp. 43–44). *Successful Fundraising for Higher Education: The Advancement of Learning.* © 1997. The American Council on Education.

ing in a typical focus group and the open-ended nature of the discussion prevent using the technique in isolation, since the results will not be statistically valid in the strictest sense. See **Exhibit 7-1** for an example.

Participant Observation

Perhaps the most important trait that any fundraiser should have is the ability to talk to potential donors and, in return, listen to what they have to say about the organization. A development officer often works outside of the office, attending meetings, participating in civic functions, or following up with a prospective donor. A good fundraiser can be seen recording observations, taking notes, soliciting feedback, and paying close attention to the surroundings, taking into account all of the variables that play a part in the situational landscape. Fundraisers must be constantly aware of the situations in which they find themselves and make the most of each situation as it applies to the distinct needs of their organization.

Prospect Information

Researchers use several traditional sources to locate prospect information, including print materials such as *Who's Who in America*, the *Guide to American Directories*, newspapers and periodicals (*New York Times, Wall Street Journal*), social registers, and alumni files and records (Broce, 1986). The Internet also provides a host of resources, so much so that there is often too much information about a prospect (see **Exhibit 7-2**). Determining the most relevant information will involve an analysis of the particular needs of the fundraisers in a particular setting.

Exhibit 7-2 Top Internet Sources

Lexis/Nexis for Development Professionals (fee)	bizjournals.com
silobreaker.com/Network.aspx	theyrule.net
dnb.com (Dun & Bradstreet; fee)	Legacy.com
Hoovers (fee)	Social Security Death Index
Edgaronlinepro or Tenkwizard (fee)	theultimates.com
Bigcharts.com	pulawski.com
Alumnifinder (fee)	Zillow.com
Research bookmarks collections (free)	salary.com

(continues)

Exhibit 7-2 (*continued*)

Guidestar (free and fee)	careers-in-business.com
CQMoneyline.com	Opensecrets.org
Foundation Center (fee and free): http://www.foundationcenter.org/	
Chronicle of Philanthropy: http://philanthropy.com/	
http://www.development.northwestern.edu/research/bookmark.html	
(sample of research bookmarks collection—see above)	

Source: C. Pulawski, personal communication, September 20, 2008.

Prospect researchers should create and index computer or hard-copy files on each prospect for easy reference. Prospect information sheets provide a way to organize background information on a prospect for the purpose of cultivation of a donation. Note the suggested high level of detail on the sheet (see **Exhibit 7-3**). While it may be impossible to gather all of the information requested on the sheet, gathering as much relevant information as possible will maximize the chance of successfully soliciting a gift to the organization.

Exhibit 7-3 Sample Prospect Information Sheet

Prospect Name

Date of Birth:	To help identify
Contact Info:	Address, phone, e-mail
Spouse:	Name, occupation
Children:	Names, ages, schools attended
Education:	Prospect's alma mater
Company:	Current employment
	Past employment
Directorship:	Director of either for-profit company or a nonprofit or civic organization
Salary:	May be based on company records; should also include any bonuses received from the company, etc.
Stock Holdings:	Any public stock holdings or sales
Real Estate:	Any current or recently sold real estate property
Other:	Additional information that may prove to be relevant when cultivating the prospect
Summary of Relationship:	What is the current state of the relationship between the prospect and the organization?

Electronic Screening

> At best, electronic screening is a quick way for a nonprofit to find wealthy persons in its database of names and to discover connections between those who serve together on corporate boards. (Helen Bergan, 2002, ¶ 3)

As demands on the fundraiser's time continue to increase, prospect research is often forced to take a back seat to other immediate issues. For this reason, the electronic screening method is becoming popular throughout the fundraising community. At some point in time, every organization will realize its need for a list of screened prospects toward which it might target fundraising initiatives. While this process may be done in-house by a one-by-one research process, it may be more time and cost effective for the organization to outsource the process to a company that specializes in electronic screening.

As outlined by Helen Bergan (2002), the process of electronic screening works particularly well for organizations that have only rudimentary information on their potential prospects. Once available in only a limited capacity, the databases against which these names are screened are becoming increasingly sophisticated. Prospect names may be matched against a variety of databases, some of which may include information regarding indicators of wealth, social status, or even alumni connections. If used correctly, and in a timely manner, the information generated from an electronic screening can be well worth the money spent on the process.

The process starts with an internal data file from the organization's computer system. Identifying information for each prospect is used to create a match to the vendor's files. Social Security numbers work best, but this information is available only to universities and colleges for each alum through student records. Date of birth would also be helpful. Full names and current addresses represent the typical identifying information, which can lead to an occasional mismatch. The vendor takes the data and matches to a national database of possibly over 90 million households. Once a match is found the computer is directed to select data regarding income range at the census track or zip code level and other characteristics.

Even though the collection of data by vendors is legal, the resulting consolidated report on an individual represents a more in-depth portrait of the prospect than one might expect. Ethical issues may surface in some situations. Should donors be told where their information came from? Should certain data be excluded from the analysis, even if they are easily available? How to handle sensitive data is not always evident. Chapter 11 discusses a methodology for ethical decision making that involves conversation with colleagues and the use of a structured analysis of possible alternative actions. Acting ethically will help to build good relationships with donors over the years.

The final part of the process involves sending the new information on prospects back to the organization. The new data are loaded into the organization's internal computer system. Sorts and selects can provide reports that prioritize the prospects. Cultivation and eventual solicitation are determined in part because of the prospect potential identified in this way.

Rating and Screening

Similar in its basic concept to electronic screening, rating and screening gathers prospect information from real-live people rather than from an impersonal national database. While this process is used most often in a university setting with a focus on alumni, it is also possible to apply the concept to a more generalized fundraising initiative. Most often performed in a peer-to-peer format, the idea behind rating and screening is to take a lengthy list of donors and, with the help of peer volunteers, shorten the list to make it both manageable and targeted, so the "best" (or most likely) prospects receive the greatest amount of attention from the fundraising staff.

The rating events themselves should be fairly structured. When the event is announced, the development team will personally recruit volunteers to participate in the event, first making sure they are apprised of the situation. On the evening of the event, the staff distributes a list of names to each of the volunteers. Most lists will also include questions about the prospects and may even ask that the volunteers categorize their relationship with the prospect, including their comfort level in asking the prospect to make a gift to the organization—though this is usually optional. It is important that the screeners know personally at least some of the names on the review lists. Otherwise, the reviewers will be providing information that is very speculative in nature and may not provide a sound basis for later decision making. While this technique may work well for one organization, it is important to take into account the organization's possible volunteer pool before attempting a rating-and-screening event. These types of events work best when the pool of volunteers is relatively similar to the potential donor pool. Although a rating-

and-screening session is usually considered ethical by the major organizations involved in fundraising (e.g., AFP, AHP, and CASE), the process could quickly become unethical if participants were not aware of how the information was going to be used, if confidentiality was compromised in the use of the information, or if the development office was not transparent regarding how they answer questions about the process.

Understanding the Fundraising Environment

While so far we have focused largely on individual prospect research, it is also important to research the overall fundraising environment. The organization should take into account not only what it is looking to gain from its fundraising efforts but also the current landscape of the fundraising community. For example, if an organization has set a goal of raising $500,000 in donations from a fundraising drive, it should take the time before implementing the campaign to determine if any competing organizations may be planning to launch campaign initiatives within the same time period. If the research shows that another organization will be launching an initiative within the same period, the organization may want to consider readjusting its fundraising goals to coincide with the current landscape.

Although researching the campaign environment may seem like a small piece of the puzzle, it is truly an integral factor within the overall scheme of the fundraising initiative. The more an organization knows about the non-profit landscape in which it operates, the more successful it will be in the end.

Understanding the Organization

Most fundraisers assume they know enough about their organizations and cases for support to ignore formally this aspect of research. Because fundraising involves relationships between the organization and the donors, understanding the organization at a deep level is crucial to success. To reach this understanding might involve interviewing key leaders in the organization to learn more about its history. There may be historical documents that are available that could be used to identify key concepts, values, or ideas that could be used in developing a case for support—or to contrast the past with a new direction that needs to be articulated to donors. In a large organization, such as a major medical center or nationally based organization with many regional offices around the world, there may simply be enough going on in many different departments or regions for the fundraiser to seek out the latest and most relevant information. Fundraisers could then use this information in conversation with donors as they strengthen the relationship in the cultivation process or as input to the fundraising planning process.

Preparedness Process

An organization can determine in a variety of ways its level of preparedness for a capital campaign or other new fundraising initiative. A widely used preparedness index is the Dove Preparedness Index (DPI; Dove, 2000, pp. 33–34), which considers a variety of factors when scoring an organization's preparedness before launching a capital campaign (see **Exhibit 7-4**). In conjunction with a feasibility study, any organization that is considering participating in a capital campaign should also complete a DPI to determine its level of preparedness.

Exhibit 7-4 Dove Preparedness Index

The DPI considers 10 prerequisites for capital campaign success, each scored on a scale of 1 (the lowest) to 10 (the highest). Items 4, 6, and 7 are considered the "key three."

1. Commitments of time and support from all key participants (board, CEO, prospective major donors, key volunteer leaders, staff, organizational family).
2. A clear organizational self-image and strategic plan for organizational growth and improvement.
3. Fundraising objectives based on important and legitimate institutional plans, goals, budgets, and needs.
4. A written document that makes a compelling case for supporting the campaign.
5. An assessment of the institutional development program and a market survey addressing internal and external preparedness.
6. Enlistment and education of volunteer leaders.
7. Ability and readiness of major donors to give substantial lead gifts.
8. Competent staff and, perhaps, external professional counsel.
9. Adequate, even liberal, funds for expenses.
10. Other factors (age of the organization, caliber of the constituency, range of the institution's giving program, size and geographical distribution of the constituency, previous fundraising success, quality of the program and impact of its services, location of the organization, human factors, state of the economy, competing and conflicting campaigns, trends in the nonprofit sector, unfavorable publicity, local issues).

Source: Capital Campaigns (2006).

Henry Rosso (2003) defines a feasibility study as "an in-depth examination and assessment of the fund raising potential of an institution or agency, conducted by fundraising counsel and presented in the form of a written report setting forth various conclusions, recommendations, and proposed plans" (p. 500). The foundation for a successfully implemented capital campaign is the feasibility study. Designed to determine an organization's readiness to ask its constituency for donations and the constituency's willingness to make the necessary contributions to the organization, the feasibility study can become the single most important step that an organization makes during the capital campaign planning process. While it is possible for an organization to conduct its own feasibility study, I recommend that organizations outsource the process so that they may receive unbiased information regarding their readiness to proceed and so that they will not compromise the ongoing fundraising activity by diverting internal staff resources to the feasibility process.

The feasibility study consists of several components, some of which may differ based on the particular consulting agency used. However, several strategic pieces of the study tend to remain constant across consultants. As outlined by Rosso (2003), these tactics may include, but are not limited to, "questioning, measuring, qualifying, verifying, listening to hard answers to hard questions, and weighing judgments expressed by potential key volunteer leaders and potential key contributors" (p. 120).

When performing the interviews for the study, it is important to take into consideration which donors the organization considers their "top donors." Weinstein (2004) suggests that the top 10 donations to an organization generally account for one-third of the total campaign funds. Hence, approximately 30 to 50 of the top prospects should be interviewed as potential pacesetters for the campaign as a part of the feasibility study. These interviews will make it possible to determine if the organization will have the ability to reach its desired fundraising goal.

In addition to determining an organization's fundraising preparedness, a feasibility study may also reveal underlying problems with the current fundraising plans. For example, one feasibility study that was completed for a Chicago-area nonprofit determined that although the organization had the support of the community overall, due to the relative newness of the organization it had not yet "paid [its] dues" within the community, and it would have to wait its turn behind the other organizations that had "paid their dues." The organization did that and went on to complete a successful campaign a couple of years later than originally planned.

PLANNING FOR FUNDRAISING

Information derived from a comprehensive research effort is essential to the overall fundraising process. Typically, the next step after research is taking the information and developing a strong plan to guide the fundraising process. Our steps are not always in sequence, however, and fundraisers may find that the planning process comes first and it determines the level and scope of research that follows. Fundraising is not a lockstep process.

What is clear in sequencing is that planning for fundraising needs to follow—or work hand in hand with—a planning process for the organization itself. Given the resulting action steps for the organization, which steps are relevant to fundraising? Different organizations may create different planning frameworks. Some may include fundraising issues within the context of organizational planning; others may split the process into two distinct settings. In either case, there are planning tools that are useful in the process. One of the tools used in the planning process is what is referred to as the SWOT (Strengths, Weaknesses, Opportunities, and Threats) analysis.

SWOT Analysis

When discussing the strengths that an organization must possess before beginning the fundraising process, Eugene Tempel offers the following remark: "For an organization to be successful in fund raising, it must be connected to its external environment. It must understand the changing needs of that environment and its ability to respond to the organization's need for human and financial resources to remain functional" (quoted in Rosso, 2003, p. 31).

In order for an organization to determine its external environment, it can first perform a SWOT analysis, which can be applied across several levels of any organization. Not only can it be used to determine the direction in which an organization will move forward, but it can also be used at a departmental level as a way for the department staff to organize themselves before moving forward with the strategic planning process. As stated by Kelly (1998), SWOT "starts by identifying opportunities and threats in the external environment that could affect fund raising" (p. 397). Kelly goes on to say that through the course of the analysis, "as each opportunity and threat is identified, related internal factors are weighed" (p. 397). Because the SWOT analysis is presented in progressive steps, it should start by identifying opportunities and threats that may affect fundraising in the external environment.

In order to get a more targeted read on a situation, the person conducting the analysis may also choose to map the issues in a two-by-two matrix

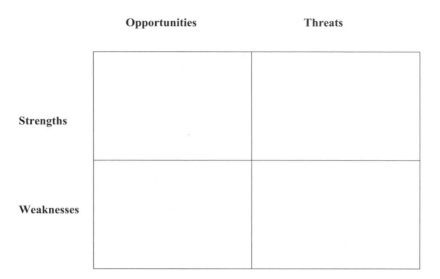

Figure 7-1. SWOT analysis table

format, focusing on the opportunities and threats via their organizations' strengths and weaknesses. As shown in **Figure 7-1**, once the situations that are involved in the process are defined as strategic issues, they are then divided up into four different types. These types can be classified as: (1) Comparative Advantage (Opportunities/Strengths), (2) Mobilization (Threats/Strengths), (3) Investment/Divestment (Opportunities/Weaknesses), and (4) Damage Control (Threats/Weaknesses).

The next step in the SWOT analysis process is the clarification of the issues at hand. This clarification "helps the department reach agreement on a set of questions that will reflect the critical choices facing it" (Kelly, 1998, p. 399).

The final step in the analysis process is the ranking of issues. As the majority of nonprofit organizations do not have the resources that would be necessary to resolve all of the issues brought to light through the analysis, they must establish priorities for resolving issues accordingly so that resources are not spread thin moving forward.

GOAL SETTING

Out of the SWOT analysis come the general goals and specific objectives for the organization, some of which bear directly on fundraising efforts. For example, the organization may have as a goal to build a new health clinic for the region. Unless there is already funding set aside for this goal, fundraising will bear directly on this goal. A list of fundraising goals is produced within the context of the organizational goals. These can be stated in the following example format:

- *Facilities goal*: Over the next five years $10,000,000 will be raised from all sources for a new health clinic.
- *Endowment goal*: Over the next five years $1,000,000 will be raised from all sources for new endowments.
- *Operating goal*: Over the next five years $500,000 in cash will be raised annually from all sources for general operations.

Objectives are subgoals. They can be combinations of process and outcome objectives. A process objective is an objective whose achievement depends on the organization's internal resources, staff competence, and management ability. For example, under the operating goal (from above) the objective of sending out 50,000 direct mail pieces annually for five years may be created. Even if no one gives a dime to this direct mail campaign, the internal organization will be able to say it was successful in completing this process objective. An outcome objective is an objective whose achievement depends on the organization's external constituency to do their part in the process. Successful organizations must mobilize their prospects in the fundraising process to convert them into donors. Continuing our example, one possible outcome objective is to raise $100,000 annually from the direct mail campaign.

Action Plans

Given general goals and specific objectives, the fundraising operations staff needs to develop specific action plans that, if implemented, will most likely cause the achievement of the objectives and goals. The action steps need to be within the resource constraints of the organization and its environment. They need to be realistic yet imaginative. The action plan will set the blueprint for activity in the coming year(s). When alternative fundraising ideas arise in the months ahead, the plan will help to guide and direct.

Fundraising involves using a variety of techniques within the action plan. Which combination of techniques will produce the greatest amount of support? (See **Exhibit 7-5** for an example of the effect of change in alloca-

Exhibit 7-5 Resource Allocation

Lindahl's model for resource allocation (1992) predicted that Northwestern University could have raised an additional $16.4M in 1987–1988 beyond the base case of $63.7M if $2.5M in fundraising costs were better reallocated across the range of possible fundraising techniques and markets.

tion.) The resource allocation issue can drive the development of an action plan. See Chapter 12 for a full discussion of this topic as a part of the budgeting process.

CULTIVATION FOR FUNDRAISING

> Recognition and cultivation go hand-in-hand. Most donors will tell you that they are not looking for recognition. They get all the satisfaction they need just by giving to your organization. That may be only partially true. (Terry Axelrod, 2004, p. 135)

Defined by the Association of Fundraising Professionals as a process in which a fundraiser may "engage and maintain the interest and involvement of (a donor, prospective donor, or volunteer) with an organization's people, programs, and plans" (AFP, 2003), cultivation can be seen as a pivotal piece of the fundraising process. Some ways to cultivate donors include face-to-face contact, direct mail, Web site, newsletters, and special events. Public relations may also play a role in cultivating donors, if press releases, video clips, and human-interest stories appear in the press describing the organization's programs and special fundraising initiatives.

In his book *Nine Cardinal Principles*, Thomas Broce states, "Cultivation is the key to successful solicitation" (1986, p. 24). Broce goes on to say that the "cultivation of prospects and potential prospects is a process, not a one-time effort. It must be as deliberate and well planned as all other phases of fund raising" (1986, p. 24). Skipping this step in the process would make the actual act of soliciting a prospect very difficult. Donor cultivation is the foundation of successful solicitation.

The process of cultivating relationships with donors is often lengthy and highly involved. It can connect back to the research phase, since cultivation can bring in new information about the prospect. It can connect back to the planning phase, since uncovering a relationship with a particular high-level donor can cause an organization to adjust the priorities for planning.

Before the solicitor takes the first step toward asking for a major dona-tion, it helps to form a personal, face-to-face relationship with the donor. But what is the best way to create this working bond? First, the fundraiser must seek to create a solid relationship with the donor. This relationship should not be forced, but rather should develop naturally. Seasoned fundraiser David Dunlop (1993) recommends the following way to create lasting donor relationships: "Let your friendships grow naturally. Don't assume familiarity that is not based on the experience of your relationship with the prospect" (p. 109). Once these friendships have taken hold, then the solicitation process will begin to flow on a much more natural level.

Another idea that the fundraiser can employ in the cultivation process is managed communication. According to Kelly (1998), cultivation on the part of the fundraiser can best be defined as "managed communication by which fund raisers continually seek to *inform* prospective donors about and *involve* them in a charitable organization's work" (p. 421). But what does managed communication really mean? As we noted above, relationships with donors should develop naturally, and at their own pace. Through the employment of managed communication, the fundraiser may share pieces of information, stories, or facts with the prospect as they are relevant to the relationship, thereby strengthening the bond but not overwhelming the donor.

Fundraisers may use many different tactics to cultivate prospects. While one tactic may work better in a specific situation, another may need to be employed in a different situation. Terry Axelrod (2004) has outlined four key variables to be applied for the successful cultivation of a donor prospect. Each contact with the prospect must be:

1. Personal,
2. Relevant to the donor's unique interests and needs,
3. Timed to the pace and style of the donor, and
4. Delivered via each donor's preferred medium (p. 130)

Each of these steps is necessary for effective donor cultivation. Just as the contacts between the fundraiser and the donor must take place on a per-sonal level, they also need to be relevant to the donor's needs. For example, you would not discuss the college football team with school alumni who had no interest in the sport. However, if an alumnus is an avid sports fan, the topic may be the perfect jumping-off point for a conversation between the fundraiser and the donor.

Timing is often overlooked, but it often proves to be a high-impact fundraising tool. When managing contact with donors, always aim for a timely response to all communications. These communications, however, should be timed to the pace of the donor. To quote Axelrod (2004), "Prompt turnaround time tells them [donors], first, that they are important enough to you that you moved quickly to respond to their concerns. Second, it does not let too much time pass so that they begin to forget your organization" (p. 131).

This brings us to the preferred mode of communicating. It is important to understand how to communicate effectively with prospects. While one prospect may communicate best via e-mail, another may crave a more personal telephone conversation. And face-to-face contact might be preferred as well, especially for more senior prospects.

In *The Complete Guide to Corporate Fund Raising* (1982), Podesta advises fund-seeking groups to present their best case in a businesslike manner with adequate presentation to potential corporate donors. In addition to researching corporate data, Podesta highly recommends cultivating the relationship with key corporate personnel indentified during the research process. Podesta points out that an organization's *compelling story* personally told and understood is essential to effective solicitation (p. 33). Therefore, it is important to maintain and broaden these personal contacts. Podesta's suggestions include:

1. *One-on-one contacts:* A formal visit, a simple phone call, or a brief discussion at a reception can accomplish this.
2. *Small luncheon or breakfast meetings:* Have an informal gathering at the organization's office or a restaurant to discuss the organization's programs and needs. The agenda may include a PowerPoint presentation, slides, or a video on the organization.
3. *Larger luncheon or dinner meetings:* In some cases, some corporations will host a larger luncheon meeting for a group presentation. The need for support should be mentioned, but the individual requests for support should not be made at the meeting.
4. *Site tour:* Give a tour of the site of the proposed project or program area to the potential corporate donor(s). This can be very helpful for them to better understand the grant proposal. (Podesta, 1982, pp. 34–35)

Podesta (1982) states that the process of cultivation is "sound public relations" (p. 33) and makes the following suggestions:

1. Make a presentation at the time the grant request is submitted, if possible. This way, the potential donor is updated on all aspects of the organization's activities, needs, and objectives.

2. Submit updated information if a lapse of several months occurs.
3. Send an appropriate acknowledgment when the grant is received. It is unforgivable not to acknowledge a gift. If you do not, it will highly diminish the chances for future funding.
4. Keep the donor informed by sending a periodic progress report. This will enhance the communication between the donor and the nonprofit organization and keep you in the donor's "radar screen" for future funding. (p. 33)

Part of cultivating the donor-recipient relationship is to maintain "transparency." That is, be an open book; do not maintain "secret agendas," but rather demonstrate integrity, trustworthiness, and high ethical and professional standards. A good model to follow is the Donor Bill of Rights, developed by the Association of Fundraising Professionals (AFP), the Association for Healthcare Philanthropy (AHP), the Council for Advancement and Support of Education (CASE), and the Giving Institute. Kelly (1998) considers the Donor Bill of Rights "stronger than the codes of ethics of the individual associations" (see Chapter 11) because it "acknowledges the dual levels of accountability to the 'general public' as well as to the specific publics of donors and prospective donors. Finally, it advances self-regulation by assuming that charitable organizations must continually demonstrate their worthiness of confidence and trust" (p. 307).

Why Is Cultivation Important?

What factors make donor cultivation so important? First, it is important that donors feel they have a stake in the organization. The majority of donors will give to a cause that they have connected with on a personal level. One of the best examples of this sort of giving is the donor that gives to his or her alma mater. "Culbertson (1992) warned, however, that genuine involvement exists only when the person feels that he or she has done or at least can do useful things for the organization" (Kelly, 1998, p. 422). In Francie Ostrower's book, when a donor who gave a large sum of money to his alma mater was asked why he did so, he responded simply by saying, "I consider that not to be generosity; I consider that to be almost an obligation. It's like repaying a student loan. . . . You really should do something if you can" (1995, p. 88).

In addition to the connection that donors feel with the organization, many donors also enjoy the attention that comes along with their gift. With smaller dollar amounts, donors may give simply for the act of giving, but usually the large-scale donors expect attention. In this case, the solicitor must make sure to take the time to work with these donors, giving them the attention that they desire, while continuing to cultivate future gifts to the organization.

> Cultivation is not sucking up or "schmoozing." Prospective donors, especially those for major gifts, resent unwanted and inappropriate attention. (Kathleen Kelly, 1998, p. 421)

Special Events Fundraising

One of the most effective ways in which fundraisers cultivate prospects is through special events fundraising initiatives. These events can take on a variety of forms, from full-scale, black-tie evening events to a speaker series or silent auction. The type of special event held should coincide to both the needs of the organization and the organizational capacity for holding such an event. When planning a special event, is it important to take into account the number of prospects and their ability to give. As Kelly states, "Programming differs by gift capacity and number of prospects. Whereas prospects for major gifts are cultivated through both involvement and information, annual giving prospects are cultivated primarily through information" (Kelly, 1998, p. 423). This idea is important to note when you are planning a special event for an organization. More often than not, special events are used to cultivate higher-level, major gift donors. If the development staff is assigned the task of planning special events for their organization, they must first make sure to take into account the donor base of the organization. For example, a non-profit organization that has 20 employees and attempts to raise $20,000 in funds may not be best served in holding a black-tie, $200-a-plate dinner, as the overall costs may overwhelm the organization before they begin. This organization may be best served by holding a series of smaller, more casual events that are designed to showcase the organization at a personal level.

It is also important for larger organizations not to get in over their heads when planning an event. One director of development at a private, educational institute in the Midwest relays the multiple issues that her organization faced with an annual large-scale silent auction: "After paying the rental on the space, paying the entertainment fee, security, and catering costs, we were lucky to break even at the end of the night." If the organization relies on only one event per year for the majority of their funding dollars, then it is in the best interest of the organization to create a detailed cost-benefit analysis to discern if their resources are on par with their needs.

When holding a special event, it is important for the fundraisers to remain distinctly aware of the timetable within which they are required to operate. As Broce emphasizes, "It is important that the solicitation comes as soon as possible on the heels of the major event" (1986, p. 94). This way, not only will the event and the organization be fresh in the donors' minds, but donors may also be compelled to give a bit more to the cause if they are reminded of the importance of the organization's work through an engaging conversation with the organizational representative. While special events often bring in the dollar amount that was set as the original goal, there have been some high-profile examples of large-scale special events that have called into question their viability as fundraising initiatives. See **Exhibit 7-6** for an example. However, keep in mind the multiple goals of fundraising events. The goal is not just to raise funds but also to raise the visibility of the organization and to provide networking opportunities with donors and prospective donors.

Point-of-Entry Event

Terry Axelrod has described another type of special event used to cultivate potential donors, what she calls the "point-of-entry" event. Point-of-entry events are especially useful for smaller organizations that do not have a natural prospect pool. Designed to bring donors into the fold, such events give

Exhibit 7-6 Farm Aid: Good Idea, Poor Execution

One example of a high-profile event that did not live up to its promise in regard to helping the population that it was created to serve was the Farm Aid concert. Farm Aid concerts were originally designed to both raise awareness regarding the plight of the American farmer and also raise money that would later be distributed in the form of grants to the same farmers to assist them in avoiding foreclosure on their farms.

While the causes for which the organization and event were created are noble, after tax documents for the 2002 and 2003 concerts were reviewed, a disturbing realization came to light: the actual concert itself brings in very little money after the expenses for the show are tabulated. The 2003 concert earned $1,013,087 through the sale of tickets, programs, and merchandise, but after the $853,833 in expenses were paid, only $159,254 was left to be given out in the form of grants to the farmers.

With an expense ratio of close to 74 percent, it would appear to the general public that the Farm Aid Foundation is not following through on the principles on which it was founded. If they are truly out to help the farmers save their farms from government foreclosure, then steps must be taken to ensure that a drastically larger percentage of the show revenue is directed at its intended recipients: the American farmer.

Source: George (2005).

the fundraiser an opportunity to introduce them to the organization. Axelrod goes on to state that as a fundraiser, "Your point of entry must give people a sense of how the work of your organization changes lives. . . . *As individuals, we are emotional donors looking for rational reasons to justify our emotional decision to give*" [italics in original] (2004, p. 65).

It is up to the fundraiser to develop the ability to appeal to each of the donors on their most basic, emotional level. This type of appeal is known as an "emotional hook."

Axelrod (2004) suggests including the following three components when developing a point-of-entry event:

1. The basic Facts 101 about your organization, including the vision and needs;
2. An "emotional hook" so compelling people will never forget it; and
3. A system for capturing the names, addresses, phone numbers, and e-mails of the guests who attend, with their permission. (p. 64)

As a follow-up to a point-of-entry event, fundraisers need to place phone calls to all attendees to determine further interest in the organization. The screening will let you know who to drop from further cultivation and who to continue to look for ways to connect with the organization. This process takes time, but it is crucial to follow up.

Cultivating Major Gift Donors

Major gift donors are in many ways the most important donors to any nonprofit organization. While the donations received via annual gift donors boost the organization's operating budget, the gifts that come from the organization's major donors provide the basis for truly advancing the organization's programs to new levels over the course of many years. But what, exactly, constitutes a major gift? As stated by Rosso, "The definitions of a major gift vary as greatly as the institutions themselves. One thing is certain: major gifts are inspired that have a significant impact on the development program and the institution" (2003, p. 89).

As discussed earlier in this chapter, a development professional may go about cultivating donor gifts in a variety of ways. See **Exhibit 7-7** for an example of an unusual cultivation story. However, what is it that makes the major gift donor different from the annual fund donor, and how should these donors be cultivated? Simply put, the major gift donor will give a larger gift to your organization. These relationships should be cultivated through the tactics that we have discussed throughout this section. When it comes time to begin the cultivation process, the fundraiser should pay close attention to each of the high-level donors on an individual level, and the organization will reap the rewards that come along with carefully cultivated relationships.

While major gifts may come in a monetary form, it is also important to note that this is only one form that they may take. According to Rosso et al. (2003), "Gifts of significance come in many forms. They may be substantial cash contributions, gifts of appreciated securities, or in-kind gifts such as contributions of valuable art or tangible personal property" (p. 89). These gifts should be received and acknowledged like monetary gifts, and cultivation of the relationship should be continued.

Moves Management

Moves management is "a series of initiatives or moves to develop each prospect's awareness of, knowledge of, interest in, involvement with, and commitment to the institution and its mission" (Dunlop & Ryan, 1990, p. 32). Developed by David Dunlop and G. Taylor "Bunky" Smith, moves management was created "to help large development staffs monitor relationships with numerous perspective donors. . . . Thoughtful 'moves management' is a system that helps the organization maintain gracious and meaningful relationships with its supporters" (Weinstein, 2004, p. 116). The concept of moves management is important in cultivating major donors.

Over the course of several years, the true meaning behind moves management has come to be widely misinterpreted throughout the development community. While many fundraisers view it as a form of manipulation, those who understand the concept fully can learn to use it ethically to build a strong and honest relationship between the donor and the organization. The

Exhibit 7-7 Cultivating Major Gifts: The Rose Bowl

Cultivating donors doesn't always need to be face to face. A major gift to Northwestern University Dental School was raised essentially through extended monthly phone calls with an elderly donor over many months. The relationship was further developed when a dozen roses was sent to the donor during the Rose Bowl game weekend in 1996. Northwestern had not been to the Rose Bowl (or any bowl game) since 1946. Later in the month of January, the donor gave close to $5M to the Dental School—most likely the largest gift ever given to a dental school at the time.

management of these relationships can take many forms, from a simple phone call to a personal visit to the donor's home. The most important thing to remember within the context of moves management is that the relationships cultivated by the fundraiser must be respected and maintained at the highest level possible.

Capital Campaigns

Kent Dove (2000) says, "A capital campaign is an organized, intensive fundraising effort on the part of a third-sector institution or organization to secure extraordinary gifts and pledges for a specific purpose or purposes (such as building construction, renovation, equipment acquisition, or endowment funds) during a specified period" (p. 5). See **Exhibit 7-8** for an example of a successful campaign. Once an organization has determined that it is indeed prepared to institute a capital campaign, it must then determine how to set the stage for garnering donations from its supporters. According to Stanley Weinstein, potential donors should be encouraged to participate in planning sessions prior to the launch of the campaign. He encourages organizations to "invite stakeholders and potential donors to planning sessions, briefings that include real question-and-answer periods, open houses, and breakfast or lunch meetings with organizational leaders. Encourage dialogue. Listen. Seriously consider the advice offered. And when your campaign gets underway, offer opportunities for people to participate as donors and volunteers" (Weinstein, 2004, p. 33).

By giving your potential donors the opportunity to play a part in the fundraising process, you will automatically be setting the stage for them to participate in the process later. Through encouragement and open lines of communication, they will feel as though they are directly involved in the process. They will in return be more likely to give generously to the cause when the time comes to make a donation.

As a part of planning for a capital campaign initiative, you should construct a gifts table. The construction of this table should be based on the mathematical principle of the 90/10 rule that states that 90% of the money for the campaign will come from 10% of the donors. **Table 7-1**, taken from Dove, illustrates a traditional gift table based on the following premise: "The lead major gift—the single largest gift needed—is calculated to be 10 percent of the campaign goal" (Dove, 2000, p. 69).

As discussed in the research section of this chapter, a capital campaign is a fundraising initiative not to be started without advanced planning. Once

Table 7-1 Standards of Giving Necessary for Success in a $2 Million Campaign

Gift Type	Gift Range	Number of Gifts	Total
Major gifts	$400,000	1	$400,000
	250,000	1	250,000
	150,000	1	150,000
	100,000	2	200,000
	50,000	2	100,000
Special gifts	25,000	10	250,000
	10,000	15	150,000
	5,000	25	125,000
General gifts	less than 5,000	all others	375,000
			$2,000,000

Source: Dove (2000, p. 69).

the campaign initiative starts, the process should be closely monitored, from the small, daily workings of the campaign to the "big picture." While all of the donors that contribute to the campaign are important to the process, ultimately the major gift donors will play the greatest role in the success of the initiative.

SOLICITATION FOR FUNDRAISING

Fundraising is much bigger than solicitation. Solicitation is the asking component of fundraising, and it involves only a small portion of the process. A survey of AFP fundraisers shows that only 15% of the time allocated to fundraising by professionals involves asking (Kelly, 1998). The rest of the time involves research, planning, cultivation, stewardship, and evaluation. However, do not think the lack of time involved means that solicitation is not important. Without asking people for financial support, giving will not be

Exhibit 7-8 Case Study: Hampton University Capital Campaign

In 1982 Hampton College conducted a major fund-raising campaign with a goal of $30 million. The purpose of the campaign was to provide a firm foundation for the future advancement of the university, for the development of innovative programs to meet student and societal needs, for the provision of scholarships for needy and deserving students, for the payment of adequate salaries to obtain and retain able faculty and staff, and for the construction of buildings to provide first-class facilities for efficient quality instruction.

The $30 million campaign generated $46.4 million. This campaign, the largest fundraising effort in the university's history, was completed in less than three years and exceeded its goal by more than 50%. During the campaign, the university received its largest gift ever from a foundation (a gift of $7.5 million) and its largest federal grant (an award of $2.25 million). Other seven-figure gifts included one for $4 million and another for $1.25 million. The successful completion of the campaign raised Hampton's endowment to $70 million.

The campaign's unprecedented success is documented in a number of tangible developments during the early 1980s. A marine science center, the Hattie McGrew Towers and Conference Center, a science and technology building, the Olin Engineering Building, and a storage/warehouse building were erected. The University Book Store, dormitories, classrooms, and faculty offices were renovated. Twenty-four new degree-granting programs were initiated. Twenty university-endowed professorships and several endowed student scholarships were established.

During the early to mid-1980s, Hampton's fundraising enterprise was characterized by challenge and progress. Overall, the university greatly increased its share in the philanthropic market. Contributions from all of the university's constituencies also grew sharply. Private gifts consistently reflected dramatic increases in the amount of funds generated. Foundation gifts rose by more than 1,400%, and corporate gifts increased by more than 400%.

Source: Harvey (1997, p. 136). *Successful Fund Raising for Higher Education: The Advancement of Learning.* © 1997. The American Council on Education.

encouraged. A few people do give without asking, but for most others, asking is the key ingredient in transforming someone on the sidelines to an active financial supporter of the mission of the nonprofit organization. Approximately a third of all respondents to a U.S.-based Independent Sector phone survey bring up "being asked" as a reason for making a gift (Mixer, 1993). Considering all the other reasons possible for giving a gift, solicitation is certainly one of the most important and can be leveraged by the organization in a big way by allocating resources to the task.

Solicitation takes many different forms, each geared to the type and level of gift expected. Annual gifts that may be in the range of $10 to $10,000 are usually solicited via letters and reply cards, phone calls from volunteers, special events, or e-mails that allow the prospect to link to a secured Web site for making a gift. Major outright gifts that may be in the range of $10,000 to $1,000,000+ are almost always solicited in person by someone high up in the organization. Planned gifts (trusts and bequests) at any dollar level are usually solicited via discussion with a professional with special knowledge of the tax issues that surround the details of these gifts. The following discussion divides along these three basic situations.

Annual Fund Solicitation

Direct mail forms the foundation of annual fund solicitation, although Internet fundraising is close behind and growing fast—especially for causes of deep national interest such as disaster relief. Direct mail involves several components. The organization can adjust these components to achieve the best results. The database containing the names and addresses of the prospects can consist of either an internal file or an external file purchased or rented from the market. The internal file contains past donors and prospects that have some relationship with the organization. Hospitals will have former patients, although new government regulations such as the Health Insurance Portability and Accountability Act of 1996 (HIPAA) prevent identification of the particular treatments provided to the patients. Schools will have former students and relatives of students. Museums and churches will keep track of attendees. Maintaining an up-to-date file of all donors and prospects is very important to a direct mail program—if the mail does not reach the audience, it does not matter how creative the message contained inside the envelope.

The letter forms the basic creative content of the piece. The letter should be written with the reader in mind and should not be simply a description of the organization and its programs. The more customized the letter, the better—for example, using an appropriate salutation that matches the writer and the reader. Be careful, though, of becoming too fancy. Using nicknames from college days may not be the most appropriate, even if those data are available (see **Exhibit 7-9**). The letter should be exciting to read with plenty of great examples and stories of how the mission relates to the reader. The one thing to remember is to always "ask" sometime in the letter. Do not beat around the bush—ask for "the order" with a particular amount that is appropriate to this reader. You may need to segment the file to allow for variations. Many times, giving clubs with different levels and names are used to help in the asking process. Regardless of how this is done, make sure to actually ask the prospect for the gift. The postscript (PS) section of the letter is the first thing the prospect will read. Anything you want to highlight should go in the PS.

The outside envelope is also key to developing a successful direct mail piece. The prospect will look at the outside for less than a second. Direct mailers have traditionally used "teaser copy" on the outside to encourage the recipient to look further. Others have used plain white envelopes with no return address to increase the curiosity of the potential reader. Still other organizations will provide a see-through window that exposes a gift for the reader (e.g., return mail stamps). Whether or not the envelope has a postal

Exhibit 7-9 Watch Out for Nicknames!

An older (very tall) alumnus of a university where I worked had a nickname, "Shorty," that he used as an 18-year-old student. He confided to me a few years ago that he had not used that name for over 40 years and was upset that it was used in the salutation of all letters coming from the university. Needless to say, what was supposed to be warm and friendly was neither to this reader. I quickly changed his salutation in the computer system and went through the system with staff to look for unusual nicknames that needed expunging!

stamp placed in the corner or is just machine stamped is also considered and determined. Using first class or nonprofit class, which has a longer delivery time, must be determined in advance. All of these different options can be tested by sending out two or three variations and comparing the results. Statistics need to be used to make sure the differences are actually significant. Generally, each category should have at least 40 responses.

The return envelope can be either postage paid or not. We did some extensive testing whether or not this mattered for annual fund donors to Northwestern University in the 1990s. The results were mixed. For donors who had never given before, it was very helpful to have the postage paid by Northwestern. Donors who had repeatedly given over the years did not seem to mind adding the extra cost of a stamp to their gift. Other organizations can run tests for this component to determine a pattern of giving for various return-envelope situations. Envelopes that go through the BRE (business reply envelope) process at the postal center can be delayed compared with a donor-provided standard first-class stamp on a regular envelope. At North Park University, we noticed that BREs would come in batches and include those with dates ranging from one to three weeks, which adds a further twist to consider.

Reply cards are another important ingredient in the direct mail packet. The card needs to contain the pre-printed name and address of the prospect and needs to have the name and address of the organization in case the card is inadvertently separated from the return envelope. There should be notes about how to make out the check, what level gift, and possibly how to match this gift at the prospect's work—if they have a corporate matching gift program. The card can be pre-coded for data entry of the gift information (e.g., donor id number and identifying mailing codes).

As you can see from the above discussion, direct mail has become a science in many ways. Still, remember that the solicitor is communicating with a real person and make sure the person's experience giving through direct mail is a good one. Direct mail solicitations should be creative, friendly, and welcoming.

Online fundraising is poised to surpass direct mail in the coming years, but the transition has been slow. At first, organizations expected all donors to respond instantly to e-mail solicitation. At Northwestern University we tested our first e-mail solicitation on our engineering alumni. We sent half direct mail and half an e-mail with a link to a Web site that accepted donations. The results showed that direct mail was the bigger draw—by far! It is clear that online fundraising is not the silver bullet it was thought to be. However, as Web sites become more sophisticated, donors become more familiar with handling various transactions online (e.g., banking, purchasing, research), and disaster relief fundraising continues to lead the way, the interest in online giving will increase.

Online gift systems can benefit from putting into practice three general ideas. First, an organization's online presence should reflect the look and feel of the materials being sent in the mail or appearing in the media. Create an integrated communication strategy. The logos should match. The case for support should be consistent. There should be links mentioned in written materials that would provide a way for the reader to access the Web site. Online giving should not be done in a vacuum. Second, the organization needs to make giving easy. Do not make the donor go through multiple layers to make a gift. Put the "giving button" in key locations and make it obvious. Third, make the online system as interactive and up-to-date as possible. Include a way for the donor to respond to the organization through a survey, comment board, or blog. Allow the donor to send things quickly and easily to others in his or her network. These three basic ideas provide the framework for a successful online giving program.

Major Gift Solicitation

Asking for outright major gifts from $10,000 to over $1,000,000 almost always involves a personal approach. Prospects for major outright gifts are known to the key people in the organization. They most often will have given gifts at the $1,000-plus level annually. The cultivation of the relationship with the prospect needs to be authentic and extensive. Asking the prospect for a major gift need not be "arm twisting" but more like a "tap on the shoulder" reminding the person of this new opportunity to continue support to the organization through an additional gift at a new, higher level.

The solicitation process for a major gift begins with the development of a solicitation plan. The development officer will assemble a small group consisting of the executive director or chief executive officer (CEO) of the organization (or head of the unit represented, such as a dean of a school within a university) and the key volunteer or staff member assigned to help with the solicitation. Everyone (CEO, director of development, and volunteer/staff) needs to have already committed to a gift at the same proportional level as they will ask the prospect to give. The group will develop a specific plan that answers the following questions: When will the prospect be asked? Where will the proposal be presented? Who will actually say the asking words? What specifically will be in the proposal? How will objections be handled?

The timing of the ask is sometimes neglected in the planning process. How about the timing from the prospect's point of view? Research may have shown that the prospect has recently sold his or her company—in which a delay is warranted to allow the financial details of the transaction to be firmer. The prospect might have something going on in her or his personal life, such as a child's wedding. This needs to be considered and may necessitate a delay by three to five months. What day of the week to meet? The common untested wisdom is to stay away from a Monday or Friday. How about lunch or dinner time? This may not be the best, because waiters may interrupt the conversation at the wrong moment and it is difficult to control the noise level.

Where to meet is also important to determine ahead of time. If the proposal is for a building under construction, the asking event could involve the construction site in a creative way. Looking at the plans and considering naming a particular room fits perfectly into a tour situation. Proposals that do not involve naming "turf" could be presented at the prospect's office, at a coffee shop near the prospect's office, at the prospect's home (especially if a spouse is involved), or at the CEO/executive director's office. The key is to provide a place that is comfortable for the prospect, somewhat controllable by the development officer, and certainly quiet enough for easy conversation.

Who should ask is always open to debate. Just because a volunteer is a very close friend of the prospect does not mean that he or she is the best one to do the asking. Often the best friend is not willing to be direct about the level of gift requested, and their friendship may prevent the prospect from being honest about the reasons for not funding the proposal. The head of the organization or unit within a large organization is the very best default solicitor for any major gift proposal. The CEO/executive director will be signaling to the prospect that the major gift purpose is the very highest priority for the organization. The resource commitment of the organization to the purpose is very important. Suppose the major gift would help to fund the construction of a new building. The donor needs to know that his or her gift will not be out there "alone" and that the organization will do all it can to complete the project. So what is the function of a volunteer in the process? Just being in the room and then briefly commenting on the gift he or she gave and how excited he or she is about the project is perfect. This reduced role may even help convince a nervous volunteer to participate! The director of development's usual role would be in managing the entire process, figuring out the logistics, and following up at the end of the meeting.

So what project or purpose do you ask for? What is in the proposal? Certainly, each organization must figure out the particulars. Development research staff can help with understanding the donor—how much money is possible, what interests they have that match with the organization, the possible pledge arrangements, and so on. Even so, the proposal (one to three pages describing the purpose and expected gift level) should have "draft" written clearly at the top (Kelly, 1998). This allows the donor to participate in the process and allows the organization to make adjustments following the donor conversation.

It is a great idea to think of possible objections in advance of the meeting. The most common objections are (1) can't afford the gift, (2) need to involve someone else in the process, (3) not a good time to give, and (4) don't like that particular purpose. Typical responses to these objections are as follows (in the same order as above): (1) you can spread the payments out over three to five years, reduce the amount, or switch to a deferred gift, (2) make an appointment for a meeting that includes the other people, (3) make an appointment for three to six months later or make the pledge a deferred pledge with payment due in one year, or (4) modify the purpose within the organization.

So with the plan set, how does this play out? First, a letter is sent from the person who will do the asking requesting a meeting. The letter is short but does indicate that the prospect will be given an opportunity to participate in a giving program or campaign. The person (or the development officer) calls to make the appointment. Getting the appointment is the most difficult, since most active wealthy individuals often have restrictive calendars. Prospects may also use the scheduling problems as an excuse or will try to discuss the gift over the phone. This is not the best situation. Work to get an appointment, even for just 10 minutes, and you will be more successful. Once the appointment is set, send a short letter that confirms the details.

At the meeting, the person from the organization who signed the letter welcomes the prospects and briefly mentions the purpose of the meeting—to ask for support to the organization. This reduces the tension in the room. Small talk can follow, including questions about the prospect's thoughts about the organization. Once the meeting moves into the proposal phase, the development officer may participate by explaining the details about the proposal. Once all questions are answered, the person assigned to asking will ask using some form of the following language, "Would you consider a gift of XXX to help fund the YYY proposal?" After the ask, the soliciting party needs to be quiet and wait for a response. This is not easy to do. Conventional wisdom says that "the next party to speak loses!" This, of course, is not really the case. The organization's mission is hopefully shared by the prospect, the prospect can afford the gift, the gift continues a strong relationship with the organization, and making the gift will help achieve the philanthropic goals of the prospect. Therefore, when the prospect responds—philanthropy happens—and our world becomes a better place for everyone.

If the prospect responds in the positive, then the organization's representatives thank the prospect (first of several thank yous) and leave shortly after. Final written documents can be exchanged in the mail after the donor makes this oral commitment. If the prospect has objections, they are met per the plan. If a further meeting is needed, the development officer handles the arrangements and maintains control of the situation as much as possible. Do not leave it in the hands of the prospect to "get back to you" in the future.

So much has been written about the solicitation process over the years that readers may think that all solicitations follow the pattern suggested by the various writers. Most readers think most proposals will be funded. However, each assumption is incorrect. Having worked in fundraising for most of my career, I can honestly say that very few major gift solicitations follow the exact pattern found in books—including this one! Serendipity takes over in most of the cases. If the development officer meets with a variety of prospects face to face over a year and works to lead them ever closer to the organization, good things will happen. Donors will suggest some major gifts themselves; special projects will be tailor-made to certain donors, and volunteer contacts will make the major gifts happen without the official solicitation ever happening. Finally, what percentage of "asks" are funded? There are no national statistics on this, but certainly most professionals would agree that only 10% to 25% of all major gift solicitations are funded at the level suggested. Professional development officers need to understand that rejection is a part of the process, and they need to consider solicitation as a true challenge and not at all a sure thing. In addition, a rejection can be the start of a new conversation about a gift down the road. Fundraisers need to see the glass as half full even during challenging times.

Planned Giving Solicitation

Professional planned giving officers typically do not even think of their meetings with donors as "soliciting" planned gifts. Prospect meetings to discuss planned (i.e., deferred or estate) gifts, because of the financial benefits to the donors, are much closer to financial planning sessions than major gift "asks." Potential donors reveal many financial details regarding assets, income, and dependents. Planned giving officers are trained to know something about tax implications of gifts as well as the charitable purposes and mission of the nonprofit organization. Often the charitable purpose is general or unrestricted support of the organization. No one knows what the particular needs will be for an organization 20 or 30 years in the future. In addition, many planned gifts are revocable, and an organization may not want to risk starting a specific program without a secure financial foundation of support. A bequest may specify setting up an endowment fund for general support, for example, but rarely would it mention creating a new department that would be endowed by the bequest. The exception would be irrevocable charitable trusts in which the assets are precisely identified and the gift is irrevocable. These might be more specific in charitable purpose, and the organization could take out an equivalent loan from a bank to implement the purpose before the money from the trust is finally available.

Meetings with planned giving prospects are usually one-on-one. The professional planned giving officer meets alone and develops a relationship that includes financial issues. The officer sends out a letter requesting a visit and follows up with a phone call to set up an appointment. Often the prospect list is determined through a direct mail program that includes a reply card the prospect sends back to the organization looking for more information on planned giving. Planned giving prospects are not always past donors, however, based on statistical analysis many will be repeat planned giving donors—setting up multiple trusts or gift annuities over several years (Lindahl, 1995).

The meetings are usually at the prospect's home or at a restaurant nearby. Listening to the donor is the key to the solicitation process. Once the officer understands the prospect, the officer develops a proposal that includes an extensive tax component. These proposals usually come from a purchased proprietary software package that includes the latest tax rates and describes in detail what the donor will contribute, how much the donor can deduct for income taxes, and how much the donor will expect annually in payments until the donor (and spouse) dies.

If the prospect agrees to the terms of the proposal, the officer implements the plan using specialized staff or outside services. In every case, the donor should be instructed that he or she needs to consult his or her own attorney and financial adviser before signing off on the planned gift. The thank-you process and even much of the donor recognition should be similar to that used with other major gift donors.

STEWARDSHIP FOR FUNDRAISING

In 2002 the Cooper-Hewitt, National Design Museum, Smithsonian Institution, made a discovery that would set the art world abuzz. A drawing by Michelangelo was found among the museum's holdings that had been previously misidentified. Essentially, no one knew the drawing existed until a Scottish museum director visiting Cooper-Hewitt on sabbatical unearthed the artwork while sifting through a box of drawings that sat in storage (Michelangelo drawing found, 2002). Initial estimates valued this work around $10 million to $12 million. This was an impressive find considering the museum purchased the artwork as part of a collection of drawings in 1942 for $60.

Is this a case of good fortune or poor management? Peter Frumkin (2002) raised this issue by describing the news as troubling. How could such a significant artifact sit in storage for 60 years? As Frumkin pointed out, how would people react "if a cash-strapped nonprofit community health clinic discovered it had a 'forgotten endowment' that it had neglected to draw upon for decades" (p. 35)? Although the impacts of these scenarios differ widely, the point is essentially the same. It matters how nonprofits take care of the resources entrusted to them. Nonprofits, as recipients of public faith, trust, and resources, have a responsibility to manage gifts in a responsible manner. In short, stewardship matters.

Stewardship: What Is It?

Stewardship is one of those practices that sounds like such a good idea. What exactly is it, though? The evolution of the concept comes through a variety of sources. In the religious realm, Christianity teaches that all things are a gift from God. People, therefore, are entrusted to use these gifts to do good deeds and to honor God. In the end, Christians believe that God holds accountable the stewards of his creation for their action or inaction.

The actual term *steward* morphed from the Old English word *stiweard* or *stigweard*. One root of the word, *sty*, means hall or a pen for livestock. The other root, *weard*, carries the meaning of keeper or guard (Gove et al., 1986). Pulling the roots together gives the literal meaning "keeper of the hall." Stewards were entrusted with and responsible for keeping, managing, even guarding their masters' belongings.

How Does Stewardship Apply to the Nonprofit World?

The Association of Fundraising Professionals (2003) defines stewardship as "A process whereby an organization seeks to be worthy of continued philanthropic support, including the acknowledgment of gifts, donor recognition, the honoring of donor intent, prudent investment of gifts, and the effective and efficient use of funds to further the mission of the organization."

People working in the nonprofit world are often entrusted with resources not their own. They serve as stewards who ultimately answer to someone else. The "someone else" is often a host of donors who support their nonprofit organization not only financially but also with their personal talent, their good reputations, and precious time. At the heart of stewardship is an attitude that drives the philanthropic spirit and compels many to give. It is a two-way street. The same attitude that compels a donor to give should drive those in the nonprofit arena to graciously accept these gifts and see that they are used to maximum impact for the giver.

"Stewardship is the conscience of philanthropy, a sentinel centering the organization on responsible action at all times." (Henry Rosso, quoted in Conway, 1997, p. 11)

Nonprofits exist to serve the public—or at least "common"—good, and they voluntarily accept the trust of the public and various stakeholders when they charter their organizations. The role of steward and the practice of stewardship apply to anyone who serves in a position where the management and accounting of financial resources is part of their job (Conway, 1997). Rosso sees this calling of stewardship as so vital that the very integrity of the organization is on the line (Conway, 1997). Maintaining public trust should always be an overriding priority as nonprofit managers and employees seek to fulfill the mission of their organizations.

Stewardship also helps to close the loop in the relationship best modeled as a social exchange (Blau, 1968). Donors who support an organization are provided "satisfactions" that encourage a continued relationship and possible future support. Some of the satisfactions can be considered a part of the stewardship of a gift. Not only the public at large but also individual donors develop a sense of trust over time as they repeat their giving behavior in an environment that values their support and shows it in a variety of ways.

Stewardship: Where Do We Start?

We have been talking about the theoretical side of stewardship, and it is time to cross over into practice. Yet organizations always need to keep the *why* in mind as the *how* is being considered. Mission and stewardship are vitally connected. So often the particular tasks of a stewardship program quickly become the focal point of any discussion on stewardship. Remember to determine tasks within the context of overall purpose of stewardship.

> The wisest move any non-profit agency can make is keeping on top of stewardship. (Don Fey, 1995, p. 42)

Planning and Policy

The first step toward implementing a stewardship program starts with planning and setting policy. Naturally, most nonprofit organizations already practice stewardship to varying degrees. However, certain advantages exist in making it a formalized practice. In creating a plan and setting policy, an organization hopes to answer the question: How do we accept, handle, manage, and invest our gifts (Dove, 2001)? In short: Who does what and when?

For example, what is the organization's policy regarding the naming of programs, buildings, positions, rooms, and so on in recognition of donors? Who will send out a thank-you note when someone donates $20 to the organization? What about $20,000? Will you create a system of donor societies where differing levels of gifts entitle the donor to various membership privileges? Who will be responsible for assuring donors that the organization used their gift in the manner they intended? Who will handle public relations for announcing the gift? What is the stewardship program budget? Can you spend $1,500 on a reception you are throwing your major supporters? These questions and many more are all policy considerations and should be included in the planning process.

Implementing the Program

The moment a donor makes a gift is the starting point in the stewardship process. From this moment, the organization is responsible for acknowledging the gift, donor recognition, honoring of donor intent, and wise gift investment all aimed toward an effective and efficient use of resources to further the mission of the organization (AFP, 2003). In the end, most nonprofits hope their diligent efforts will lead to closer donor relationships and continued support. These processes can be broken down into four categories: Response and Recognition; Responsible Gift Use; Reporting; and Relationship Building.

Response and Recognition

The term *reciprocity* used in a fundraising context is the response an organization makes after receiving a gift. A mutual exchange should occur between the donor and the organization. The donor relationship seems out of balance when nonprofit organizations fail to respond. However, a timely and sincere response—most often just a simple thank you—creates balance in the relationship. The donor feels satisfied with the exchange and may respond by making another donation in the future.

> At the applied level, reciprocity simply means that organizational recipients show gratitude for gifts. (Katherine Kelly, 1998, p. 435)

Saying thank you should be the first response an organization makes after receiving a donation. Showing appreciation should be timely and appropriate to the size of the gift. Kent Dove favors a thank you that is "personal, informative, and meaty" (2001, p. 350). Whatever the style, here are a few suggestions for getting the most from a thank you:

- Make a 48-hour goal. Send a thank you within 48 hours of receiving the gift. Do not take any longer than a week or two at the very most. Some donors will wonder if you received the gift if the response takes too long. Avoid the embarrassment of a donor getting his or her canceled check before receiving a thank you.
- Use wisdom and prudence. Significant gifts warrant more attention from the appropriate staff and volunteers. However, an excessive number of thank-you notes are not necessary. Ironically, "holding back" a significant

gift from the regular process can actually cause delays in responding to the gift as you wait for special text or the signature of a busy senior executive.

- Compose the thank-you notes at the same time that you create your annual fund drive solicitation materials so that they are ready to go when the donations arrive.
- Be creative. A thoughtful thank you can come in a variety of formats, messages, messengers, and gestures. See **Exhibit 7-10** for a creative example.
- For major gifts and planned giving, a more personalized letter may be appropriate. The person responsible for soliciting the gift should include a personal thank you and discuss how the nonprofit intends to use the gift. Final details and any terms for transfer of assets should also be included (Jordan, 2000).

The following details how a hypothetical arts organization might show appreciation to donors at various levels of giving:

- $50–$99 MEMBER
  - ○ Free subscription to the donor newsletter, priority ticket brochure, discounts on preview lectures, discount at the gift shop, and advance notice of special events
- $100–$499 PATRON
  - ○ All benefits listed above plus:
  - ○ Invitation for two complimentary admissions to a special concert, seating for one at an open rehearsal, invitation to a backstage tour
- $500–$4,999 FRIEND
  - ○ All benefits listed above plus:
  - ○ Two open rehearsal passes per season, listing in the program, priority invitations to special events, priority ticket service
- $5,000–$9,999 BENEFACTOR
  - ○ All benefits listed above plus:
  - ○ Listing in the annual report, use of a private dining room for a special event, five free valet parking vouchers per season

Exhibit 7-10 Thanking Donors

While in charge of annual giving for the University of Maryland, Katherine Kelly (1998) remembers stamping each check with "Thanks Again" in red ink. The hope was that the donor would receive the canceled check, see "Thanks Again," and remember the gift and the organization's gratitude.

- $10,000–$49,999 GRAND BENEFACTOR
  - All benefits listed above plus:
  - Invitation for you and a guest to a special dinner hosted by the executive director, one free designated compact disc of music
- $50,000–$99,999 IDEAL GRAND BENEFACTOR
  - All benefits listed above plus:
  - Invitation for you and a guest to a private dinner with the executive director, premier listing in the program, annual report, and at the special donor's annual meeting

In addition to showing appreciation, recognition is equally important. In most instances, recognition goes hand in hand with showing appreciation. Many people are honored by the recognition given in return for their gift. A word of caution: some donors prefer anonymity. It is best to involve donors when talking about recognition to receive input and address their needs. Err on the side of providing too much recognition if there is any question. People tend to say they do not want recognition, even when they really do want to be recognized. However, the key is to get to know your donors well enough to have a clear discussion as the recognition plan develops.

Common forms of recognition include:

- *Donor societies:* At predetermined levels, a gift grants the donor membership to a society. Membership has certain benefits for the donor like invitations to social gatherings, updates and newsletters, special rates or fees, and so on.
- *Small events and receptions:* Hosting a reception, commemorating a building, holding a ceremony, and other small events are means of recognizing the contributions of one or many. The point is to make people feel special and to honor their support. Small events give donors and recipients an opportunity to express appreciation. The intimate environment also furthers relationships and a growing sense of commitment (Jordan, 2000).
- *List of donor names in organizational publication:* Listing names in a publication is an easy way to recognize donors and is a common practice among nonprofits. Obtain permission from the donor. It is a good idea to include with the donor receipt a self-addressed stamped envelope and a card indicating permission to publish his or her name and a place to write the preferred spelling (Jordan, 2000).
- *"Premium" gifts:* The use of token gifts requires common sense, good taste, and knowledge of donor publics. Gifts range from donor pins and coffee

mugs to umbrellas and benefit tickets. Some organizations have a storied history of using inexpensive gifts as forms of recognition and appreciation. Their donors come to expect it. However, other donors feel that the gifts are unnecessary and in some cases, wasteful (Kelly, 1998). The last thing any nonprofit wants is to communicate that it does not need or is not worthy of support by giving out tacky or extravagant gifts. Also, be aware of IRS guidelines involving the receipting of "premium" gifts (see Chapter 6).

- *Plaques and naming privileges:* As dictated by policy, certain gifts are recognized by placing plaques and/or naming buildings, rooms, positions, and so on after someone. Give the donor a photograph of the moment or better yet, for a significant gift, present the donor with a small photo album with notations by each picture a few weeks after the event.
- *Media coverage:* For substantial gifts, alert and invite the media to ceremonies or receptions, but unless the gift is truly unusual (e.g., all-time largest gift made in the state of Iowa) the press will usually not participate in such events.

See **Table 7-2** for a helpful chart in organizing the recognition process (Dove, 2001, p. 354).

Responsible Gift Use

After receiving a donation, showing appreciation, and recognizing the donor, the next phase is using the gift responsibly. What does that mean? Well, this is the point where issues of integrity and ethics become very important. Will we use our assets to fulfill our mission efficiently and effectively? Can donors trust us to honor their intentions and keep our promises? James Greenfield calls stewardship "the 'bottom-line' of accountability" (2001, p. 187). As stewards entrusted with resources given to us, we are obligated to follow through with our promises.

"A steward is one called to exercise responsible care over possessions entrusted to him or her. Stewardship is therefore a trust and involves a sense of being accountable to someone or something higher than self." (G. F. Maynard III & J. A. Rice, quoted in Greenfield, 2001, p. 247)

The question of using gifts appropriately takes many ethical twists. For instance, what is appropriate spending on travel and entertainment? Would

Table 7-2 Donor Recognition at Various Giving Levels

	$100	$500	$1,000	$2,500	$5,000	$10,000	$25,000	$50,000	$75,000	$100,000
Acknowledgement letter	X	X	X	X	X	X	X	X	X	X
Information (newsletters, e-mails)	X	X	X	X	X	X	X	X	X	X
Mementos	X	X	X	X	X	X	X	X	X	X
Holiday card		X	X	X	X	X	X	X	X	X
Special events (cultural, academic, athletic, black tie)			X	X	X	X	X	X	X	X
Holiday gift				X	X	X	X	X	X	X
Birthday card				X	X	X	X	X	X	X
Personal letter or phone call from key volunteers or staff					X	X	X	X	X	X
Personalized site visit					X	X	X	X	X	X
Personal letter/or phone call from the chief executive officer						X	X	X	X	X
Reception with chief executive officer and key volunteers						X	X	X	X	X
Letter from recipient of endowment						X	X	X	X	X
Personal report on endowment						X	X	X	X	X
Personal report on annual giving amounts and cumulative lifetime giving								X	X	X
Publicity								X	X	X
Personalized donor recognition event								X	X	X
Personal visit from chief executive officer										X

Source: Dove (2001, p. 354).

donors approve of alcohol purchases? How exactly does the organization account for discretionary funds? Major gifts present other issues. What happens to named gifts when they become outdated or when the named building is torn down to make room for a new facility? What if an entire named unit or program is closed down due to a changing marketplace for clients? These are not easy questions to answer, and the potential for hurt relationships with donors is very real. The more upfront thinking by leaders, the better able the organization will be to maintain strong donor relationships during stressful situations.

Reporting

Reporting to donors is a key component in all responsible gift use, especially in terms of accountability. At its basic level, reporting involves informing donors how your organization used their gifts. It can be as simple as a quick update or as complete as a multi-page annual report and site visit. Regardless, reporting takes time and energy away from other fundraising activities. Sometimes the significance of this activity is easy to miss.

Henry Rosso (1991) advises fundraisers to see donors like investors. Investors want to see a return on their investment. Furthermore, a timely report fulfills the organization's obligation in the exchange relationship. Public trust is at stake. Reporting is also a chance for an organization to win over skeptics and is fuel for their future support. The words of Don Fey express it best: "Never pass up an opportunity to let your donors know how vital they are to your success" (1995, p. 42).

The audience should be the first consideration when composing reports. It affects style and content. For example, many foundations and grant-making agencies require specific accounting of their grant money. In his article "The Stewardship Report: Keeping in Touch with Friends," Fey (1995, p. 42) outlines a few basic elements to include when writing progress reports for grants:

- Cover letter
- Title page
- Needed background
- Summary of key points contained in the report
- Body of report
- Conclusion
- Necessary financial statements

For many donors, newsletters and annual reports are the most common reporting mechanisms. The essential aim for these outlets is to communicate the difference made and the impact achieved because of their continued support of the organization. Often the strong temptation to paint a glossy picture of the nonprofit leads many organizations to "fudge" the numbers. Obscuring expenses, misallocating costs, and inflating outcomes threaten the future of *all* nonprofit organizations. Organizations should use diligence and maintain the highest ethical standards.

Relationship Building

Contemporary fundraising has added a relationship-building element to the stewardship process. In the past, acknowledgment of the gift and responsible use dominated the discussion and practice of stewardship (Rosso, 1991). However, in the present, nonprofits have much to gain from nurturing donor relationships and pursuing further involvement after gifts are made. This makes intuitive sense and fits into the model of a social exchange. If the development of donors includes increasing levels of involvement with the organization and its mission, why wouldn't donors desire to sustain their contact?

A sense of ownership, feelings of attachment, and deep satisfaction describe a few benefits donors receive after making a gift. These are typical emotions of people who have become highly identified with the organization. By taking care of them, nonprofits can count on continuing support. Cultivating gifts from donors who already give their support is easier and cheaper than finding new donors (Kelly, 1998). Past outright donors are by far the most likely to give outright gifts in the future (Lindahl & Winship, 1992). Short-changing this part of the process is shortsighted. Organizations might think they should be concentrating on the "asking," but in reality there needs to be a balance with the "thanking."

Continuing, nurturing, and growing relationships is not rocket science. Rosso (1991) described fundraising as a "contact sport" (p. 159). Establishing contact with current donors should receive the same priority as new, potential donors. Phone calls, invitations to special events or meetings, providing opportunities to volunteer, birthday cards, and personal visits are all avenues toward growing relationships. This contact makes the fundraiser more aware of the preferences, interests, and needs of the donor. Creating networking opportunities can also be effective. With this in mind, nonprofit organizations should organize events where connections happen. For instance, allow board members a chance to mingle with donors at social events, or pair key volunteers with key donors during serving opportunities. Expanding the number of relationships donors have within the organization is a good strategy. It allows genuine, mutually beneficial relationships to develop outside the solicitation mode.

> Good stewardship leads quite naturally to stronger existing relationships and to the development of new ones with the organization. (Kent Dove, 2001, p. 249)

Stewardship: Final Considerations

Implementing a stewardship program or fine-tuning an existing one is a worthwhile objective. Starting from scratch may require a better record-keeping system, recruiting new volunteers, hiring and training staff, and locating funds, whereas fine-tuning could range from minor attitude adjustment to thorough evaluation of the program. Educating key players, stakeholders, and board members to gain their buy-in is paramount (Rosso, 1991).

Stewardship is not an option; it is a necessary part of the development process. Through careful planning and thoughtful policy, you can build the infrastructure of a great program. Carefully managing all aspects of response and recognition, using gifts responsibly, and building relationships will not only increase the contributions to an organization but will make a nonprofit more effective and efficient at fulfilling its mission. Stewardship is more than an idea—it is the driving force behind the spirit of philanthropy.

EVALUATION FOR FUNDRAISING

The final piece in the fundraising process is evaluation. Did the research, planning, cultivation, solicitation, and stewardship lead to successful achievement of all goals? What was accomplished? What was not finished? Why were the dollar goals met for major gifts and not the goals for the number of new donors to the annual fund? Were there human resource issues that came into play in the process? Did the organizational leadership and board members, and other volunteers, participate at the levels needed for success? Did the general economic conditions, both locally and globally, help or hinder the results? Finally, was the organization lifted forward through the fundraising process to new heights of success, nearer to the shared vision?

Process and Outcome Objectives

The planning process should be set up with evaluation in mind. Each year (or other period within the strategic time frame), the basic evaluation process should compare goals and objectives with final results. One of the objectives may have been to send out 50,000 direct mail pieces to prospects throughout the year. The results need to be tracked using the same framework. So the results may report that 55,000 direct mail pieces were actually sent out. The process objectives are the most easy to evaluate and explain the results, since they do not depend on donors to do their part in the process. If the direct mail was not sent, the analysis will quickly show what happened—someone was not doing his or her job, there was a postal strike, or plans were changed midstream. Adjustments to the organization as a whole or to the development operation specifically can be made based on this analysis.

The outcome objectives are also easy to track but much more difficult to analyze. The number of dollars raised via the direct mail program can be determined (if using a coding system for the gifts) with a high level of accuracy. However, determining why only $45,000 in gifts came in versus an objective of $100,000 is not always easy to do. Given the nature of nonprofit organizations, the board of trustees tends to focus on what can be easily quantified. Since mission success is often difficult to quantify, they tend to look at the dollar fundraising goals and can see what happened when comparing goals and results. Sometimes this is a very superficial comparison. They may then make employment decisions based on whether or not these outcome objectives were met—without always understanding the dynamics involved.

To get around the problem, the board should always look at evaluation of both the process and outcome objectives. A development office achieving its outcome objectives for the year but failing miserably on achieving its process objectives may represent a situation that does not bode well for coming years. The development officers need to demonstrate, for example, that they can make their visits, present proposals, send out direct mail, and create an online fundraising environment. In contrast, a development office might complete all of the process objectives and still not raise the dollar goals. If it is a one- or two-year "blip," then the development staff should be encouraged and not fired. However, if these results continue there needs to be a much closer look at what is happening. An outside consultant may be helpful in evaluating the situation.

Another problem with outcomes objectives is the way gifts are typically counted. Organizations tend to want to count as much as is legally and ethically possible in each category of objectives. This is fine from an organizational viewpoint. However, to better track success of the development operation, some adjustments are needed to the gift reports for internal evaluative use. First, the report should remove gifts that are received without much involvement from the development office. This is difficult to do philosophically, let alone logistically. Every time a gift comes in that was solicited outside of the regular development channels, the gift should be tagged in the computer and eliminated from the monthly/yearly internal fundraising report. Second, pledges should be recorded and pledge payments eliminated. Why? The effort to raise a major gift pledge is concentrated during the year the pledge is made. Counting the pledge (after adjusting for the time value of the pledge and possible default amount) will make the dollar results more closely aligned to the effort expended to get the pledge. Third, irrevocable charitable trusts should be counted at a reduced level. Considering the cost of money, a gift that will not be available to use for 5 to 20 years should not be counted at the same level as a cash gift. Obviously, when the donor dies and the money becomes available, it should not be double counted. Finally, bequest expectancies should be counted at a reduced level (determined by the life expectancy of the donor and the default rate) at the time the organization finds out about them. They should not be re-counted when the person dies (even if the amount is much more or less than expected). If organizations make these adjustments to their fundraising reports, the reports will better reflect the success or failure of the development operation.

The Importance of Evaluation

Evaluation is perhaps the easiest piece of the process to short-change. It takes time away from solicitation and cultivation. If goals are not reached, it may seem simpler just to ignore and create new goals for the coming year. However, if you look at fundraising as a systems process, the only way to improve is to understand the success and failure. Providing feedback into the system will improve the system over time and provide the support needed to help the organization achieve its mission.

FUNDRAISING AS A NONLINEAR PROCESS

The fundraising process goes well beyond solicitation to include research, planning, cultivation, stewardship, and evaluation. It is also not necessarily a linear process. Research on a prospect might be developed progressively as the phases are encountered through the process. During the solicitation, for example, the fundraiser might be gathering research that helps guide the solicitation or perhaps will guide future solicitation of this prospect. Solicitation might not just occur at the traditional single meeting set aside for this purpose. Instead, a prospect might have a preliminary meeting with the fundraiser just to get to know each other (research phase). The discussion of a possible gift might actually be brought up by the prospect at this early point in the relationship and a pledge made on the spot! And certainly evaluation occurs at each part of the process in an informal way. The fundraising process described in this chapter provides a framework for operations rather than a prescription to follow precisely. That is what makes fundraising both art and science.

REFERENCES

Association of Fundraising Professionals. (2003). *The AFP fundraising dictionary online.* Retrieved January 15, 2006, from http://www.afpnet.org/content_documents/AFP_Dictionary_A-Z_final_6-9-03.pdf

Association of Professional Researchers for Advancement. (APRA). (1998). Position paper: The strategic role of research in the development process. Retrieved January 15, 2006, from http://www.aprahome.org/TheStrategicRoleofResearchintheDevelopment/tabid/226/Default.aspx

Axelrod, T. (2004). *Raising more money, a step-by-step guide to building lifelong donor* (3rd ed.). Seattle, WA: Raising More Money Publications.

Bergan, H. (2002). Rating and screening prospects. *The Granstmanship Center Magazine Online.* Retrieved January 15, 2006, from http://www.tgci.com/magazine/Rating%20and%20Screening%20Prospects.pdf

Blau, P. M. (1968). Social exchange. In D. L. Sills (Ed.), *International encyclopedia of the social sciences.* New York: Macmillan.

Broce, T. E. (1986). *Fund raising: The guide to raising money from private sources* (2nd ed.). Englewood Cliffs, NJ: Prentice-Hall.

Broom, G. M., & Dozier, D. M. (1990). *Using research in public relations: Applications to program management.* Englewood Cliffs, NJ: Prentice-Hall.

Capital campaigns—Here's your initial checklist. (2006). *The NonProfit Times.* Retrieved August 5, 2008, from http://www.nptimes.com/enews/tips/capital.html

Conway, D. (1997). Interview with Henry Rosso on stewardship and fundraising. In D. F. Burlingame, T. L. Seiler, E. R. Tempel, D. Conway, & C. H. Price (Eds.), *The practice of stewardship in religious fundraising* (pp. 11–20). San Francisco, CA: Jossey-Bass.

Dove, K. E. (2000). *Conducting a successful capital campaign: The new, revised and expanded edition of the leading guide to planning and implementing a capital campaign* (2nd ed). San Francisco, CA: Jossey-Bass.

Dove, K. E. (2001). *Conducting a successful fundraising program: A comprehensive guide and resource.* San Francisco, CA: Jossey-Bass.

Dunlop, D. (1993). Major gift programs. In M. J. Worth (Ed.), *Educational fund raising: Principles and practice* (pp. 96–116). Phoenix, AZ: American Council on Education and Oryx Press.

Dunlop, D., & Ryan, E. (1990, November/December). Thirty years in fund raising: Master fund raiser David Dunlop tells what he's learned about the staff's role in dealing with donors. *CASE CURRENTS.*

Fey, D. (1995). The stewardship report: Keeping in touch with friends. *Fund Raising Management, 26*(9), 42–43. Retrieved October 11, 2004, from Business Source Elite database.

Frumkin, P. (2002, August 8). Museum's $10-million lesson: Stewardship matters. *Chronicle of Philanthropy, 14*(20), 35–36. Retrieved October 11, 2004, from Academic Search Premier database.

George, J. (2005, September 17). Farm aid: Expenses eat away donations. *Chicago Tribune.* Retrieved April 7, 2006, from LexisNexis database.

Gove, P. B., et al. (Eds.). (1986). *Webster's third new international dictionary of the English language, unabridged.* Springfield, MA: Merriam-Webster.

Greenfield, J. M. (2001). Accountability: Delivering community benefits. In J. Greenfield (Ed.), *The nonprofit handbook* (3rd ed., pp. 153–190). New York: John Wiley and Sons.

Harvey, W. R. (1997). Successful fund raising at a historically black university: Hampton University. In F. H. T. Rhodes (Ed.), *Successful fund raising for higher education: The advancement of learning.* Phoenix, AZ: Oryx Press.

Jordan, R. R., & Quynn, K. L. (2000). *Planned giving: Management, marketing, and the law.* New York: John Wiley and Sons.

Kelly, K. S. (1998). *Effective fund-raising management.* Mahwah, NJ: Lawrence Erlbaum Associates.

Lindahl, W. E. (1992). *Strategic planning for fund raising.* San Francisco, CA: Jossey-Bass.

Lindahl, W. E. (1995). The major gift donor relationship: An analysis of donors and contributions. *Nonprofit management and leadership, 5*(4). San Francisco, CA: Jossey-Bass.

Lindahl, W. E., & Winship, C. (1992). Predictive models for annual fundraising and major gift fundraising. *Nonprofit Management and Leadership, 3*(1), 43–64.

Maynard III, G. F., & Rice, J. A. (2001). Good governance: Requisites for successful philanthropy. In J. Greenfield (Ed.), *The nonprofit handbook* (3rd ed., pp. 242–289). New York: John Wiley and Sons.

Michelangelo drawing found at Cooper-Hewitt. (2002, July 11). Retrieved October 11, 2004, from http://www.culturekiosque.com/art/news/michelangelo.htm

Mixer, J. R. (1993). *Principles of professional fundraising: Useful foundations for successful practice.* San Francisco, CA: Jossey-Bass.

Ostrower, F. (1995). *Why the wealthy give.* Princeton, NJ: Princeton University Press.

Podesta, A. C. (1982). Organizing a corporate campaign: From first principles to final thank yous. In J. Dermer & S. Wertheimer (Eds.), *The complete guide to corporate fund raising.* Hartsdale, NY: Public Service Materials Center.

Rosso, H. A. (1991). *Achieving excellence in fund raising: A comprehensive guide to principles, strategies, and methods.* San Francisco, CA: Jossey-Bass.

Rosso, H. A. (2003). *Achieving excellence in fund raising* (2nd ed). San Francisco, CA: Jossey-Bass.

Weinstein, S. (2004). *Capital campaigns from the ground up.* Hoboken, NJ: John Wiley & Sons.

Young, C. E. (1997). Successful fund raising at a large public research university with a foundation: The University of California, Los Angeles. In F. H. T. Rhodes (Ed.), *Successful fund raising for higher education: The advancement of learning.* Phoenix, AZ: Oryx Press.

chapter eight

Boards and Fundraising

Organizationally, nonprofit boards provide a mixture of positive and negative for the fundraising operation. In 2006 the former executive director of the United Way of Metropolitan Chicago, Janet Froetscher, spoke at the Axelson Center Symposium, where she raved about her board. Membership included, among other business superstars, the CEOs of Motorola, Tribune Company, and Northern Trust Company. And these memberships are not in name only. She said they had great attendance at meetings and she works with them directly and personally to fundraise for the organization. Consider as well the executive director of a small women's shelter on the south side of Chicago. At a meeting where a fundraising consultant was brought in to meet with the board of directors, only two board members showed up—even though the executive director had been asked by the board to bring in a consultant! One board member brought along a two-year-old child who captured the attention of everyone in the room. So boards can be curses and blessings, but the key is learning how to get the most out of a board.

EFFECTIVE BOARDS

A board that is successful in fundraising must be an effective board more broadly defined. In order to set a course toward effectiveness when first forming a board, it is important to set a few things in place: creating a mission for the board, generating a job description for board members, and ensuring that all board members understand the mission of the organization. It is also important for a board that is already formed to revisit these critical criteria. "Over the course of time, the board of a nonprofit corporation may require structural adjustments to enable the corporation to continue to meet its mission" (Overton & Frey, 2002, p. 233).

Create a Mission for the Board

Begin by setting a mission for the board. What will be the main purpose of the board? Will they act as just a fundraising board? Will they oversee operations? How involved will they be in the daily operations of the organization? Part of the problems that boards face is the very structure itself. The board's roles are such that they both officially monitor the organization—especially regarding fiscal matters—yet they also are expected to perform fundraising tasks that are assigned to them by the very staff they are to monitor.

In their award-winning book *Governance as Leadership: Reframing the Work of Nonprofit Boards*, Chait, Ryan, and Taylor (2005) talk about three modes of board leadership. The first is the fiduciary mode. This is the mode required by the laws that govern nonprofit organizations. The board needs to make sure the organization is led by competent staff—through the hiring and firing of the executive director—and that the monies coming into and out of the organization's coffers are well accounted for and responsibly spent. If boards stayed permanently in this mode, fundraising would suffer. Board members would become bored simply "watching the dials." Their lack of engagement would make fundraising through them difficult at best. When they are stuck in this mode, it might even signal a very negative period of time in the life of the nonprofit.

The second mode of board leadership is the strategic mode, according to Chait et al. (2005). This mode can be characterized by the traditional annual strategic planning retreat. "Whether in the form of retreats or otherwise, many of the most successful nonprofit corporations require the board and staff members to engage in regular (often annual) strategic planning sessions" (Overton & Frey, 2002, p. 235). The staff provides the scope of the discussion and basic framework for the plans, and the board members participate by fine-tuning the plans and talking honestly about their involvement in tasks such as fundraising. Development of the specific fundraising plan might be done in a similar way by the board's development committee—staff prepares and committee members approve. Boards that can successfully move into the strategic mode are in better shape than those lingering in the fiduciary mode because they will be more engaged. Fundraising through them is possible, though more involvement at a true leadership level would be even better (Chait et al., 2005).

The final mode of board leadership—generative—is more difficult to describe. In this mode the board members are given the chance to take a stronger leadership role in the organization. Free and open discussion, not pre-organized by the staff, helps the board to set a vision for the organization. Grappling with big issues provides a setting where organizational identity can be addressed. Chait et al. (2005) give an example of a traditional museum faced with a request to allow their collection to be sent on a money-making tour of Las Vegas (pp. 109–110). By struggling with this issue, the board had to come to grips with who they were and who they were not—in the generative mode.

Boards that can move between all three modes, fiduciary, strategic, and generative, have highly engaged members who have the potential to take on strong leadership roles in areas like fundraising. Once the board adopts its working mode, it will be able to run effectively knowing its purpose within the organization.

Generate a Board Member Job Description

After the mission of the board has been set or reviewed periodically, a job description for board members should be generated or re-created to help the board achieve its mission. This will explain the time commitment, the tasks, the giving criteria, and the fundraising responsibility for each individual member on the board. It is important to set the standard up front so that each individual knows what is required of him or her. Chait et al. (2005) state, "When we discussed with 28 nonprofit governance consultants their recent engagements with troubled boards, 19 characterized the client's problem as ignorance of or confusion about roles and responsibilities" (p. 14).

One thing that should be defined clearly is the giving requirement. There is a long-standing debate whether to have a stated dollar minimum contribution required from each member. Whether or not a minimum is established, requiring that each member give proportionally should not be in debate. This

Exhibit 8-1 Sample Job Description: Board Members

1. Select, support, and evaluate the CEO.
2. Review and approve the organization's mission.
3. Participate in the organization's strategic planning process.
4. Help ensure the financial solvency of the organization.
   a. Participate in the fundraising process.
   b. Make your own gifts on a regular basis—both current gifts and by will.
   c. Oversee the fiscal management of the organization.
5. Become an ambassador for the organization. Spread the word about the organization and its mission throughout the community.
6. Communicate the perceptions of the community to the organization. Represent the community perspective to the organization to help it better serve the community.
7. Perform a periodic self-assessment and evaluation. How is the board doing?
8. Provide oversight and evaluation of the organization itself. Is the organization fulfilling its mission most effectively?

Source: Estes (1995, p. 252). Reprinted with permission of John Wiley & Sons, Inc.

can be enforced by using term limits. The amount of time a board member can serve should be clearly established.

Exhibit 8-1 provides a sample board member job description taken from Tracy Daniel Connors's *Volunteer Management Handbook* (Estes, 1995, p. 252). If a board is already in place, the board should review their overall objectives and tasks associated with their board duties. From this they should create a proper job description for members that includes fundraising and giving responsibilities.

Review the Organization's Mission

All of the board members need to clearly understand the mission of the organization in order to help the organization thrive and grow. "An effective mission statement succinctly reflects the board's agreement regarding the corporation's purposes and constituencies" (Overton & Frey, 2002, p. 7). Candace Widmer and Susan Houchin (2000) describe the importance of boards knowing the mission of the organization in their book *The Art of Trusteeship*. They state, "A clear mission is critical to building a cohesive board" (p. 7). As the board reviews current and new programs for the organization, it must evaluate if each plan properly fits within the mission of the organization.

For example, as highlighted above, the board of a traditional museum faced a request to allow their collection to be sent on a money-making tour of Las Vegas. At this point, it was crucial for the board to review the mission statement of the museum. Did the museum's mission statement align with its collection going on a tour of Las Vegas? If the tour was outside the scope of the organization's mission statement, then the board should have quickly turned down the opportunity. A strong board that properly knows its organization's mission would be able to quickly discern a solution to this issue and successfully move the organization forward. According to Overton and Frey (2002), "Confusion over mission impairs the efficiency of the board in the discharge of its duties. On the other hand, adoption or renewal (such as at an annual board retreat) of a corporate mission statement can rekindle the energies and help focus the attentions of the board members, both individually and collectively" (p. 7).

Recruit the "Right" Board Members

Once the organization has the purpose and mission of its board in place along with a job description for each board member, the "right" individuals must be recruited to join the board. An issue of *BoardSource* regarding boards' fundraising responsibilities states: "To fulfill the organization's annual and long-range goals and objectives, a board must seek quality candidates who can help the organization succeed with its fundraising programs. Finding the best people who can and will do the work is key to an organization realizing its full potential for financial success" (Greenfield, 2003, p. 19).

It is vital to take a person's ability to fundraise into account when considering him or her for the board, especially if fundraising is one of the main objectives of the board. When interviewing potential candidates, ask them how they see themselves contributing to the board, whether it be with fundraising, legal advice, marketing, accounting, and so on. Someone who is unable to think of a way that he or she can add to the board may not be a "right" fit for the board.

More important, the board should develop a recruitment strategy before even beginning to recruit new members. Robert Zimmerman and Ann Lehman (2004) discuss the importance of this in their book *Boards That Love Fundraising*, stating: "An effective recruitment process is vitally important to ensure the strength and comprehensiveness of your board of directors. Any professional recruiter will tell you that, when designing a

Table 8-1 Board Profile Grid

Skills	Board member name								
Fundraising									
Sales									
Business									
Public Relations									
Marketing or advertising									
Law									
Accounting or financial									
Other									
Traits and Backgrounds									
Fundraising experience									
Connections with people with money									
Connection with businesses									
Has personal wealth									
Is well known									
Has leadership skills									
Is a client representative									
Other									
Personal Characteristics									
Gender									
Race and ethnicity									
Disability									
Sexual orientation									
Age									
Religion									
Other characteristics of your community base									

Source: Zimmerman & Lehman (2004, p. 73). Reprinted with permission of John Wiley & Sons, Inc.

recruitment strategy, the first thing to do is to identify the required skills and traits" (p. 70).

The board needs to begin by evaluating the current status of its makeup, checking for weaknesses and gaps in its design. Any shortcomings should be outlined in a profile highlighting the required skills needed to complete the board's makeup. **Table 8-1** shows a sample grid to help identify the strengths and weaknesses of a board (Zimmerman & Lehman, 2004, p. 73). When identifying new candidates, the participants need to look for the abilities shown in the created profile and also the ability to "help the board move away from entrenched attitudes and assumptions, and to meet changing realities affecting the corporation and its mission" (Overton & Frey, 2002, p. 233).

A few other things to consider when recruiting new members to a board are profession, status, gender, race, ethnicity, and religion. Individuals who have worked as professional or volunteer fundraisers would be an asset to the board. It is important to have at least one or two people with fundraising backgrounds on the board, if at all possible. Salespeople are also good individuals to fill the role as fundraisers for the board since they know how to communicate the message and close a deal. People with public relations, marketing, and advertising backgrounds are always beneficial as well as those with law, accounting, or finance expertise. They can lend their talents by serving the organization in these areas.

Once potential nominees have been found, the board must review the criteria set for each board member. At this time they should discuss the board member job description. Maureen Robinson's book *Nonprofit Boards That Work* outlines the importance of stating the board member's requirements from the beginning. "If board members are expected to be personally generous, that ought to be stated during the recruitment stage, not at the orientation. If board members are expected to participate in fund raising, that must also be clearly spelled out and some thought given to what it will actually mean" (2001, p. 90). The organization will have a much stronger working board if all of the requirements for the board members are set from the start. Then each individual will know from the beginning what is required of her or him and as a result will make the most of her or his time on the board.

Educating the Board

In a discussion of boards with performance problems, Chait et al. (2005) say, "Board members are frequently faulted for being disengaged. They are faulted for not knowing what is going on in their organizations and for not demonstrating much desire to find out" (p. 13). Once the board is in place, a consultant should be hired to teach the board about the importance of their role within the organization. The consultant should encourage the board members to get involved with fundraising and help in some capacity, from writing thank-you notes to engaging potential donors. All board members can pitch in. Even though the executive director can say this to the board, sometimes it helps to hear it from a consultant. As Fisher Howe put it in *The Board Member's Guide to Fund Raising*, "Wise heads have said that consultants can tell boards and executives what nobody else dares to. Boards listen to consultants when they can't hear the same message from the staff" (1991, p. 124). Educating the board is a wise investment because the organization will most likely see a good return on the investment through increased participation of board members in fundraising.

An orientation meeting should take place for new board members in order to provide them with sufficient information about the organization and the board. "Effective use of a new board member requires that she or he learn as much as possible about the organization, its mission, history and hopes, as quickly as possible" (Overton & Frey, 2002, p. 229). The more knowledgeable the board members are about the organization, the easier it will be for them to effectively raise funds for the organization.

BOARD FUNDRAISING

Even when board members are fully engaged and educated, however, fundraising may still be a problem. Boards of well-established nonprofits tend to leave operations to the staff, but fundraising is often the exception. "Board members are often good at fundraising and community relations; they generally perform these roles ably and willingly" (Chait et al., 2005, p. 22). Because of their personal gift potential and their potential to contact individuals of wealth or influence, boards are asked to step into operations and aid in fundraising. How this is handled is important. The best example might be from a work setting where the boss decides to help the floor manager with a project—not by directing the project but by actually helping in the operations. How does the manager direct the boss who is suddenly "on the assembly line"? Very carefully! The same care goes into asking the board member to assist the fundraising department with donor contacts. A staff member should make sure to clarify for the member what the task will be and get agreement to participate. Encourage participation by pointing to examples.

Involve the board member in the planning strategy for the donor contact. Always follow up on commitments. Essentially, follow the guidelines for effective volunteer management as described by authors such as McCurley and Lynch (1989).

Developing a culture among board members for giving and getting will help tremendously as staff involves the board in fundraising operations. The key to involving board members in fundraising is to make them feel like they are a part of the organizational team. In G. Douglass Alexander and Kristina Carlson's book *Essential Principles for Fundraising Success*, they state, "An important educational role of the successful fundraiser is to get board members to view themselves as advocates, donors, askers, and stewards of the organization" (2005, p. 19).

Make board members feel like they are part of the team and ensure that they clearly understand and believe in the mission of the nonprofit. Asking for money is a very difficult thing to do, so the board members must have complete faith in the organization. Maureen Robinson, in her book *Nonprofit Boards That Work*, states: "There is only one thing that will get us over the fear of asking. . . . The one thing that will take a board member right up to the line and help him cross it is a belief in the power of the mission that overcomes all doubt and hesitation, a clear understanding of what the organization does that makes a difference for the good" (2001, p. 91).

And for the board members to clearly understand the mission of the organization, they must get involved and become part of it, observing and taking part in some of the daily activities—interacting with the clients. Robinson goes on to say: "The only board member who can achieve vertical takeoff on the matter of fund raising is a board member who is fully committed to the organization, has found a part of its work that has meaning for him, can connect his work on the board with the success of the organization, understands what the money will be used for, and can assure the fund-raising prospect that the money will be well spent" (2001, pp. 91–92). With that knowledge and belief in the organization the board member is well on the way to asking for money.

Before any board member asks for a donation, it is important that he or she has already contributed financially to the organization. Board members cannot expect others to give if they have not given themselves. Giving also instills confidence in the individual to ask others to contribute. A *Board-Source* report on fearless fundraising states, "Contributing also performs a psychological function; *it gives board members confidence to ask others to give*" (George, 2003, p. 3).

Once board members are ready to help with fundraising, they can start out slowly by thanking donors for their support. Convincing a board member to make five "thank-you" calls is easier if this activity is a part of the expectations for board members. This is where having a good job description set and explained to members before they join is helpful. However, if much of the board has been involved for a while and has not been expected to help with fundraising, convincing them to do this may take a little time and work. Achieving this culture change is not impossible, but it does take time—several years perhaps. The key is getting the leadership involved and clarifying the expectations on all relevant communications to the board members.

Fundraising tasks assigned to board members can vary by the particular interests and skills of the board member and the needs of the organization. Some tasks can be assigned to almost any member—for example, signing thank-you cards. Here are a few tasks that board members could do: (1) calling donors to thank them for recent gifts, (2) inviting their friends to fundraising events, (3) making lead gifts, (4) allowing the organization to use their names publicly regarding their gifts, (5) writing special thank-you notes by hand, (6) calling and asking prospects for annual gifts, (7) attending a face-to-face solicitation without saying a word, (8) attending a face-to-face solicitation and telling their story, (9) providing a list of potential prospects, and (10) going alone to solicit a prospect for a major gift. Many of these tasks are not difficult, but some do take training and skill, while others take a great deal of courage. No one on the board has an excuse for not participating at some level once the expectations are a part of the board culture.

Auxiliary Boards

Another way to expand the reach of an organization, increase its funds, and involve more donors is to create a separate fundraising board. Many nonprofits have additional boards such as an auxiliary board to oversee a fundraising event or generate additional funds and publicity for the organization.

Auxiliary boards come in many forms: a women's board composed of all women, a junior board made up of younger people in their 20s and 30s, or an auxiliary board that focuses on fundraising as a whole that is made up of all different types of individuals. All of these boards supplement the work of the main board of directors by bringing in more funds and awareness for the organization. Most of them aid the nonprofit in creating, managing, and overseeing fundraising events for the organization. These volunteer boards

Exhibit 8-2 Auxiliary Board Mission and Job Description

Kids' Club Junior Board Mission

The Kids' Club Junior Board strives to increase awareness about Kids' Club and raise new funds for the ministry.

Criteria for Junior Board Members
- Young professionals
- Good work ethic
- Mature Christian
- Connects to the mission of Heart for Kids' Club
- Willingness to give relative to their income
- Access to network for other volunteers and donors

Time Commitment
- Attend one monthly Junior Board Meeting
- Serve on a Junior Board Committee (i.e., publicity, event, sponsorship, etc.)

Junior Board Goal
- To create a distinct Kids' Club Fall 2007 fun, casual fundraising event that caters to all Kids' Club volunteers and donors, includes our children, and raises $30,000 for the ministry.

Source: S. Schwarcz (personal communication, 2006).

are very helpful to nonprofits, especially those with small development staffs that are unable to allocate much time to fundraising events.

Similar to forming a board of directors, the forming of an auxiliary board must begin with a board mission and board member job description. These help define the board and keep it on course. See **Exhibit 8-2** for an example of a board mission and job description. It is important to have at least one development staff person designated to work with the board so that the board has structured direction from the nonprofit. Once the board mission and job member description have been created the new board can be formed.

Women's Boards

One of the most popular types of auxiliary boards is the women's board. Susan Blankenbaker Noyes writes about Chicago women's boards in her article titled "A League of Their Own." Noyes (2005) states,

Women's boards, a powerful concept unique to the Chicago area, have been the institutional backbones of arts, museums, zoos and medical organizations for more than a century. . . . In fact, those who closely watch Chicago's philanthropic scene commonly believe that the overall health of a Chicago civic organization can best be measured by a) whether it has a women's board and b) the level of activity of the board. One thing is clear: The more successful the women's board, the more successful the organization is overall. (p. 65)

Women's boards in Chicago have done a great job of raising additional funds for Chicago nonprofits. The Joffrey Ballet Gala, put on by the Joffrey Ballet Women's Board consisting of 145 ladies, netted over a million dollars at the 2005 gala (Noyes, 2005). Many other women's boards for Chicago's well-known institutions such as the Lyric Opera, Chicago Symphony Orchestra, Lincoln Park Zoo, Field Museum, Ravinia, and others have netted over half a million dollars each at their fundraising galas (Noyes, 2005). All of these women's boards exist to plan and oversee an annual benefit to raise money and awareness for the nonprofit. Some of these boards, like the successful Joffrey Ballet Board, were formed by volunteers such as Maureen Dwyer Smith, a philanthropic volunteer (Noyes, 2005). **Exhibit 8-3** discusses how she successfully started a women's board. Without the assistance and backing of these women, many of these fine institutions would miss out on extra funds and publicity for their organizations.

Exhibit 8-3 How to Start a Women's Board

Maureen Dwyer Smith's strategy for building a successful women's board includes:

1. *Gain the confidence and cooperation of the board of trustees.* The female trustees and the wives of male trustees will likely be your first members.
2. *Call in your friends.* Smith credits many with incredible support.
3. *Give it roots and wings.* Start with a small group that loves to give back. Expand the board to accomplish high-flying dreams.
4. *Make your cause emotionally acceptable.* Joffrey creates events that fuel the universal dream of girls to become prima ballerinas.
5. *Make no small plans.* Next year's gala, an extravaganza in Millennium Park, promises to bring dance into the hearts of Chicagoans of all ages and backgrounds.

Source: Noyes (2005, p. 68).

Not only do these auxiliary boards help the organization generate revenue and awareness, but they also get donors more involved and connected to the organization. Auxiliary boards are a great tool for fundraisers to use as a way of cultivating their donors. Individuals consider it an honor and privilege to be asked to serve on a board, especially for the more prestigious organizations. Once on the board, the donor begins to take more ownership of the organization and will usually increase his or her giving level. For example, the Kids' Club Junior Board began as an auxiliary board to help create and plan a fall fundraising event for an after-school organization, although part of the strategy behind forming the new board was to involve younger up-and-coming professionals in the organization. Two months after the birth of the junior board, one of the junior board members, a 26-year-old, wrote a check for $15,000 to Kids' Club. Had the board member never been asked to join the board, he most likely would not have written such a large check. So, auxiliary boards are a great way to raise funds and awareness for the nonprofit as well as cultivate current donors (S. Schwarcz, personal communication, 2006).

PRESTIGE AND BOARD INVOLVEMENT

Finally, does it matter how prestigious the organization is when trying to inspire board involvement and success in fundraising? Unfortunately, yes, it does matter. Ostrower's book *Why the Wealthy Give* demonstrates that philanthropy and involvement with nonprofit organizations as a whole, and board membership in particular, provide the social elite with a framework that helps to define their culture (1995, p. 28). Membership on certain boards— large prestigious universities, hospitals, cultural institutions, and so on—are highly sought after by the social elite. In order to be "players" they will make the appropriate-level gifts and involve others when the time comes to ask for money to the cause. That is one of the reasons why larger, well-known institutions' women's boards such as those of the Joffrey Ballet, Lyric Opera, Chicago Symphony Orchestra, and others raise so much money—because "philanthropy is itself a mark of privilege and high social status" (Ostrower, 1995, p. 36). Membership on boards of smaller, human services organizations, in contrast, are not as sought after by the social elite. Some wealthy individuals from the Ostrower study felt that they contributed enough through payment of high taxes for the support of human services. These organizations will have a more difficult time recruiting board members who would be able to make a big difference in their fundraising success. Referring back to the opening example of the United Way of Metropolitan Chicago shows that it does help to have a strong name to recruit star power for the board. However, even a small nonprofit can recruit a high-quality board of dedicated volunteers, albeit with fewer social elite, if they understand the board development process and work hard to achieve their goals.

REFERENCES

Alexander, G. D., & Carlson, K. J. (2005). *Essential principles for fundraising success.* San Francisco, CA: Jossey-Bass.

Chait, R. P., Ryan, W. P., & Taylor, B. E. (2005). *Governance as leadership: Reframing the work of nonprofit boards.* Hoboken, NJ: John Wiley & Sons.

Estes, E. G. (1995). The role of volunteers in fund-raising. In T. D. Connors (Ed.), *The volunteer management handbook.* New York: John Wiley & Sons.

George, W. (2003). *Fearless fundraising for nonprofit boards* (rev. ed.). Washington, DC: BoardSource.

Greenfield, J. M. (2003). *Fundraising responsibilities of nonprofit boards.* Washington, DC: BoardSource.

Howe, F. (1991). *The board member's guide to fund raising.* San Francisco, CA: Jossey-Bass.

McCurley, S., & Lynch, R. (1989). *Essential volunteer management.* Downers Grove, IL: Heritage Arts.

Noyes, S. B. (2005, September). A league of their own. *NorthShore,* 65–69.

Ostrower, F. (1995). *Why the wealthy give: The culture of elite philanthropy.* Princeton, NJ: Princeton University Press.

Overton, G. W., & Frey, J. C. (Eds). (2002). *Guidebook for directors of nonprofit corporations* (2nd ed.). Chicago: American Bar Association.

Robinson, M. K. (2001). *Nonprofit boards that work: The end of one-size-fits-all governance.* New York: John Wiley & Sons.

Widmer, C., & Houchin, S. (2000). *The art of trusteeship: The nonprofit board member's guide to effective governance.* San Francisco, CA: Jossey-Bass.

Zimmerman, R. M., & Lehman, A. W. (2004). *Boards that love fundraising: A how-to guide for your board.* San Francisco, CA: Jossey-Bass.

chapter nine

Religious Fundraising

Religious organizations hold a unique status as the recipients of the largest slice of philanthropic giving. The Giving USA Foundation reports that in 2007, religious organizations received $102.3 billion, which amounts to slightly over 33% of the estimated total of charitable giving. Adjusted for inflation, gifts to religious organizations grew approximately 1.8% in 2007 (Giving USA Foundation, 2008). At the same time, though, giving to religious organizations may be less popular since it has risen more slowly than increases in other subsectors, and giving to religious organizations is below its 40-year average of 44.9% (Giving USA Foundation, 2004). **Table 9-1** provides an estimate of how many people adhere to the major religions. We will now consider the question: Are there aspects of fundraising that are particular to giving to religion? This chapter will provide a look into the distinctive fundraising and giving issues in religious organizations and compares them with the rest of the nonprofit sector.

Table 9-1 Followers of Abrahamic Religions

	Adherents	Countries
Christianity	2 billion	260
Islam	1.3 billion	184
Judaism	15 million	134

Source: Huebler (n.d., p. 1).

ISLAMIC FUNDRAISING AND GIVING

Islam is one of the "Abrahamic" religions of the world, so named because it, like Christianity and Judaism, descended from the prophet Abraham. Moses (associated with Judaism) and Jesus (associated with Christianity) are descended from Abraham's son Isaac, while Muhammad (associated with Islam) is descended from Abraham's son Ishmael (Huebler, n.d., ¶ 5).

The word *Islam* is the name of the religion and may be used as an adjective, as in "Islamic philanthropy." *Muslim* is the name given to an adherent of the religion and refers to a person of the Islamic faith. Care must be taken not to confuse religion with ethnicity. *Arab* is an ethnic identity. Arabs can be either Muslims or Christians. Conversely, many non-Arabs are Muslims. Examples of non-Arab Muslims are most people of Pakistan, Indonesia, and Afghanistan, as well as many people of India (Huebler, n.d., ¶ 13).

Judaism, Christianity, and Islam have similarities in messages, messengers, and doctrines that provide a basic understanding of giving:

- Each has a canonized written form believed to be divinely revealed: Torah (Judaism), Old and New Testaments (Christianity), and Qur'an (Islam).
- Each professes belief in a single God.
- Each subscribes to the belief that all people are God's creation and at most, humans are collaborative procreators.
- Humans are only the trustees of God's creation.
- Humans have no claims to Earth's bounty beyond what is necessary to sustain their own existence.
- The classical documents of all three religions agree that the responsibility to share wealth and other resources has both a voluntary and an obligatory component. (Smurl, 1991, pp. 2–3)

Islam is not a monolithic religion. As with other traditions, there is wide variance in the beliefs and practices of Muslims the world over. "Hakan

Yavuz of the University of Utah suggests that there are seven distinct 'zones of Islam': Arab, Iranian, Turkish, African, South Asian, Southeast Asian and Diaspora (i.e., non-Muslim majority countries)" (Alterman & Hunter, 2004, p. 4). Regardless of regional variations, Muslims all share certain common bases of faith.

Islamic Philanthropy

Muslim philanthropy needs no Western referents since philanthropy is a long-standing idea in Muslim communities (Alterman & Hunter, 2004, p. 1). The Islamic concept of *takafful* is the notion that each Muslim is responsible for every other Muslim, making charity not so much a matter of piety but obligation (p. 3).

Zakat, or "concern for the needy" is third of the five pillars of Islam (see **Exhibit 9-1**), and it means "giving back to Allah (God) a portion of His bounty as a means of avoiding the sufferings of the next life" (Alawan, 2006, ¶ 1). It is given annually at the conclusion of the feast of Ramadan and is generally 2.5% of one's annual income. It may be distributed to individuals, institutions, or relatives not in the ascending or descending line. Zakat is a norm of Islamic law, making Islam unique among the world's religions. "No other world religion prior to Islam has required charity in the form of a positive norm of law" (¶ 3). "Contributions are normally given at, or to, a mosque for collective distribution" (Huebler, n.d., ¶ 8). Muslims with incomes below a certain fixed threshold do not have to pay zakat (Benthall, 1999, p. 29). In modern times the state enforcement of zakat is almost unheard of, although many Muslims continue to make contributions voluntarily (Kozlowski, 1998, p. 282).

The Qur'an Surah 9–Verse 60 provides the key reference to zakat (see **Exhibit 9-2**). It specifies eight permitted classes of beneficiaries of alms:

Exhibit 9-1 The Five Pillars of Islam

- Belief in God and the Prophet Muhammad
- Prayer
- Charity
- Fasting
- Pilgrimage to Mecca (Hajj)

Source: Alterman and Hunter (2004, p. 3), Huebler (n.d., p. 1).

Exhibit 9-2 Qu'ran Surah 9–Verse 60

Alms are for the poor
and the needy, and those
employed to administer the [funds]; for
those whose hearts have recently been reconciled;
for those in bondage and in debt;
in the cause of God, and for the wayfarer;
thus it is ordained by God,
and God is full of knowledge and wisdom.

Source: Benthall (1999, p. 30).

- The poor
- The very poor
- Administrators of the alms
- Those recently or about to be converted to Islam
- Muslims in captivity (some scholars disagree on this and believe it refers to men from other tribes enslaved by the Meccans and Medinans)
- Debtors
- Those engaged in God's causes (fighters, teachers, etc.)
- "Sons of the road" or travelers (Benthall, 1991, pp. 30–31)

Besides zakat, Islam has several other forms of charity. The other major charitable forms of Islam are:

- *sadaqah:* a voluntary or discretionary charity, not necessarily monetary in nature
- *kaffara:* a penitential charitable contribution for the breaking of an oath
- *khoms:* a charitable obligation of Shi'a Muslims, calculated at 20% of annual profits, or 20% of income above and beyond living requirements (Alterman & Hunter, 2004, p. 5)

The Qur'anic reference for sadaqah comes from Qur'an 57:18:

Let those who give alms, both men and women, and lend unto Allah a goodly loan, it will be doubled for them, and theirs will be a rich reward. (Alawan, 2006, ¶ 8)

Likewise, the Qur'an tells that good deeds are also treated as a charity equal to sadaqah:

God is never unjust
In the least degree
If there is any good done,
He doubleth it,
And giveth from his own
Presence a great reward.
(Qur'an 4:40, Alawan, 2006, ¶ 11)

The Ja'afari school's observance of the 20% levy on the individual's surplus is based on the following:

Know that whatever of a thing you acquire,
a fifth is for Allah, for the Messenger,
for the near relatives, the orphans, the needy,
and the wayfarer. (Qur'an 8:41, Alawan, 2006, ¶ 14)

The Qur'an also addresses the manner in which charity should be given. Ostentation in the presentation of charitable gifts may make the gift unacceptable in the sight of God.

Nor those who spend
Of their substance, to be seen
of men, but have no faith
In God and the last day:
If any take the Evil One
for their intimate,
What a dreadful intimate he is! (Qur'an 4:38, Alawan, 2006, ¶ 16)

Objects of Islamic philanthropy have been relatively consistent across all regions of the world. These are:

- Mosques
- Schools (sometimes connected to a mosque)
- Hospitals and clinics
- Support for the poor, women, and orphans
- Aid to communities in distress
- Informal practices (ad hoc in nature, these are some of the most developed and impressive of all Islamic philanthropic activities—i.e., responses to natural disasters) (Alterman & Hunter, 2004, pp. 9–11)

Awqaf or "Endowments"

Awqaf (singular: *waqf*) are institutional religious foundations. They can be endowed by individuals, families, or institutions and usually do have income-producing activities. A *waqf ahli* is similar to a Western-style family trust, serving as something of a tax shelter for the transmission of wealth from one generation to the next. A *waqf khayri* is principally established to further the public good, to establish and maintain hospitals, clinics, schools, baths, and other institutions (Alterman & Hunter, 2004, pp. 6–7).

With the discovery of the Sasanian law book "Book of the Thousand Judgements," it has been firmly established that the roots of waqf lie in pre-Islamic Iranian law. Islamic jurists who developed waqf in the eighth and ninth centuries did not derive it from zakat, which had become corrupt and fallen into desuetude. Rather, they based waqf on the system discovered by invading Muslims when they conquered the Sasanian capital, located in what is now Iran (Arjomand, 1998, pp. 110–111).

Initially, awqaf were used by members of the patrician class to fund *madrasas*, or institutions of learning dedicated to Islamic sciences, traditions, jurisprudence, and theology. An added benefit to the patricians was that it allowed them to maintain control of family wealth. Badr B. Hasanuya, the Buyid governor of several provinces in western Iran, used awqaf as a tool of public policy when he used them to endow bridges, hostels, and wells (Arjomand, 1998, pp. 113–114).

Badr's endowment of hostels was an important philanthropic innovation. He attached them to teaching mosques, thus providing housing for out-of-town students who were visiting the mosques. The awqaf also provided for a small stipend. This model of the "teaching mosque/hostel/stipend" was later built into the madrasa of the eleventh century (Arjomand, 1998, p. 114).

During the tenth and eleventh centuries libraries or "houses of knowledge" were added to the list of public works funded by awqaf. They were used for lectures, research, and learned gatherings. Teaching hospitals were another type of public work funded, with a primary focus on health care training and research. Public works now began to take on the form of a larger project, often incorporating several kinds of public works into a single project. A mosque, a madrasa, and a hostel might be combined into a single complex, all funded by appropriate awqaf (Arjomand, 1998, pp. 113–115).

By the middle of the thirteenth century, very large projects had arisen, taking the form of the "educational-charitable complex." They might contain a madrasa, a mosque, a hospital, a pharmacy, a hostel, a library, and so forth. Scholars speculate that at some stage of their development, the educational-charitable complex was observed by Knights Templar who carried the concept back to western Europe, possibly even influencing the endowment and establishment of the first three colleges of Oxford in the mid-thirteenth century (Arjomand, 1998, pp. 114, 120).

The differentiation of state and nonstate activity is murky, especially in patrimonial societies. This is especially true in premodern societies because the interests of the state and ruler are often indistinguishable (Ilchman, Katz, & Queen, 1998, p. xii). Some scholars such as Makdisi, Bulliet, and Schacht view awqaf as strictly private acts. While this is technically true under Islamic law, it is not possible to separate the awqaf from public policy given the patrimonial nature of the prevailing society (Arjomand, 1998, pp. 116–117).

The Mongol invasion of 1219 began a long period of Mongol rule. Islam was disestablished as the state religion, but the Mongols permitted the awqaf to continue, even exempting them from taxation, thus making awqaf even more attractive as instruments of public policy. State revenues and land were freely mixed with private revenues and land in the same waqf without hesitation. Vizier Rashid-al-Din (d. 1318) was a stupendous builder of awqaf projects and viewed himself merely as an intermediary in the work of God (Arjomand, 1998, pp. 118–125). By the fourteenth century, awqaf had become the Islamic world's most common philanthropic institution (Kozlowski, 1998, p. 283).

With the rise of the Ottoman Empire, the awqaf remained an instrument of public policy. The Ottomans made two significant innovations in the awqaf: first, they extended the creation of pious foundations endowed by awqaf to non-Muslims, and second, they permitted the establishment of cash awqaf that loaned money at interest, thus circumventing the categorical prohibition against usury in the Qur'an. These cash awqaf became major credit institutions in the Ottoman Empire and were especially attractive to men and women of modest means (Arjomand, 1998, pp. 125–126).

By the early nineteenth century, the British had become the dominant power in India and were drawn more and more into disputes over awqaf. Although they would have preferred to remain apart from such disputes, eventually both British and French colonial courts ruled that in order to be legally valid, awqaf had to be primarily for religious and charitable purposes. These rulings became guiding principles for many post-imperial nation-states in the Muslim world (Kozlowski, 1998, pp. 287–288).

In modern Islamic states there is no single relationship between religious endowments and state institutions that prevails (Alterman & Hunter, 2004, p. 7). Legal reforms and modernization of the state have made the law of waqf obsolete as an instrument of public policy, thus reducing the public purpose of the endowments (Arjomand, 1998, pp. 126–127). In the early twentieth century many states nationalized awqaf in order to remove the shelter enjoyed by these institutions and as a response to confrontations between traditional wealth and modernizing bureaucrats (Alterman & Hunter, 2004, p. 8). Egypt, Libya, Syria, and Turkey seized the assets of all awqaf. Those that benefited families were abolished, while those that benefited historic preservation, education, or charity were preserved (Kozlowski, 1998, pp. 288–289).

These events have led to a number of significant constraints on Islamic philanthropy, all related to state control:

- Awqaf have been nationalized and are under the control of the state.
- Many states have appropriated religious authority.
- The state determines who can organize and for what purposes.
- The state has introduced government-organized nongovernmental organizations (GONGOs) (Alterman & Hunter, 2004, pp. 11–12).

Modern Islamic Philanthropy

The estimated worldwide giving to Islamic philanthropies is estimated to be between $250 billion and $1 trillion annually (Alterman & Hunter, 2004, p. 1). "Large Islamic charities such as the IIRO [International Islamic Relief Organization] now use fundraising techniques borrowed from the West" (Benthall, 1999, p. 37). Islamic philanthropy has seen some recent innovations and significant growth. Some of these experiences are documented below:

In Turkey over the past 30 years a new kind of waqf has appeared, founded by Turkey's wealthiest industrialists and financiers. The Western word *foundation* is often used to describe these awqaf, especially in English-language materials. These new awqaf engage in many philanthropies that are similar to Western-style foundations (Kozlowski, 1998, pp. 289–290).

In India, a few individuals have begun making strides in transforming small awqaf into thriving enterprises dedicated to public needs. On a larger scale, Hakim Muhammad Said's Hamdard Laboratories has established an Islamic research institute. Then, leaving his brother in charge of the Indian company, Said moved to Pakistan, where he established another Hamdard company. Subsequently, he converted the Pakistani company into a waqf that supports an impressive array of educational projects. He has succeeded in getting otherwise contentious factions of Islam to at least grudgingly work together for philanthropic purposes (Kozlowski, 1998, pp. 293–297).

With the influx of oil money, King Faisal of Saudi Arabia has emerged as a leading philanthropist. The Faisal Foundation, named in his honor, is always referred to as a waqf. The Faisal Foundation's activities resemble those of most Western foundations, with this exception: most of its grants are focused on Islam. Many projects involve building mosques and Islamic schools. India is a major recipient of the Foundation's funding. However, Chicago's Bilal Institute has also received support from the Foundation, as have projects in the United Kingdom, the Netherlands, New York, and New Jersey. Worldwide activity is roughly distributed as:

- 50% Asia
- 24% Africa
- 16% United States
- 10% Europe (Kozlowski, 1998, pp. 298–300)

CHRISTIAN FUNDRAISING AND GIVING

The term *fundraising* is not typically used in churches. A church needs funding to support its mission, but talk about money and financing in a church can be uncomfortable, and *fundraising* sounds too materialistic. More often, parishioners hear about *stewardship*. The *American Heritage Dictionary* (2000) defines *steward* as "one who manages another's property, finances or other affairs." In the context of the church, parishioners are asked to become the stewards of God's gifts, and they are encouraged to return some of those gifts to God through the church. The term *stewardship* was first used between 1870 and 1900 when church leaders "latched onto the word *stewardship* trying to get church members to become steady, regular supporters of mission endeavors" (Mead, 1998, p. 88). Regardless of the origination or interpretation of the term, *stewardship* is still recognized as a more acceptable word for fundraising within a church setting.

In the Christian tradition, congregants are encouraged to give as an expression of their faith. The Bible encourages readers to "Give, and it will be given to you" (Luke 6:38, New International Version; hereafter NIV), and it declares that "God loves a cheerful giver" (2 Corinthians 9:7). Most churches are different in size, governance, theology, and method of raising money, although there are general patterns relating these factors. Some depend upon weekly offerings; others hold annual pledge drives. Some emphasize stewardship, and others encourage tithing (giving a tenth of all income to the church). Unlike most secular nonprofit organizations, which have to do research to identify their potential donors, the donor pool for a church is already identified as the congregation's membership and active attendees. Church fundraising is unique for several reasons. The members are both the providers (through their financial support and volunteer labor) and the recipients of many of the services that the church offers. They are the board members, the Sunday school teachers, and the ushers. They sing in the choir, help out with the soup kitchen, and sometimes even pay the bills. Churches depend almost solely upon individual contributions. Volunteers usually do church fundraising. Only large churches with memberships of over 1,000 typically have staff fundraisers or development directors. Although not typical, some churches have set up a separate nonprofit organization as the human services arm to provide community support. This related nonprofit would then ask for support from foundations and government sources. An example of this relationship between a church and a human service nonprofit is the Fresno Covenant Foundation, which is partnered with several churches and schools in Fresno, California. The Foundation works with low-income families in the city of Fresno and receives government and corporate support (Fresno Covenant Foundation, n.d.).

Like most nonprofit organizations, churches are subject to the 80/20 rule of "skewness": 20% of the members contribute 80% of the funds, and 80% of the congregation contribute 20% of the funds, though the ratios vary among churches. Uneven giving holds across all congregations and is consistent with experiences of giving to nonprofit organizations as a whole (Iannaccone, 1999).

Research has shown that a positive relationship exists between donor age and religious giving but that no relationship exists between donor age and nonreligious giving. Religious giving most likely dominated past research that found a relationship between age and total giving (Hrung, 2004). People between the ages of 50 and 65 give the highest amounts. Giving decreases after age 65 because of a decrease in income. Additionally, older people tend to give a higher percentage of their income. Presumably, this relates to how people of various ages view "disposable income" (Hoge, Zech, McNamara, & Donahue, 1996).

In 1996 Dean Hoge, Michael Donahue, Patrick McNamara, and Charles Zech published a study on giving in five religious denominations: Assemblies of God, Baptist, Catholic, Lutheran, and Presbyterian. They found considerable differences in the level of giving to churches depending upon the denomination. "Members of some denominations give five times as much as members of others, in terms of percentage of household income" (p. 11). They conclude that the differences in giving are related to "how religious groups differ from one another, both theologically and organizationally" (p. 11). Hoge, Zech, McNamara, and Donahue classified denominations into five giving categories:

> Conservative Protestant, black Protestant, mainline Protestant, Catholic, and other. Conservative Protestants give the most—over 3 percent of their household income. Black Protestants give about 2.5 percent, and mainline Protestants follow at about 2 percent. Catholic giving is lower, at less than 1.5 percent. At the very bottom are smaller and newer religious groups—the Christian Scientists and the Unitarian-Universalists. In general, the more sectlike the denomination (that is, the more it maintains a clear distinctiveness from the prevailing culture), the higher the percentage given. (p. 13)

Hoge, Zech, McNamara, and Donahue (1996) identify the five factors most associated with high levels of giving to the church as: (1) high family income, (2) a high level of involvement in the church or parish, (3) conservative theology, (4) planning one's giving by the year, as in tithing or pledging, and (5) small congregation size.

All research has demonstrated a correlation between the level of family income and the level of giving to the church. Those with a high level of income give higher amounts, and those with lower levels of income give lower amounts. However, there is an inverse relationship between the percentage of household income given and the level of income. Households with a higher level of income tend to contribute a lower percentage of their annual income (Hoge, Zech, McNamara, & Donahue, 1996).

Research clearly shows that increased giving is associated with the level of involvement in an organization, and the church environment is no different. There is a correlation between the level of giving and the level of involvement in the congregation. Hoge, Zech, McNamara, and Donahue (1996) found that "church attendance and hours spent volunteering for church work are highly predictive of giving" (p. 70). Others have also found this correlation of regular churchgoing and high levels of giving (Santoro, 1995).

Another predictor of higher levels of giving is the practice of tithing or making an annual pledge for giving to the church. Those who decide to contribute a percentage of their annual income give more than those who decide to contribute a fixed amount annually. Those who plan their giving week by week contribute less than those who plan their giving by the year or the month. Church attendance correlates to this disposition toward systematic giving. The strongest predictor of tithing and annual planning of individual church giving is church attendance. Those who attend church regularly are much more likely to tithe or plan their giving annually, while those who do not regularly attend church usually give what they wish each week (Hoge, Zech, McNamara, & Donahue, 1996). It could be said that those who plan their giving strive to give what they consider to be "right" rather than what is left.

Research shows a positive relationship between involvement in religious organizations and contributions to secular nonprofit organizations. Perhaps the church fosters altruism, since there is also a positive correlation between contributions of time and money to nonreligious charitable organizations and contributions to religious organizations (Clain & Zech, 1999). An excellent resource for information about the relationship between religious giving, volunteering, and secular giving is *Faith and Philanthropy: The Connection Between Charitable Behavior and Giving to Religion* (Independent Sector, 2002). The data gathered and summarized in this special report support other studies that show positive relationships between giving and volunteering to religious organizations and secular organizations. The report includes data on people from all income categories and regions of the country.

While several studies have found a correlation between marriage and higher levels of giving to the church, Hoge, Zech, McNamara, and Donahue (1996) made a further connection. They noted: "Married members give far more than those who are single, divorced, or widowed. Moreover, in four of the [five] denominations [studied], married people give far more if their partner attends the same congregation as they do. But Catholics are an exception; married Catholics whose spouses do not attend the same parish give slightly more" (p. 65).

In their book *Plain Talk About Churches and Money*, Hoge, McNamara, and Zech (1997) identify four basic motivations for religious giving:

1. *Reciprocity with a social group.* This speaks mostly to the individual relationships that develop among the members of a congregation who call on

each other for favors. It is often said that people give to people, and this is true of the church environment as well. These reciprocal relationships are precious because they develop strong bonds over time and include both trust and support of one another.

2. *Reciprocity with God.* This is giving for the sake of salvation or for the belief that gifts are repaid through spiritual blessings. This could be a very potent motive indeed if the theology of the church encourages the belief that God is mindful of gifts and will reward the givers.

3. *Giving to extensions of the self.* For some members, the church becomes an extended family and as such becomes a part of their "extended self." The idea that we give to extensions of ourselves is in keeping with the finding that people who are active participants in their congregations tend to give more. Just as one may define identity in terms of one's occupation, one may also define identity in terms of faith and the church community. This analysis highlights the importance of having church leaders who are able to nurture feelings of love and a sense of belonging among the members.

4. *Thankfulness.* Giving back or repaying is a frequently cited motivation for giving to nonprofit organizations. Stewardship theology stresses that we are always receiving gifts from God, and it encourages giving gifts in thankfulness.

Surprisingly, Hoge, McNamara, and Zech (1997) do not list altruism as a separate motivation. Rather, they view altruism as being an integral part of each of the other four motivations.

Types of fundraising activities in a congregation range from small (bingo nights or sales of items such as baked goods, T-shirts, or Christmas wreaths) to large (multimillion-dollar capital campaigns). Some churches segment their budgets—that is, operating costs and missions—and therefore segment their fundraising accordingly. Occasionally, churches engage in joint ventures with for-profit companies. For example, Catholic Telecom is a long-distance and Internet service reseller that promises that a portion of every dollar billed will go to the subscriber's favorite church (McMenamin, 1997). However, virtually all churches rely upon individual contributions as their primary source of funding.

Tithing refers to the concept of giving 10% of an individual's annual income to the church. There are different interpretations of tithing. Some say that the tithe should be to one's church. Others suggest that the tithe should include all charitable giving, not just giving to one's congregation. Either way, tithing is not a typical example of church fundraising. "In fact, tithing began to be actively promoted in American Protestantism only in the nineteenth century, after [other methods of raising church funds] failed to produce enough revenue. Preaching to tithe may have produced more income, but few major religious groups in American history have ever succeeded in getting its adherents, on average, to give anything close to one tenth of their incomes" (Hudnut-Beumler, 1999, p. 51).

Hodgkinson (1999) found substantial differences in fundraising strategies between small, medium, and large congregations. Large churches tend to make use of more strategies, including hiring outside fundraising specialists and emphasizing long-range planning. Hodgkinson found that the most common fundraising strategies among all congregations are "making extensive use of board members in fund-raising (30 percent); developing a long-range strategy to increase individual giving (26 percent); using special events like carnivals or dinners (24 percent); giving existing staff responsibility for fund-raising (23 percent); and using sales of products such as T-shirts and baked goods (18 percent)" (p. 85).

Not all churches rely upon an annual pledge drive, although research has shown there is a clear benefit to annual giving campaigns. The members of many mainline Protestant churches and many Catholic parishes are opposed to making an annual financial pledge (Hoge, Zech, McNamara, & Donahue, 1996).

An annual pledge campaign can be conducted in several ways: one-on-one in person, one-on-one over the phone, in a small group or focus group, or by mail. In a one-on-one campaign, a group of member volunteers (usually from the stewardship committee) is recruited to visit the members, talk with them about their experiences with the church community, and ultimately ask them to make a financial commitment. A one-on-one strategy is the most effective way of conducting a successful campaign because it strengthens the relationships among the church members. It has already been noted that the reciprocal relationships that develop create strong bonds among the members. A one-on-one strategy is also one of the most difficult because of the numbers of volunteers needed. The phone campaign is slightly less personal, so the opportunity for building relationships is not as great. Small groups or focus groups can take the form of a social gathering or a meeting. This type of approach has the advantage of reinforcing the sense of belonging, or as Hoge, McNamara, and Zech (1997) call it, an "extension of self." The mail campaign is probably the most common and usually involves a form letter sent to every member of the congregation. This type of campaign is the least effective because the letter usually appeals to only a small segment of the population, and it misses the opportunity for relationship building. Annual fundraising appeals often use combinations of these approaches.

Regardless of the approach taken, the church stewardship committee usually conducts these campaigns. As stated before, only the largest churches have staff fundraisers, so the stewardship committee is usually made up of all volunteers. There are many resources available for conducting annual stewardship campaigns. For example, the guide *Fundraising with a Vision* by Edward Landreth (1997) is published by the Unitarian Universalist Association.

One might expect that the minister would provide a great deal of leadership in the stewardship campaign. In fact, many ministers do not receive much training in the area of stewardship campaigns and are uncomfortable with them. "Today's pastors are, at best, reluctant stewards of their churches' human, physical, and financial resources. Although their hearts are in the right place, pastors, by their own admission, frequently lack the knowledge and experience that is required to oversee the development and management of resources" (Conway, 1999, p. 101).

No matter what kind of church fundraising campaign is used, the most important element is to create a favorable giving climate in the congregation. Since Clain and Zech's (1999) research indicates that there is a correlation between church attendance and volunteerism and higher levels of contributions, they make the following suggestion: "A church that is feeling a financial crisis may in fact be suffering from an involvement crisis. Rather than running a campaign to increase member contributions through sermons, home visitations, and other fundraising techniques, churches feeling a financial pinch might be better served by focusing on increasing member involvement" (p. 940).

According to Clain and Zeck, another way for churches to create a favorable giving climate is to collaborate with nonreligious charities. "Since contributions to both groups tend to be complementary, church policies that entice members to contribute to nonreligious charities ultimately pay off in more resources contributed to the church" (1999, p. 942).

While the church provides a unique environment for fundraising, we find that perhaps the most important factor is creating a generous or giving community. The basis of effective fundraising is relationship building, and this is true for church fundraising as well. It is the sense of love and belonging to one's religious community that creates the bond of devotion to the mission of the church.

The Bible and Giving

In order to understand Christian fundraising, it helps to understand what the Christian scripture says about it. The theme of giving runs throughout the Bible, both the Old and New Testaments. The Bible speaks about the importance of giving, who is worthy of gifts, as well as how and why people should give. Although the Bible is certainly not a handbook for fundraising, it does help us to understand those prospects who read and follow the Bible's directives regarding giving and whose understanding of giving is developed through the lens of scripture. This section will focus on the New Testament text as representing the main teachings of the Christian faith. The Hebrew scriptures, the Old Testament, will be discussed at the end of the section on Jewish fundraising.

The New Testament

There is no doubt that Jesus is the central figure of the New Testament. Therefore, we will begin by looking at the Gospels, the four books of the New Testament that tell the story of Jesus' life and ministry. Luke 4:14–21 is an extremely important text for understanding who Jesus is and what his ministry would entail:

> Then Jesus, filled with the power of the Spirit, returned to Galilee, and a report about him spread through all the surrounding country. He began to teach in their synagogues and everyone praised him. When he came to Nazareth, where he had been brought up, he went to the synagogue on the Sabbath day, as was his custom. He stood up to read, and the scroll of the prophet Isaiah was given to him. He unrolled the scroll and found the place where it was written: "The Spirit of the Lord is upon me, because he has anointed me to bring good news to the poor. He has sent me to proclaim release to the captives and recovery of sight to the blind, to let the oppressed go free, to proclaim the year of the Lord's favor." And he rolled up the scroll, gave it back to the attendant, and sat down. The eyes of all in the synagogue were fixed on him. Then he began to say to them, "Today this scripture has been fulfilled in your hearing." (New Revised Standard Version; hereafter NRSV)

This text tells us many things about Jesus. By standing up in the synagogue and reading this passage of scripture and by claiming that the spirit of the Lord is upon him, Jesus is identifying who he is. He is the one who is able to bring this good news, this gospel, to the people. The second point is that this good news is aimed toward the poor. It allows the captives to be set free and the oppressed to go free. Proclaiming the year of the Lord's favor is a reference to the year of the Jubilee from the Old Testament. Jesus is claiming to have the ability to give those held captive freedom. This short text gives us insight into the purpose of Jesus' ministry by telling us why he is here and what he has come to do. Through an understanding of why Jesus came, along with knowledge of the purpose of his ministry, we are given a window into what the New Testament says about giving. This text is not direct in stating that giving should be focused on those less fortunate, but it certainly seems to imply this.

Other Gospel texts share this idea. The Sermon on the Mount in the book of Matthew provides a background for understanding Jesus' ministry. The very first words Jesus speaks are familiar ones, "Blessed are the poor in spirit" (Matthew 5:3, NIV). These words are directly in line with the theme of God's concern for the poor. As Jesus continues, he blesses those who mourn and those who are persecuted. The Sermon on the Mount even presupposes giving to the needy. Matthew 6:2 begins with these words, "So when you give to the needy." Verse 3 repeats these words. Giving to the needy is not an option, it is assumed. Jesus goes on to say that people should give to the needy not in order to receive praise from others but because it is part of Jesus' mission and purpose.

Matthew 6:19–21 (NIV) further illustrates the concept of giving and the relative importance of the temporal over the eternal: "Do not store up for yourselves treasures on earth, where moth and rust destroy, and where thieves break in and steal. But store up for yourselves treasures in heaven, where moth and rust do not destroy, and where thieves do not break in and steal. For where your treasure is, there your heart will be also."

Personal patterns of giving reveal the things that are important to people. Giving could be called a window into one's spirituality (Vincent, 2001). How people spend their money and whom they choose to give it to reveal the things that are important to them. The writer of 1 John puts it this way, "If anyone has material possessions and sees his brother in need but has no pity on him, how can the love of God be in him? Dear children, let us not love with words or tongue but with actions and in truth" (1 John 3:17–18, NIV).

Jesus shows how to put this love, this giving, into action while at the house of a Pharisee. He tells the host that whenever he has a luncheon or a dinner not to invite his friends, relatives, or rich neighbors because they may some day return the favor. He should invite the poor, the crippled, the lame, and the blind because these people cannot repay him (Luke 14:12–14,

NRSV). Jesus is expecting giving to occur without the receiving of rewards or benefits. The benefits are future in nature. Jesus' words here are, "You will be repaid at the resurrection of the righteous" (Luke 14:14). Dietrich Bonhoeffer, a famous German Christian theologian who was martyred during World War II for standing up against Hitler, puts it this way, "When we love those who love us, our brethren, our nation, our friends, yes, and even our own congregation, we are no better than the heathen and the publicans. Such love is ordinary and natural, and not distinctively Christian" (1963, p. 169). It would seem that giving, according to Bonhoeffer and according to the scripture we have looked at so far, must not be characterized by selfish motivation or gain. For a Christian, giving should be characterized by a concern for those less fortunate.

There are a few remaining texts in the Gospels that must be considered before we proceed to the remainder of the New Testament. The first is the story of a rich young man, told in each of the first three Gospels of the New Testament. In this lesson, Jesus recounts the story of a young man who comes to Jesus wondering what it takes to inherit eternal life. Jesus tells him that he must obey the commandments, and he lists a portion of the Ten Commandments. The man replies that he has done this since he was a boy. Jesus responds by telling him there is one thing he still lacks; he must sell all he has and give it to the poor. At Jesus' statement the man became very sad because of his great wealth. Jesus replies, "How hard it is for the rich to enter the kingdom of God!" (Luke 18:23–25, NRSV). "Indeed, it is easier for a camel to go through the eye of a needle than for a rich man to enter the kingdom of God." In Matthew 6:24, Jesus had said, "You cannot serve God and Money." Jesus held this man up as an example of how not to give. His giving was based on what he perceived his needs to be now, not laying up treasures in heaven. A similar parable is found in Luke 12:16–21:

Then he told them a parable: "The land of a rich man produced abundantly. And he thought to himself, 'what should I do, for I have no place to store my crops?' Then he said, 'I will do this: I will pull down my barns and build larger ones, and there I will store all my grain and my goods. And I will say to my soul, Soul, you have ample goods laid up for many years; relax, eat, drink, be merry.' But God said to him, 'You fool! This very night your life is being demanded of you. And the things you have prepared, whose will they be?' So it is with those who store up treasures for themselves but are not rich toward God." (NRSV)

The man is condemned because he planned only for himself; he was rich in his giving toward neither others nor God. The opposite of these two characters is seen in two other individuals in Luke 19 and 21. In Luke 19 Jesus meets Zacchaeus, a wealthy tax collector. After having an encounter with Jesus, Zacchaeus vows to give half of his money to the poor, and he vows to pay back anyone whom he has cheated at four times the amount. In Luke 21 Jesus contrasts the rich who give their gifts with a poor widow who put in two small copper coins. Jesus praises the woman's gift. Unlike the rich described earlier who gave out of their wealth, or out of a surplus, this woman gave out of her poverty, despite the fact that this was all she had to live on. C. S. Lewis offers insight into the woman's giving. He is also helpful in answering the question, how much is an appropriate amount to give?

> Charity—giving to the poor—is an essential part of Christian morality. . . . I do not believe one can settle how much we ought to give. I am afraid the only safe rule is to give more than we can spare. In other words, if our expenditure on comforts, luxuries, amusements, etc., is up to the standard common among those with the same income as our own, we are probably giving away too little. If our charities do not at all pinch or hamper us, I should say they are too small. There ought to be things we should like to do and cannot do because our charities expenditure excludes them. (Lewis, 1952, p. 86)

The final Gospel passage that helps us understand giving and the poor is Matthew 25. Here Jesus speaks of his return when he will separate people from one another based on whether they have given him something to drink when he was thirsty or something to eat when he was hungry. When he was a stranger did they invite him in, when he was naked, did they clothe him? Finally, when he was sick or in prison did they visit him? The righteous respond, wondering when they have seen him, hungry, thirsty, naked, or sick. Jesus' response is that whatever has been done to the least of those people has been done to him. The opposite is also true; whatever has not been done to the least of these people has not been done to him. "In Jesus, the service of God and the service of the least of the brethren were one" (Bonhoeffer, 1963, p. 146). How Christians give, how they spend their resources, and to whom they give are matters that are thought by believers as important to Jesus. There is a strong focus on giving to the poor in the Gospels, and this theme will continue to be prevalent as we turn to the remainder of the New Testament.

The book of Acts follows the Gospels chronologically. It tells the story of the early Christian movement after the death and resurrection of Jesus. Acts continues to show that God cares about one's giving. Acts 2:44–45 describes the church as having all things in common. They sold their goods and possessions and gave to anyone as was needed. Many have used this passage to support a divine version of communism or socialism. The passage does not need to be taken to this conclusion; it is not necessarily prescriptive for how the church should be run today (MacArthur, 1982). Nevertheless, it is descriptive for how this early Jerusalem church chose to take care of those in need. This idea of having everything in common is repeated in Acts 4:32–37: "There were no needy persons among them. For from time to time those who owned lands or houses sold them, brought the money from the sales and put it at the apostles' feet, and it was distributed to anyone as he had need" (Acts 4:34–35, NIV).

These verses do not ensure that if this model of giving is followed that there will never be any in need, nor are they mandates for how the Bible says one should give. Still, they are an important testimony to the lengths the early Christians went in order to care for their neighbors. They seem especially radical when we compare them with patterns of giving today. Paul's words to the Corinthian church are appropriate here: "What do you have that you did not receive?" (1 Corinthians 4:7, NIV). These people viewed everything as coming from God and it was only natural for them to share it with those in need.

Immediately following this story in the fourth chapter of Acts is the story of Ananias and Sapphira. Ananias and Sapphira sold a piece of property; they gave a portion of the proceeds to the apostles as was customary but withheld some of the money for themselves. The apostle Peter assumed the fact that the land belonged to Ananias before it was sold, and he also assumed that the money from the sale belonged to Ananias. This illustrates an important point. Having possessions or money is not evil: nowhere in our survey of scripture has this been the case. The Bible says that the love of money is the root of all evil; it does not say that money is the root of all evil (1 Timothy 6:10, King James Version). Money and possessions are neutral. However, the way that possessions and resources are used is not neutral. We have already heard Jesus' words: "You cannot serve both God and Money" (Matthew 6:24, NIV). The problem with the gift given by Ananias and Sapphira is that they attempted to deceive God with their gift (Acts 5:4, NIV).

Up to this point, we have gathered scripture from the Gospels and the book of Acts to show some common themes of giving in the Bible. Let us conclude by looking at 2 Corinthians 8–9, which is the most concentrated discourse on giving in the Bible. This passage will also help sum up some of the themes of giving that we have already seen:

- Giving is motivated by God's grace; it is done joyfully as an act of worship and submission.
- Giving should be generous no matter what the circumstances; it requires proportionate sacrifice.
- Giving is voluntary; it is a choice.
- Giving is aimed toward love and equality. (MacArthur, 2000)

Giving is motivated by God's grace; it is done joyfully as an act of worship and submission. In 2 Corinthians 8:1, Paul speaks of the grace that has been given to the Macedonian churches. Here Paul is urging the Corinthian church to model their giving after the Macedonian church that has given in response to God's grace. 2 Corinthians 9:7 says, "God loves a cheerful giver." Earlier it says, "They gave themselves first to the Lord" (2 Corinthians 8:5). The one distinction that separates biblical giving from other forms of good-natured giving is that it is an act of worship. Gifts are offered in gratitude to a gracious God.

Giving should be generous no matter what the circumstances; it requires proportionate sacrifice. Recall the widow who gave everything she had even though she was poor (Luke 21:1–4). 2 Corinthians 8:2 tells how the Macedonian church gave despite experiencing severe trials; their extreme poverty welled up into extreme generosity.

Giving is voluntary; it is a choice. This theme runs throughout 2 Corinthians 8–9. 2 Corinthians 8:3 speaks of the Macedonians giving out of their own accord. Verse 4 says that they urgently pleaded for the privilege of sharing in this giving. They may have been familiar with Jesus' words "it is more blessed to give than to receive" (Acts 20:35). Finally, 2 Corinthians 9:7 further cements the theme of voluntary giving, "Each man should give what he has decided in his heart to give, not reluctantly or under compulsion."

We should aim our giving toward love and equality. If there is one point that has been stressed repeatedly, it is that the Bible speaks often about giving directed toward the poor. When distinct missions were set up to the Jews and the Gentiles, the one thing that was insisted upon was that they "remember the poor" (Galatians 2:9–10). 2 Corinthians 8:13 puts it this way, "Our desire is not that others might be relieved while you are hard pressed, but that there might be equality." The God of the Bible strives for equality; concern for the poor and the oppressed was an important part of Jesus' ministry. He came to "bring good news to the poor" (Luke 4:18). Any plan for giving that wants to follow the patterns of giving in the Bible should include giving to the poor or the marginalized members of society.

JEWISH FUNDRAISING AND GIVING

According to Mead (1998), the Christian concept of stewardship of God's gifts is unknown to the members of a typical Jewish synagogue. In an article in *Forbes* magazine, Lee and Foster (1997) quote Rabbi Roy Rosenbaum as saying that "the Hebrew word for charity literally means justice or what is proper. It is your obligation as a human." In contrast, Christian traditions tend to view giving as a matter of spiritual growth. "Though different, both are religious motivations based on one's relationship to the divine, made manifest in community. Both address the question, what kind of people are we, and what kind of people do we wish to become over the course of our lives?" (Durall, 1998, p. 5). In the Jewish tradition, giving is "expressed differently through the concept of *tzedakah*, handed down from generation to generation. Translated from the Hebrew, *tzedakah* means "righteous giving," in which sharing is not a matter of individual preference, prayer, or reflection but rather a duty and an expectation, a matter of honor and justice. Many Jews believe that not giving would be like failing to provide for their children—an unthinkable dereliction" (Durall, 1998, p. 4).

The Jewish community has two kinds of communal organizations: synagogues and federations. Federations are similar to the United Way in that they raise money for a variety of charitable causes such as social services and relief efforts. Most Jewish households contribute the bulk of their charitable giving to the local federation. "The federation system's prowess at annual fundraising is already clear: More than $850 million is raised annually by 159 federations, which reach out yearly to hundreds of thousands of donors in an extraordinary fundraising achievement" (Edelsberg, 1999, p. 31). The motivation to give is not usually because there is any personal involvement with the federation, but because there is a sense of obligation or an expectation to give. "Donors spoke of this gift as an obligation they felt they had as Jews. In doing so, their emphasis was on a sense of ethnic identity and membership in a particular community, rather than religiosity" (Ostrower, 1995, p. 56). Peer pressure and visibility in the Jewish business and social communities are important factors in giving to

Exhibit 9-3 Jewish Federation Fundraising "Caucus" Dinner

Each year, during the annual fundraising campaign, the Jewish Federation holds its major donor "caucus" dinner. This dinner brings together a community's key leadership and major donors to launch the campaign. There is a strict "pecking order" among the donors, with the most prosperous donors expected to lead the way with a leadership level pledge. These annual pledges are $100,000 or more. Many communities, including most major cities, have annual gifts in the range of $500,000 to $1.5 million. All other donors follow suit with a major commitment, commensurate with their giving ability.

These donors, sometimes representing their extended families, stand, talk about what the Federation means to them, their history of involvement and giving in the community, and so on, followed by their announcement of their commitment, all followed by a round of applause. Since these donor families have, for the most part, been part of the community for many years, everyone in the room knows each other's profession, business, and wealth. Each leader—chairman, vice chairmen, campaign chairman, committee chairmen (endowment, social planning, allocations, etc.)—are expected to "pay to play": in other words, earn the right to be a community leader through philanthropy. There is added excitement when a new donor (for example, a young accomplished entrepreneur) joins the ranks of the major donors. Federations build new leadership by carefully choosing their annual campaign chairs.

Source: N. K. Winship (2005, personal communication).

Jewish federations (see **Exhibit 9-3**). "Federation fund drives are major community events, and in every city there is social pressure on affluent Jewish families to make large gifts" (Hoge, McNamara, & Zech, 1997, p. 34).

Jewish synagogues, in contrast, are supported through dues, fees for seats, and tuition. Synagogues sell memberships, and synagogue giving is not viewed as charity. Most charitable contributions are made to the federations. The typical synagogue raises two-thirds to three-fourths of its budget through dues (see **Exhibit 9-4**). The rest is usually raised through social events (Hoge, McNamara, & Zech, 1997).

The Old Testament and Giving

When people think about the topic of giving in the Bible, the first place their mind often jumps is to the tithe. The tithe, which simply means a tenth, is prevalent throughout the Hebrew scriptures, occurring first in Genesis 14:20 when Abraham gave a tenth of all he received to the priestly figure Melchizedek. Its final occurrence in the Old Testament is in Malachi 3:8, the book that brings the Hebrew scriptures to a close. In Malachi, the people were being indicted for failing to give God their entire tithes and offering. They

Exhibit 9-4 The Synagogue Membership Dues System

new year

it was sometime afterward
my father & i
went to a temple to hear
the services
        sat down in time
        to hear that haunting
        language for just a moment
when someone told us we had to
        stand in the back—
we had chosen 'reserved seats'
seats that had been paid for
we left & it was thus i completed
my external jewish education

my father was right
we never visited another temple
& now i wonder how many jews are
  destroyed in this country each year
  my father with his lonely eyes
  trying to return home
  only to have the american god of money
  slapped in his face

Excerpt from the poem "new year" by d.a. levy, originally printed in *Quixote Magazine* (Jan.–Mar. 1969).

were holding back from God, and God was expressing his displeasure with them. In Genesis 28:22, the tithe is given as "an offering of a part of the spoils of war" (Johnson, 1984, p. 24). The tithe as a system that all of Israel was expected to follow is not revealed until Deuteronomy 14:22–23 with these words: "Set apart a tithe of all the yield of your seed that is brought in yearly from the field. In the presence of the Lord your God, in the place that he will choose as a dwelling for his name, you shall eat the tithe of your grain, your wine, and your oil, as well as the firstlings of your herd and flock, so that you may learn to fear the Lord your God always" (NRSV).

This passage is insightful for what it tells us about God's purposes regarding a tithe. The Israelites are to set aside a tenth of what they produce in order that they might learn to fear God always. Here, as in many cases in scripture, fear is referring to a healthy reverence and respect for God.

God calls for the firstborn of the herds and flock. This theme is elaborated again in Deuteronomy 15:19–21. God desires the best of what we have to offer; in these verses God specifically says that he will not accept animal sacrifices that have any defect or flaw. This idea of giving a person's best is repeated in Numbers 18:25–32, where God reminds the Levites, the priestly class, to make sure the offerings they make are the best of what they have been given.

The idea of tithing is mentioned again in Deuteronomy 26. This time the reason for giving is further elaborated. Specifically, the Israelites are reminded of their deliverance out of captivity in Egypt. God has delivered them and set them free; therefore, as a reminder, they are to give these offerings to God in thanksgiving for what he has done. As these texts reveal, one of the principles for biblical giving is that it should be motivated by the grace God has shown to his people.

In Deuteronomy 26:12, the Israelites are also told that every third year they must offer a special tithe to the Levites, foreigners, orphans, and widows. The Levites were the priests of Israel who did not have land set aside for them off of which they could live. By offering a special tithe to the Levites, foreigners, orphans, and widows, God was looking out for those who often were not able to care for their material needs on their own. This theme of focusing on the poor or the needy is the most dominant theme of giving in scripture. It begins here in the Old Testament. In order to make sure that the poor would not be forgotten, the Israelites were given specific laws that ensured they would care for the poor.

Exodus 23 talks about these laws of justice and mercy. Verses 10–11 describe what are commonly referred to as Sabbath laws. The Israelites are told that for six years they can sow their fields and harvest their crops, but during the seventh year they are to let the land lie unplowed and unused. The purpose of this was that the poor might be able to receive food from the land. The same commandment was given regarding their vineyards and olive groves. These Sabbath laws were a smaller part of what was known as the sabbatical year. Three things took place during this year. The first was the command for the land to lie fallow (Exodus 23:10–11), the second was that all debts were to be released (Deuteronomy 15:1–2), and finally, the third was that all slaves were to be offered release (Deuteronomy 15:1–6, 12–18) (Pilgrim, 1981). Once again, these laws were given with the reminder from God that the Israelites were once slaves, but God has redeemed them. Scholars disagree as to how often the Israelites followed these commands, but whether or not these codes were practiced the majority of the time or not, they give insight into God's desire for giving that should be directed toward the poor. Through the establishment of these laws, God is showing his concern for justice toward the poor.

Closely related to the sabbatical laws is the year of Jubilee, which is outlined in Leviticus 25. Here the Israelites are told to count off seven sabbatical years. In other words, after seven seven-year periods, the fiftieth year will be the year of Jubilee. During this time, four things are to take place. The first three are identical to what takes place each sabbatical year: the land will lie fallow, debts will be released, and slaves will be set free. Leviticus 25:23–24 (NIV) describes the fourth thing that must take place during this year of Jubilee: "The land must not be sold permanently, because the land is mine and you are but aliens and my tenants. Throughout the country that you hold as a possession, you must provide for the redemption of the land." In other words, at the end of 50 years, land must be returned to its original owner. The purpose here is to discourage a situation where the rich become wealthier, while the poor continue to struggle to sustain themselves. This passage also reveals the theme that God gives us everything, including the land. We do not own anything, and therefore whatever we give to God is only our returning of something that ultimately is not ours. This changes a person's perspective on giving. It is not 10% that belongs to God, while 90% belongs to a person; rather, 100% belongs to God. What has been given are a "means to something greater, not . . . an end in themselves" (Hall, 1990, p. 36).

To this point, we have looked at what the Torah or Pentateuch, the first five books of the Old Testament, say about giving. The rest of the Old Testament continues and elaborates on these themes. We now turn our attention to examples from the history of Israel as well as the writings of the prophets.

The most concise summary of giving in the Old Testament may be found in the final chapter of 1 Chronicles. King David knows he is about to die and is preparing for the building of a temple dedicated to the Lord. It was David's desire to build this structure himself, but God told David that he had shed too much blood and thus was not fit to build the temple (1 Chronicles 22:8). Therefore, the responsibility was to fall to his son Solomon. 1 Chronicles 29 describes this process in detail, while giving more insight into God's view of giving. The first few verses detail the organization of the materials that are to go into the process; David is to use every resource at his command as well as his private treasure. In verses 14–16, David acknowledges that everything that they are giving comes from God. They are only giving back what God has given. See **Exhibit 9-5** for further information about King David.

Exhibit 9-5 More Information on King David and Sacrificial Giving

In 1 Chronicles 21, David is commanded by God to build an altar at the threshing floor of Araunah the Jebusite. David has sinned, and building this altar will help to atone for his mistake. It will also stop the plagues that have been killing his people. King David approached Araunah and offered to buy the land from him for the purposes that the Lord had demanded. Araunah offered the land to King David free of charge. We cannot know his motives, but he may have hoped to gain favor in King David's sight, or he may simply have felt pressured speaking directly with someone as powerful as David. David again offers to pay full price for the land, but a second time Araunah tells David that he will give it to him. He will even give him the oxen and the tools necessary to build the fire. Once again David declines the generous offer and insists on paying for the materials and the land in full. His response is that he cannot offer God something that belongs to Araunah; he must offer something of his own. David adds, *I will not offer a burnt offering that has cost me nothing.* David's story supports sacrificial giving. It is also a testimony that we can only give what is ours. As we have seen, later in his life, near death, David would give all that he had to the building of the Lord's temple. Although David was wealthy, he did not only give out of his surplus, but he gave richly of his possessions.

From David we switch our focus to giving seen through the eyes of the Hebrew prophets. As has been shown, a significant portion of biblical giving is looking out for the poor and the oppressed. A passage from the Torah serves as a bridge to the prophetic literature. Deuteronomy 15:10–11 says this: "Give generously to him and do so without a grudging heart; then because of this the Lord your God will bless you in all your work and in everything you put your hand to. There will always be poor people in the land. Therefore, I command you to be openhanded toward your brothers and toward the poor and needy in your land."

The prophet Isaiah echoes these ideas when he says, "Seek justice, encourage the oppressed, defend the cause of the fatherless, plead the case of the widow" (Isaiah 1:17). Isaiah's concern for the poor continues throughout his book, culminating in Isaiah 61:1–2, a text that draws back on the year of the Jubilee: "The Spirit of the Sovereign Lord is on me, because the Lord has anointed me to preach good news to the poor. He has sent me to bind up the brokenhearted, to proclaim freedom for the captives and release from darkness for the prisoners, to proclaim the year of the Lord's favor and the day of vengeance of our God, to comfort all who mourn."

The prophet Jeremiah also reflects on God's pattern for giving in the Old Testament. Jeremiah is condemning evil kings that have ruled over Judah. In Jeremiah 22:11–17, God condemns one such king, Shallum. The charges against him include building his palace by unrighteousness and injustice, and making his people work for no wages. God contrasts this with the work of his father Josiah, who was king before him and who defended the cause of the poor and the needy. In reference to the care of the poor and the needy, God asks a poignant question, "Is that not what it means to know me?" (Jeremiah 22:16, NIV). The prophet Jeremiah is asserting that supporting the cause of the poor and the needy is what it means to know God.

This theme of giving to the needy continues throughout most of the prophetic books in the Old Testament. However, in none is it more prevalent than in the book of Amos. Amos declared that sacrifices, ceremonies, and other forms of external religion were insufficient. Amos was concerned with social justice. This aspect of giving was essential to a life that was pleasing to God (Foster, 1998). Here is a passage from Amos 5:21–24 that highlights his message:

> I hate, I despise your festivals, and I take no delight in your solemn assemblies. Even though you offer me your burnt offerings and grain offerings, I will not accept them; and the offerings of well-being of your fatted animals I will not look upon. Take away from me the noise of your songs; I will not listen to the melody of your harps. But let justice roll down like waters, and righteousness like an ever-flowing stream.

Amos provides a fitting conclusion to our survey of the Old Testament regarding giving. The text tells the reader that God will not tolerate greed, nor will God tolerate injustices, but God has a passion for the poor and the oppressed and continually stresses the importance of caring for these people. The prophet Micah, who prophesized at approximately the same time as Amos, restates this conclusion as well when he answers the following question: "and what does the Lord require of you? To act justly and to love mercy and to walk humbly with your God" (Micah 6:8).

OTHER RELIGIOUS FUNDRAISING

Hinduism and Buddhism both stress "the obligations of believers to care for the poor and the sick and to promote education" (Salamon, Sokolowski, & Associates, 2004, p. 170). The term *dana* is used in both religions and means giving, generosity, or charity. "In the Buddhist religion, the concept of dana or 'selfless giving' is the first virtue among the Six Paramitas or Perfections" (Takamura, 1991, p. 79). "Giving in many forms is central to the Hindu tradition as expressed in the Vedas [Hindu scriptures]. . . . Translated variously as giving, donation, alms, etc., *dana* plays a major role within all the traditions of Hinduism" (Queen, 2005, p. 2).

Salamon, Sokolowski and Associates (2004) describe the history of religious giving in India:

> The emergence of Buddhism around 600 BC made voluntarism and the provision of social assistance and education key missions of monastic life. As a result, organized religion, especially monasteries, played an important role in providing public services, formal education, public utilities, and services to the poor and needy. Another area influenced by religion was the protection of certain trees and animals—a precursor of modern environmentalism. (p. 161)

Hindu temples in the United States, such as the Hindu Temple of Greater Chicago, raise funds through annual membership dues, donations, and sponsorships. Buddhist temples usually have charity boxes "into which the devotees drop a few coins as a contribution for the maintenance of the monks and the monastery" (Kariyawasam, 1995, p. 15).

CONCLUSION

Because religious organizations are currently the largest recipients of charitable contributions in the United States, it is important to understand what motivations and methods are involved in raising money for this group of organizations. This chapter also provided an in-depth discussion about the related religious scriptures and what they say about giving. Professional fundraisers who work with donors who are religiously motivated need to understand and be able to articulate the case for giving as found in various religious texts. Each religious faith presents particular ways of looking at giving and fundraising, but there is a clear connection among all faiths. Religious motivations from all backgrounds seem to share a common concern for giving to the poor and the needy—they all focus on gifts of compassion. Not that all religious people limit their giving to this area, but instead we find that donors motivated by religion give to both compassion and community.

REFERENCES

Alawan, C. K. (Haj). (2006). *Philanthropy in Islam* [From a religious panel discussion]. Retrieved October 11, 2006, from http://www.learningtogive.org/religiousinstructors/voices/phil_in_islam.asp

Alterman, J. B., & Hunter, S. (2004). *The idea of philanthropy in Muslim contexts.* The Center for Strategic and International Studies. Retrieved September 30, 2006, from http://www.csis.org/media/csis/pubs/idea_of_philanthropy_in_muslim_contexts.pdf

The American heritage dictionary of the English language. (2000). (4th ed.). Boston: Houghton Mifflin.

Arjomand, S. A. (1998). Philanthropy, the law, and public policy in the Islamic world before the modern era. In W. F. Ilchman, S. N. Katz, & E. L. Queen II (Eds.), *Philanthropy in the world's traditions.* Bloomington: Indiana University Press.

Benthall, J. (1999). Financial worship: The Quranic injunction to almsgiving [electronic version]. *Journal of the Royal Anthropological Institute, 5*(1), 27–42. Retrieved June 11, 2005, from the Academic Search Premier database.

Bonhoeffer, D. (1963). *The cost of discipleship.* New York: Macmillan.

Clain, S. H., & Zech, C. E. (1999, October). A household production analysis of religious and charitable activity. *American Journal of Economics & Sociology, 58*(4), 923–946. Retrieved January 17, 2005, from Business Source Elite database.

Conway, D. (1999). Clergy as reluctant stewards of congregational resources. In M. Chaves & S. Miller (Eds.), *Financing American Religion* (pp. 95–101). Walnut Creek, CA: Alta Mira Press.

Durall, M. (1998). *Creating congregations of generous people.* Bethesda, MD: The Alban Institute.

Edelsberg, C. (1999). Federation philanthropy for the future. *Journal of Jewish Communal Service, 80*(1), 31–38. Retrieved June 10, 2005, from the Academic Search Premier database.

Foster, R. J. (1998). *Streams of living water.* San Francisco, CA: HarperSanFrancisco.

Fresno Covenant Foundation. (n.d.). Retrieved August 8, 2005, from http://www.fresnocovenantfoundation.org

Giving USA Foundation. (2004). *Giving USA 2004.* Glenview, IL: Giving USA Foundation.

Giving USA Foundation. (2008). *Giving USA 2008.* Glenview, IL: Giving USA Foundation.

Hall, D. J. (1990). *The steward: A biblical symbol come of age.* Grand Rapids, MI: W. B. Eerdmans.

Hodgkinson, V. (1999). Financing religious congregations: A national view. In M. Chaves & S. Miller (Eds.), *Financing American religion* (pp. 79–86). Walnut Creek, CA: Alta Mira.

Hoge, D., McNamara, P., & Zech, C. (1997). *Plain talk about churches and money.* Bethesda, MD: The Alban Institute.

Hoge, D. R., Zech, C. E., McNamara, P. H., & Donahue, M. J. (1996). *Money matters: Personal giving in American churches.* Louisville, KY: Westminster John Knox.

Hrung, W. (2004, July). After-life consumption and charitable giving. *American Journal of Economics and Sociology, 63*(3), 731–732. Retrieved January 17, 2005, from Business Source Elite database.

Hudnut-Beumler, J. (1999). Historical myths about financing American Christianity. In M. Chaves & S. Miller (Eds.), *Financing American religion* (pp. 47–53). Walnut Creek, CA: Alta Mira Press.

Huebler, J. (n.d.). *Diversity essay: Philanthropy as a tenet of Islam.* Association of Fundraising Professionals. Retrieved October 11, 2006, from http://www.afpnet.org/ka/ka-3.cfm?content_item_id=6510&folder_id=1865

Iannaccone, L. (1999). Skewness explained. In M. Chaves & S. Miller (Eds.), *Financing American religion* (pp. 29–25). Walnut Creek, CA: Alta Mira Press.

Ilchman, W. F., Katz, S. N., & Queen II, E. L. (Eds.). (1998). *Philanthropy in the world's traditions.* Bloomington: Indiana University Press.

Independent Sector. (2002). *Faith and philanthropy: The connection between charitable behavior and giving to religion*. Washington, DC: Author.

Johnson, D. W. (1984). *The tithe: Challenge or legalism?* Nashville: Abingdon Press.

Kariyawasam, A. G. S. (1995). *Buddhist ceremonies and rituals of Sri Lanka*. Kandy, Sri Lanka: Buddhist Publication Society.

Kozlowski, G. C. (1998). *Religious authority, reform and philanthropy in the contemporary Muslim world*. In W. F. Ilchman, S. N. Katz, & E. L. Queen II (Eds.), *Philanthropy in the world's traditions*. Bloomington: Indiana University Press.

Landreth, E. (1997). *Fundraising with a vision: A canvass guide for congregations*. Boston: Unitarian Universalist Association.

Lee, S., & Foster, C. (1997, December 15). Loosen up a bit, folks. *Forbes, 160*(13), 64–85. Retrieved January 17, 2005, from ABI_INFORM database.

Lewis, C. S. (1952). *Mere Christianity*. New York: MacMillan.

MacArthur, J. (1982). *God's plan for giving*. Chicago: Moody Press.

MacArthur, J. (2000). *Whose money is it, anyway?* Nashville: Word Publishing.

McMenamin, B. (1997). Internet philanthropy. *Forbes, 160*(3), 46–47. Retrieved January 17, 2005, from Business Source Elite database.

Mead, L. (1998). *Financial meltdown in the mainline?* Bethesda, MD: The Alban Institute.

Ostrower, Francie. (1995). *Why the wealthy give: The culture of elite philanthropy*. Princeton, NJ: Princeton University Press.

Pilgrim, W. E. (1981). *Good news to the poor: Wealth and poverty in Luke–Acts*. Minneapolis: Augsburg.

Queen, E. L. (2005). *The roots of philanthropy in Hinduism, Buddhism, and Confucianism*. Unpublished manuscript, Emory University, Atlanta.

Salamon, L. M., Sokolowski, S. W., & Associates (2004). *Global civil society: Dimensions of the nonprofit sector*. Vol. 2. Bloomfield, CT: Kumarian Press.

Santoro, E. (1995, January). Religious givers want more information. *Fund Raising Management, 25*(11), 11. Retrieved January 17, 2005, from Business Source Elite database.

Smurl, J. F. (1991). *Three religious views about the responsibilities of wealth*. Indiana University Center on Philanthropy. Retrieved September 30, 2006, from http://indiamond6 .ulib.iupui.edu/cdm4/document.php?CISOROOT=/PRO&CISOPTR=32530&REC=13

Takamura, J. C. (1991). A volunteer caregivers' program in the Buddhist tradition. *Generations, 15*(4), 79. Retrieved June 11, 2005, from Academic Search Premier database.

Vincent, M. L. (2001). *Speaking about money: Reducing the tension*. Scottdale, PA: Herald Press.

chapter ten

Fundraising Among Diverse Populations

In the arena of American philanthropy, various diverse populations have been overlooked in much of the research on giving. Many nonprofit organizations have not tapped into this potential donor source (Fogal, 2002). With the emerging and growing wealth and purchasing power of this segment of our population (Berry & Chao, 2001), it is of great interest to the nonprofit sector to understand more about these cultures and to understand what motivates these groups to give.

The information available on diverse communities tends to focus on giving behavior rather than on particular associated fundraising strategies and techniques. However, as mainline nonprofit institutions begin to involve diverse communities in their organizations, a first step is to discover more about how potential donors act and think about philanthropy. This chapter represents a start for those venturing into the process of understanding and eventual engagement and partnership with communities different from themselves. In other words, the purpose of the chapter is to help fundraisers begin to think differently about how to cultivate relationships with potential donors from diverse communities.

A word of caution is included at this point. Generalizations about groups of people can be problematic. Obviously, groups are made up of individuals, and not all individuals within the group will act or think alike. Also, groups are dynamic and change through time as they interact with other groups and react to the challenges that arise. For example, an improved economic setting might provide a way for a particular group to increase their philanthropy. A downturn in the economy might encourage more giving within their own group. It is important to be cautious and always plan to do additional research as you begin to engage other cultures. Truly understanding a potential donor, regardless of race or ethnicity, quickly moves beyond the general understanding found in a textbook and requires hard work at the individual level of interaction. As fundraising centers on relationships, building relationships across cultures will allow fundraising to grow and develop over time.

A DIVERSE NATION

Before generalizing about the giving patterns of the diverse populations of the United States, it is important to examine how these populations are growing and changing. **Figure 10-1** illustrates the racial composition of the United States per the 2000 U.S. Census.

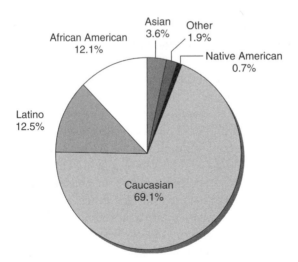

Figure 10-1. Racial composition of the U.S. population in 2000.
Source: Berry & Chao (2001, p. 6)

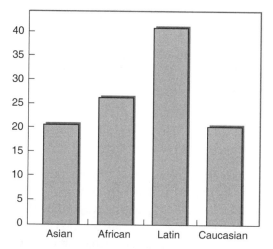

Figure 10-2. Percentage of income increase among cultural groups (1995–2000). *Source:* Fogal (2002, p. 20)

It is estimated that by the year 2050, individuals from various racial and ethnic populations will outnumber Caucasians. Some diverse populations are growing due to immigration and high birth rates. The Latino population is the most rapidly increasing. The Census Bureau has projected that by 2050, this population will constitute as much as 25% of the total U.S. population (Berry & Chao, 2001). Additionally, income levels are growing rapidly in some diverse communities. Latinos' buying power increased 84.4% to $383 billion between 1990 and 1999. This increase in income among various ethnicities is illustrated in **Figure 10-2**.

Giving to Family and Community

Philanthropy among some diverse groups is closely tied to family and relationships. Among these communities, more so than with Caucasians, giving begins at home and extends in concentric circles to extended family, friends, neighbors, fellow members of religious organizations, coworkers, other people in the ethnic community, relatives and friends in the homeland, and finally to society in general (Smith, Shue, Vest, & Villarreal, 1999). From a historical standpoint, American society was based around the family and the community. Through these networks, a "sharing and helping" tradition developed where individuals freely shared goods and services with one another. Eventually this informal system was replaced by more structured and organized government and philanthropic services. However, among ethnic groups, community and family relationships continue to be of central importance because of immigration, discrimination, and cultural factors (Smith et al., 1999). Research also shows that as a donor's wealth increases, his giving extends from the immediate family or community to a more disassociated giving through mainstream philanthropic institutions (Berry & Chao, 2001).

Similarities and Differences

The diverse population groups in the United States have shared a similar experience in that they have been isolated from mainstream philanthropy. Because of this isolation, these ethnic groups have formed their own philanthropic structures and practices (Berry & Chao, 2001). Despite these similarities, it is important to recognize that each cultural community is unique and has its own beliefs and traditions that are not shared by anyone else (Smith et al., 1999). It is important to avoid making generalizations that are too broad, which may perpetuate stereotypes. Furthermore, not all people identify strongly with their cultural background (Berry & Chao, 2001).

AFRICAN AMERICAN PHILANTHROPY

The historical context of giving for African Americans began during slavery when blacks formed strong networks of mutual aid and support. The concept of support and unity in the African American culture helped this group to survive the harsh and brutal conditions of slavery. Additionally, large extended support systems were created to replace the families torn apart by slavery. They created separate all-black neighborhoods, churches, schools, and other institutions. Informal patterns of helping and sharing were developed (Smith et al., 1999).

"The creation and evolution of the black church has been the most significant factor in the political, social, cultural, spiritual, educational, and philanthropic development of African Americans in this country" (Smith et al., 1999, p. 9). During the decades of racial segregation and inequality, the black church was one of the only entities that was run by the black community for the black community (Ellison & Sherkat, 1995). "In addition to spiritual guidance and support, churches provide human services and education to needy members, as well as social and leadership opportunities, financial assistance in emergencies, and political cohesion" (Berry & Chao, 2001, p. 31).

It is estimated that 84% of African American adults consider themselves religious and almost 70% are members of the church (Billingsley & Caldwell,

1991). Furthermore, the majority of African Americans, 59%, contribute financially to religious causes, particularly the church (Millett & Orosz, 2001, ¶ 11). Many African Americans consider contributing to the church an obligation, a concept that is instilled in its members from a young age (Holloman, Gasman, & Anderson-Thompkins, 2003).

Some observers have even gone so far as to refer to the rural southern black church as a "semi-involuntary" institution because of its role in the black community (Ellison & Sherkat, 1995). According to Emmett D. Carson, "African Americans understand that the role of the Black church—especially in the area of fundraising is legendary. We recognize that the Black church puts the force of authority and legitimacy behind its appeals to reach givers in the Black community. The Black church is a triumphant example of philanthropy among friends" (cited in Holloman et al., 2003, p. 138). In addition, many African Americans tithe to the church, regardless of their income or economic standing, as they feel it is their social and spiritual responsibility (Smith et al., 1999).

The black preacher is a powerful and influential figure within the black community. A great amount of trust is placed in the black preacher by the members of his or her congregation. Through this trusting bond, the preacher encourages church members to support the work of the church. Additionally, any organization that seeks support from the black church must first receive an endorsement from the minister. Furthermore, the black preacher is viewed as a spokesperson for the African American community in a society where this group may not have a voice otherwise. This is evidenced by many ministers becoming leaders, not only within the African American church but in our nation as well, such as Nat Turner, Malcolm X, and Martin Luther King, Jr. (Holloman et al., 2003).

An additional consideration in African American giving is whether there is an immediate need. Areas of particular interest to African Americans that receive the most support include religion, education, health, and human services. "They are motivated to give to tangible, concrete causes, especially when the appeal comes from well-respected members of their ethnic community" (Millett & Orosz, 2001, ¶ 11).

In addition to the church, social and fraternal organizations also serve as a vehicle to encourage African American giving. These organizations establish community service programs and encourage charitable giving, and the funds that are raised by these organizations typically support civil rights causes as well as scholarship funds. Although only 5% of African Americans participate in these organizations, they remain an important aspect of philanthropy by affluent, middle-class, and professional African Americans (Berry & Chao, 2001).

Exhibit 10-1 Tom Joyner

Tom Joyner, a successful radio personality, is using his influence in the black community to encourage giving among African Americans. His syndicated morning talk show blends music and celebrity interviews with serious discussions of major political and social issues affecting the black community. In 1996 Tom Joyner created the Tom Joyner Foundation, which raises money for historically black colleges and universities.

Source: Bachman (2002).

Recently, black philanthropy has begun to move outside of the black church, and a new generation of African Americans has moved philanthropy to a more individual approach (see **Exhibit 10-1** for an example). According to Emmitt Carson (2005): "African Americans no longer share a commonality of experiences even though we share history and skin color. As the axiom would suggest, the focus and direction of black philanthropy is more likely to be driven by individual interests rather than communal needs" (p. 9). Carson goes on to explain that the reasons for this include the fact that the African American community now has individuals of significant wealth, the diminished racial discrimination in America has caused philanthropy to be less race focused, and philanthropy is no longer centered just through the black church. This changing philanthropy appears to be associated with generational differences. "As people who are leaving school and starting a career, many younger donors turn their philanthropic efforts back to the educational institutions and programs that helped and supported them" (Mottino & Miller, 2005, p. 39). Understanding black philanthropy can no longer be seen exclusively through the lens of the black church. Readers interested in the most up-to-date information about African American giving should contact the following organizations: the National Center for Black Philanthropy, Washington, DC (www.ncfbp.net), and the National Black United Fund, Newark, New Jersey (www.nbuf.org).

LATINO PHILANTHROPY

It is estimated that 35 million Latinos live in the United States. Although the majority of Latinos in this country come from Mexico, other places of origin include Puerto Rico, Cuba, and Central and South America, as **Figure 10-3** illustrates.

Although Latinos in the United States are an extremely diverse group, this community's giving tends to be concentrated in three areas: family and

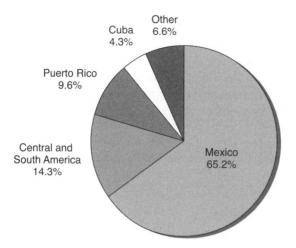

Figure 10-3. Countries of origin of Latinos in America. *Source:* Berry & Chao (2001, p. 32)

extended family members, religious organizations, and charitable organizations in the Latino community (Millett & Orosz, 2001, ¶ 14). The concept of family is very broad in the Latino community and generally includes extended family in addition to individuals who are not related biologically. Latino families are a close-knit group who give aid and support to one another. It is common for Mexican American extended families to live together, particularly because there is an expectation that older relatives will be cared for by their family (Smith et al., 1999). Many Mexican Americans financially support friends and family who remain in Mexico. It is estimated that as much as $3.8 billion is remitted to Mexico annually, much of this consisting of financial and in-kind gifts to family and friends (Berry & Chao, 2001).

The church is an important aspect in the lives of many Latinos and is often the recipient of charitable giving. In 1980 it was estimated that 73% of Latinos in this country were Catholic, and although this figure has declined somewhat, religion remains closely tied to the Latino community (Berry & Chao, 2001). For example, many Mexican families send their children to private Catholic schools, despite the significant cost. Religious giving in the church is also intertwined with various festivals that are held in celebration of a holy day (see **Exhibit 10-2**). These festivals, in the context of a community celebration, also serve as fundraisers for various charitable causes (Smith et al., 1999).

Lastly, Latinos support charitable organizations in the Latino community. Most Latino charitable organizations were formed fairly recently (Berry

Exhibit 10-2 Santos

Gifts and donations made in honor of religious icons, called *santos*, are an integral part of church giving for many Latino Catholics. Donations are often made to support festivals that celebrate the various saints. Additionally, some believers make a pilgrimage to the shrine of a specific santo, where offerings of prayer, money, and goods are made. These offerings are made in exchange for the santo's intercession (Smith et al., 1999). One Guatemalan man stated that santos "are almost like sacred [beacons] with the actual saint or the Virgin able to intercede on the asker's behalf with God. This is not entirely all. The saints, they have powers, each of them has their own, and people reward their saints accordingly for a good year, or the prosperity of the upcoming year."

Source: Smith et al. (1999, p. 60).

& Chao, 2001). Latinos generally have very strong cultural ties and often support organizations that benefit the citizens of their country of origin or fellow Latinos in the United States. For example, one analysis of Salvadoran organizational giving showed that much of the charitable giving among this community in the United States directly supported Salvadoran immigrants or aided in Salvadoran war relief (Smith et al., 1999). One Salvadoran who participated in this study reiterated the importance of helping fellow immigrants, stating, "We must help our people get informed and involved. They need to know how to use available services. A lot of times people don't know how to succeed. So it's our fault if we don't help" (Smith et al., pp. 86–87). Additionally, Latinos support organizations that promote social justice, advocating for public policies that are important to the Latino community, such as immigration policies and bilingual education (Millett & Orosz, 2001, ¶ 15).

ASIAN AMERICAN PHILANTHROPY

The 2000 Census estimated that the population of Asian Americans exceeds 10 million (Berry & Chao, 2001). The Chinese have the longest history in America of any Asian group, dating back to the late 1700s (Smith et al., 1999). Although the largest group of Asian Americans is Chinese in descent, as **Figure 10-4** illustrates, this may change as the result of significant immigration of Filipinos (Berry & Chao, 2001).

An important factor influencing Asian American giving is the discrimination this group has encountered in America. For example, within the Chinese community, the United States has a long history of implementing anti-immigration policies. These policies barred Chinese from entering this country, the earliest of which was the Exclusion Act of 1882. A further

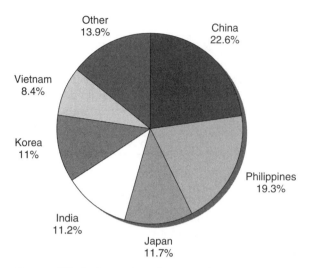

Figure 10-4. Countries of origin of Asian Americans. *Source:* Berry & Chao (2001, p. 35)

example of discrimination occurred during World War II when many Japanese Americans were forced to live in internment camps (Smith et al., 1999). Discrimination against Asians began to improve midway through the past century when, in 1952, Asian immigrants were allowed to apply for citizenship. "Nevertheless, the racially intolerant environment in American society held back Chinese economic development. Chinese immigrants and their descendants were essentially pushed into small business niches, because they were excluded from mainstream unions and other economic opportunities" (Smith et al., p. 106). Moreover, Asian immigrants relied heavily upon their community for support and protection as a result of the discrimination they encountered (Millett & Orosz, 2001, ¶ 18).

Motivations for Asian American charitable giving are strongly influenced by Confucianism and Buddhism (Smith et al., 1999). Thousands of years old, both of these traditions serve as models for charitable giving. "These wisdom traditions convey the central importance of community, oneness [and] connection with others" (Smith et al., p. 149). Traditional values in Confucianism and Buddhism teach service, compassion, and connection to the community. The principles of Buddhism and Confucianism encourage philanthropy more indirectly than do other religions (Smith et al., 1999).

Giving within this community begins first with their families and organizations that serve their families, then extends to organizations that support

Exhibit 10-3 Lulu Wang

Lulu Wang, a prominent Chinese American, is the president of a financial firm in New York and is an outspoken philanthropist in the Asian American community. In 2003 Ms. Wang donated $25 million to her alma mater, Wellesley College. Although reluctant to make this donation publicly, Ms. Wang was encouraged to do so by Wellesley College, in hopes that it would attract other donors. Ms. Wang understands that she has an important role in the Chinese American community, stating, "We have to take some form of visible leadership. Chinese are understanding that being part of a group you support lends strength to that group."

Source: Norton (2002, p. 38).

their countries of origin, and then finally extends to mainstream institutions (Millett & Orosz, 2001, ¶ 19). In the Asian community, children are taught at an early age the importance of family. Families consist of a hierarchy, and children must respect their elders. A sense of duty and obligation exists to care for one's elders (Smith et al., 1999). Additionally, it is very common for Asian Americans to send money to their countries of origin. This money, totaling billions of dollars, is given most commonly to family or to projects to improve the living conditions in their country of origin (Millett & Orosz, 2001, ¶ 17). Lastly, one of the most common areas of charitable giving outside of the Asian community is in the area of education. Asian Americans place great value on education and often support their alma maters (Berry & Chao, 2001). See **Exhibit 10-3** for an example.

NATIVE AMERICAN PHILANTHROPY

Native Americans are an extraordinarily diverse group. It is estimated that there are 2.3 million Native American and Alaska Natives living in the United States. This population consists of more than 800 different tribes, which speak more than 200 languages. These tribes differ in location, size, history, and religion. "Contrary to popular perception, in 1990 only 22 percent of all Native Americans lived on reservations and trust lands" (Berry & Chao, 2001, p. 37). Despite successful business ventures such as energy production, gaming, and resorts, many Native Americans struggle financially. It is estimated that as many as 50% of Native Americans who live on reservations live in poverty, and 25% of Native Americans who live in rural or urban areas live in poverty. However, wealth in this community is determined not by economic status but instead by how one cares for the tribe and its members (Berry & Chao, 2001). One form of giving used by some Native Americans is called the potlatch, which is a "ceremonial distribution of property and gifts to affirm or reaffirm social status, as uniquely institutionalized by the American Indians of the Northwest Pacific coast" (Potlatch, 2006). Potlatches were outlawed in Canada and the United States beginning in 1884 because "the potlatch came to serve as a means by which aspiring nobles validated often tenuous claims of high rank, increasingly through the ostentatious destruction of property" (Potlatch, 2001–2007). Potlatch ceremonies continued, however, and became legal again in 1951.

Some Native American cultures are based on the philosophy that giving should be mutual and equal for all parties (Millett & Orosz, 2001, ¶ 20). Furthermore, "sharing the abundance of the earth and its gifts are central Native American values. Because community assets are owned by the entire tribe, philanthropy is often communal" (Berry & Chao, 2001, p. 37). The concepts of giving and sharing are an integral part of this culture (Berry & Chao, 2001). Furthermore, Native Americans consider giving a way to honor future generations (Millett & Orosz, ¶ 20).

Most philanthropy in the Native American community is informal, although giving through charitable organizations is increasing. Some preferred areas of giving include nonprofits controlled by Native Americans, nonprofits that support issues related to Native Americans, intertribal networks, mutual aid societies, and professional organizations. Donations made to an organization are often anonymous, as the Native American culture does not affiliate giving with attainment of status or power like other cultures (Millett & Orosz, 2001).

BARRIERS TO GIVING

A number of barriers may limit, prevent, or discourage diverse groups from making charitable contributions to mainstream organizations. Many of the barriers stem from deep-seated institutionalized racism. Slavery, the poor treatment of immigrants from the southern hemisphere, and the legacy of Japanese internment during World War II are just a few parts of American history that contributed to the creation of barriers among societal groups in America. Moving across the barriers for fundraising is not simple. It takes hard work. Burnette (2005) describes mainstream organizations attempting to connect with the African American community: "Fundraising, not an easy business in most circumstances, is made even more difficult when fundraisers act like tourists in the neighborhood—just skipping through with limited understanding of and sensitivity to the local facts of life" (p. 113). Fundraisers working with diverse populations require an in-depth understanding of and sensitivity to the needs and interests of potential donors from those populations.

First, charitable organizations need to be sensitive to what communication preferences their donors may have (Campbell, 1999). For example, philanthropic organizations must be cautious with their terminology when referring to diverse groups. A term preferred by one person may offend another, such as "black" and "African American." Organizations should inquire about which terminology is preferred among their potential donors. Additionally, some non-English-speaking donors may be deterred from contributing if they are not able to understand written information provided by the organization. Therefore, nonprofits should consider producing bilingual marketing materials (Berry & Chao, 2001).

Second, diverse groups can be mistrustful of mainstream philanthropic institutions. Traditionally, diverse people offer assistance to family, friends, and neighbors directly (Smith et al., 1999). This informal giving creates immediate and visible results. One Guatemalan man quoted in Smith et al. states that he believes diverse populations do not give to philanthropic institutions "because they think it is a trick to separate them from their money. As the large institutions grow to become more like corporations, resembling business, they will get less because people are afraid to feed into greed" (p. 63). Furthermore, recent reports of nonprofits mismanaging money may result in increased donor skepticism and reluctance to contribute to nonprofits (Gibelman, Gelman, & Pollack, 1997). This mistrust may be minimized if organizations emphasize the immediate benefit of the contributions and devise a tangible way to show results of gifts that are made (Millett & Orosz, 2001).

An additional obstacle that may deter giving among diverse populations is their unfamiliarity with formalized philanthropy. Planned giving (such as giving through a bequest in the donor's will upon death or through a charitable trust arrangement) is an essential element to many nonprofit organizations, particularly as many large donations are planned gifts, and many endowments are funded through bequests, charitable remainder trusts, lead trusts, and charitable gift annuities (Clough, 1994). Diverse communities "are less familiar with planned giving, endowments, and the workings of mainstream philanthropy, so they are reticent to cede control of their assets to traditional institutions" (People of color, 2001, ¶ 6). Nonprofit organizations should help educate potential donors by holding informational seminars about the advantages of planned giving programs (Clough, 1994).

Lastly, organizations must have culturally diverse boards, employees, and volunteers in order to gain trust from diverse communities and to better reflect the interests of the diverse populations. Julie H. Daum, a consultant on increasing board diversity, cites several advantages of increasing board diversity that are applicable to nonprofits as well as corporations. She states, "There is a growing realization among leading companies that greater diversity among directors enriches the board's perspective, enhances understanding of customers and employees, and just makes good business sense" (Boardroom composition, 1995, p. 27). "In addition to raising sensitivity, a diverse board and staff also increase the likelihood of access to diverse social networks" (Berry & Chao, 2001, p. 28).

As nonprofits become more dependent on private donations, and competition for charitable donations increases, it will be crucial for organizations to foster relationships with diverse communities. Diverse communities are renowned for philanthropy within their own communities, exemplified by the African American philosophy "we give and then we give again, with whatever we have at hand" (Millett & Orosz, 2001, ¶ 11). In order to involve these communities in mainstream philanthropy, nonprofit organizations must be respectful of cultural differences, understand and work to eliminate barriers to giving, incorporate values that are important to diverse communities, and strive to create a diverse organization.

REFERENCES

Bachman, K. (2002). When Tom Joyner speaks, people listen. *Mediaweek, 12*(26), 18–21. Retrieved June 9, 2006, from the Wilson Select Plus database.

Berry, M. L., & Chao, J. (2001). *Engaging diverse communities for and through philanthropy.* Washington, DC: Forum of Regional Associations of Grantmakers.

Billingsley, A., & Caldwell, C. (1991). The church, the family, and the school in the African American community. *Journal of Negro Education, 60*(3). Retrieved June 9, 2006, from JSTOR Arts & Sciences database.

Boardroom composition. (1995). *Corporate Board, 16*(90), 27. Retrieved June 9, 2006, from the Business Source Elite database.

Burnette, A. G. (2005). Hopscotching in the neighborhood. In P. Rooney & L. Sherman (Eds.), *Exploring black philanthropy: New directions for philanthropic fundraising, No. 48* (pp. 113–122). San Francisco, CA: Jossey-Bass.

Campbell, B. (1999). Who are my donors? *Fund Raising Management, 30*(7), 28–29. Retrieved June 9, 2006, from the ABI/INFORM database.

Carson, E. (2005). Black philanthropy's past, present, and future. In P. Rooney & L. Sherman (Eds.), *Exploring black philanthropy: New directions for philanthropic fundraising, No. 48* (pp. 5–12). San Francisco, CA: Jossey-Bass.

Clough, L. G. (1994). Why planned giving? *Nonprofit World, 12*(2), 8–10. Retrieved June 9, 2006, from the ABI/INFORM database.

Ellison, C. G., & Sherkat, D. E. (1995). The "semi-involuntary institution" revisited: Regional variations in church participation among black Americans. *Social Forces, 73*(4), 1415–1437. Retrieved August 3, 2006, from the Academic Search database.

Fogal, R. E. (Ed.). (2002). *Fund raising in diverse cultural and giving environments: New directions for philanthropic fundraising, No. 37*. San Francisco, CA: Jossey-Bass.

Gibelman, M., Gelman, S. R., & Pollack, D. (1997). The credibility of nonprofit boards: A view from the 1990s and beyond. *Administration in Social Work, 21*(2), 21–40.

Holloman, D. B., Gasman, M., & Anderson-Thompkins, S. (2003). Motivations for philanthropic giving in the African American church: Implications for Black college fundraising. *Journal of Research on Christian Education, 12*(2), 137–169. Retrieved August 3, 2006, from the Academic Search database.

Millett, R., & Orosz, J. J. (2001). Understanding giving patterns in communities of color. *Fund Raising Management, 32*(6), 25–27. Retrieved June 9, 2006, from the ABI/INFORM database.

Mottino, F. & Miller, E. D. (2005). Philanthropy among African American donors in the New York metropolitan region: A generational analysis. In P. Rooney & L. Sherman (Eds.), *Exploring Black philanthropy: New directions for philanthropic fundraising, No. 48* (pp. 31–46). San Francisco, CA: Jossey-Bass.

Norton, L. (2002). The Chinese connection. *Barron's, 82*(49), 38.

People of color are the newest source of philanthropy. (2001). *Nonprofit World, 19*(5), 40. Retrieved August 3, 2006, from the ABI/INFORM database.

Potlatch. (2006). In *Encyclopedia Britannica*. Retrieved August 10, 2006, from Encyclopedia Britannica Online.

Potlatch. (2001–2007). In *The Columbia Electronic Encyclopedia* (6th ed.). Columbia University Press. Retrieved August 9, 2006, from www.bartleby.com/65/po/potlatch.html

Smith, B., Shue, S., Vest, J. L., & Villarreal, J. (1999). *Philanthropy in communities of color*. Bloomington: Indiana University Press.

chapter eleven

Ethical Practices in Fundraising

"The essential test of ethical behavior is 'obedience to the unenforceable,' originally described by England's Lord Justice of Appeal John Fletcher Moulton 65 years ago as obedience to self-imposed law" (Independent Sector, 1991, p. 8). The concept of ethical fundraising is multifaceted. Fundraisers serve multiple stakeholders, such as donors, their organizations, colleagues, board members, volunteers, and the community at large. Within these multiple and complicated relationships, a fundraiser is faced daily with making decisions related to truth-telling, privacy, confidentiality, financial accountability, and professionalism.

The relationships between fundraisers and their various stakeholders are critical to effective fundraising; these relationships must be based on trust. Albert Anderson (1996) cites five rules related to building enduring, trustworthy relationships:

Truth-telling: Communicate, convey, and record information truthfully, accurately, and completely; avoid misleading or deceiving.

Promise-keeping: Make and keep promises, agreements, and contracts that are consistent with organizational purposes.

> *Accountability:* Be accountable for the stewardship of donated and organizational resources, and be open to scrutiny by appropriate constituents.
>
> *Fairness:* Seek fairness and objectivity in arrangements that require the sharing of benefits and burdens, privileges and responsibilities.
>
> *Fidelity of purpose:* In all relationships, be faithful to bona fide professional and organizational purposes; avoid or disclose apparently conflicting interests, inconsistency, and hypocrisy. (p. 75)

In the for-profit sector, major corporate scandals led to the Sarbanes-Oxley Act of 2002, which requires that publicly held companies implement necessary accounting safeguards. These scandals, in which shareholders and employees lost huge amounts of investments, eroded a good portion of the trust the public had in the corporate world in general, some of which spread to the nonprofit sector. Although Sarbanes-Oxley does not apply directly to nonprofits (except for the whistleblower and document-shredding provisions; see **Exhibit 11-1**), the nonprofit sector's movement to self-regulate and

---

Exhibit 11-1 Sample Whistleblower Policy

In addition to instituting a code of ethics, nonprofit organizations should consider a formal whistleblower policy (required for nonprofits by the Sarbanes-Oxley Act of 2002). The National Council of Nonprofit Associations provides the following form as a basic template for an effective whistleblower policy:

General
{organization name} (Organization) Code of Ethics and Conduct ("Code") requires directors, officers and employees to observe high standards of business and personal ethics in the conduct of their duties and responsibilities. As employees and representatives of the Organization, we must practice honesty and integrity in fulfilling our responsibilities and comply with all applicable laws and regulations.

Reporting Responsibility
It is the responsibility of all directors, officers and employees to comply with the Code and to report violations or suspected violations in accordance with this Whistleblower Policy.

No Retaliation
No director, officer or employee who in good faith reports a violation of the Code shall suffer harassment, retaliation or adverse employment consequence. An employee who retaliates against someone who has reported a violation in good faith is subject to discipline up to and including termination of employment. This Whistleblower Policy is intended to encourage and enable employees and others to raise serious concerns within the Organization prior to seeking resolution outside the Organization.

Reporting Violations

The Code addresses the Organization's open door policy and suggests that employees share their questions, concerns, suggestions or complaints with someone who can address them properly. In most cases, an employee's supervisor is in the best position to address an area of concern. However, if you are not comfortable speaking with your supervisor or you are not satisfied with your supervisor's response, you are encouraged to speak with someone in the Human Resources Department or anyone in management whom you are comfortable in approaching. Supervisors and managers are required to report suspected violations of the Code of Conduct to the Organization's Compliance Officer, who has specific and exclusive responsibility to investigate all reported violations. For suspected fraud, or when you are not satisfied or uncomfortable with following the Organization's open door policy, individuals should contact the Organization's Compliance Officer directly.

Compliance Officer

The Organization's Compliance Officer is responsible for investigating and resolving all reported complaints and allegations concerning violations of the Code and, at his discretion, shall advise the Executive Director and/or the audit committee. The Compliance Officer has direct access to the audit committee of the board of directors and is required to report to the audit committee at least annually on compliance activity. The Organization's Compliance Officer is the chair of the audit committee.

Accounting and Auditing Matters

The audit committee of the board of directors shall address all reported concerns or complaints regarding corporate accounting practices, internal controls or auditing. The Compliance Officer shall immediately notify the audit committee of any such complaint and work with the committee until the matter is resolved.

Acting in Good Faith

Anyone filing a complaint concerning a violation or suspected violation of the Code must be acting in good faith and have reasonable grounds for believing the information disclosed indicates a violation of the Code. Any allegations that prove not to be substantiated and which prove to have been made maliciously or knowingly to be false will be viewed as a serious disciplinary offense.

Confidentiality

Violations or suspected violations may be submitted on a confidential basis by the complainant or may be submitted anonymously. Reports of violations or suspected violations will be kept confidential to the extent possible, consistent with the need to conduct an adequate investigation.

Handling of Reported Violations

The Compliance Officer will notify the sender and acknowledge receipt of the reported violation or suspected violation within five business days. All reports will be promptly investigated and appropriate corrective action will be taken if warranted by the investigation.

Audit Committee Compliance Officer

{organization name} Management Staff

Source: National Council of Nonprofits, www.councilofnonprofits.org. Copyright 2004.

attempt to rebuild trust had begun earlier, in the wake of the United Way of America scandal in the mid-1990s (discussed below). Extensive changes in accounting practices and major changes in the Financial Accounting Standards Board (FASB) accounting rules for nonprofit organizations have also played a role in the recent influx of new safeguards. In Canada, in an attempt to establish a national standard, an ethical fundraising logo was designed by the Canadian Centre for Philanthropy and has been distributed to over 600 charities that adhere to the center's stringent fundraising code (Ethical fundraising, n.d.).

"Ethical issues for fundraising cannot be easily pushed aside, for the very nature of the trust relationship among donor, institution, and society demands accountability and responsibility" (Lindahl, 1997, p. 189). We will now discuss a couple of examples of a breach of trust in fundraising: the United Way scandal and the use of honor boxes.

UNITED WAY SCANDAL

United Way of America (UWA), as well as the 2,100 local United Ways, sustained a devastating blow to their credibility with donors and the public at large in February 1992, when William Aramony, president and CEO of UWA, was forced to resign under allegations that he had conspired to defraud UWA. On April 3, 1995, Mr. Aramony was convicted in the U.S. District Court for the Eastern District of Virginia on 25 counts, including conspiracy to defraud, mail fraud, wire fraud, transportation of fraudulently acquired property, engaging in monetary transactions in unlawful activity, filing false tax returns, and aiding in the filing of false tax returns. He served 7 years in prison and was released in 2001. He was also sentenced to serve 3 years of supervised release following the expiration of his term and fined $300,000 (United Way of Central Virginia, n.d.). Board chairman Keith Bailey responded to the scandal with a call to move forward. He said, "Obviously, this is a personal tragedy for the individuals involved but a self-inflicted one. It is important that the United Way system direct its focus to the future and not dwell on the past" (Moss, 1995, last ¶).

Even though it was ultimately shown that donated dollars, for the most part, stayed in the communities in which they were raised, UWA struggled to rebuild its credibility and trust with the public. "Following the break of the scandal, the United Ways scrambled to distance themselves from the national UWA. Full-page ads signed by members of local governing boards appeared in newspapers in nearly every community. The ads referred to UWA—perhaps for the first time—as the trade association for the UWs and vehemently asserted that money raised in the community stayed in the community" (Kelly, 1998, p. 316).

Prior to the scandal, in 1991–1992 the UW system raised more than $3 billion annually, but revenues dropped an estimated 4% the first year following the scandal (Kelly, 1998, p. 317). In the wake of the scandal, it was imperative that UWA take many precautions to ensure that this type of event would not occur again. In partnership with the UWA board of governors, rigorous new audit, budget, and other financial controls have been implemented, along with a code of ethics. United Way of America is a very different organization today than it was in 1992. Over the past few years, UWA has held itself up as a model of accountability in the nonprofit sector. The United Way of the twenty-first century is a dynamic, inspiring organization that holds accountability and trustworthiness as core values (United Way of Snohonish County, 2003). "New membership standards were implemented for United Ways in 2003 and enhance the level of accountability and transparency in local operations. Annually, all United Ways must certify to United Way of America their adherence to these requirements" (Accountability, 2006). Brian Gallagher, president and CEO, has brought renewed creditability and accountability to the United Way of America, and the organization is poised for achieving its goals to address the issues of "education, financial stability, and health access" (Newsmakers, 2007, ¶ 37).

HONOR BOXES

The use of honor boxes is an example of misuse of the public's trust because the boxes mislead people into thinking their money is going directly to charity. Honor boxes have become a familiar sight at cash registers in many restaurants and retail stores over the years. Typically, customers insert bills or coins in exchange for a token item such as gum or a mint with the belief that the donation is going toward the charity or cause advertised on the front of the box.

Most people assume incorrectly that these canisters are the property of the charity and that any profits will be given to the charity featured on the device. This assumption is incorrect. Most of these boxes are sold to salespeople who secure placement, maintain the boxes, and keep the majority of the profits. Some states, such as Alabama, have laws that require that a disclosure label be displayed in a conspicuous place on all candy containers sponsored by charitable organizations stating what portion of the proceeds would go to the charity (Kelly, 1998, pp. 300–301).

ETHICAL DECISION MAKING

Anderson (1996) discusses various grounds for ethically justifying our day-to-day actions. Although he wrote that to use donor funds for purposes other than those designated by the donor is a "blatant ethical indiscretion" (p. 53), he goes on to elaborate on John Stuart Mill's and Immanuel Kant's approaches that lead people and/or organizations to do the right thing and use funds for the purposes for which they were given. The first approach, attributed to Mill and labeled utilitarianism, held that consequences are everything. Utilitarianism can be defined as *"any action that on balance is an effective means to a satisfying end, generally 'the greatest good for the greatest number,' is ethically appropriate. In this respect the end or result, if more beneficial than harmful, justifies the means"* (Anderson, 1996, p. 39). Anderson goes on to say about Mills's approach, "It doesn't pay to break a promise. Donors will lose confidence in the organization, the cause will suffer for loss of financial support, and the public good for the greatest number will not be well served" (1996, p. 53). The second guiding principle, attributed to Kant and considered a formalist theory, is that one's duty is what matters and it is simply the right thing to do. "To be morally worthy we must do our duty for its own sake, truly free of every other motivation, even the very strong feelings of sympathy and self-love" (Anderson, 1996, pp. 40–41). Although there are numerous variations on theories that guide organizations to conduct their fundraising activities in an ethical manner, these two views, by renowned leaders in the field of ethics, are considered classic examples of theories of ethical decision making.

Neither theory is faultless in helping a person make decisions in difficult situations. The utilitarian theory could potentially allow the death of innocent children from collateral damage in a retaliatory bombing raid. And the formalist approach could allow a person's enemies to take advantage of the person's refusal to ever lie—even when it might cause the person's death. So, although these theories are helpful in understanding the ethical decision-making process, they need further development to apply well in the practice of fundraising.

In her book *Ethical Decision Making in Fundraising,* Marilyn Fischer presents a model of ethical decision making that is based on two conceptual frameworks. The first framework is ethics as narrative. We need to make ethical decisions knowing the context of the ethical dilemma in an ongoing story. We need to have sympathetic understanding of the situation. "Sympathy gives access to knowledge, and emotion gives the impetus for action"

(Fischer, 2000, p. 6). Fischer explains that there is no equation or formula to employ in order to make ethically correct decisions. Rather, ethics involves judgment, and by analyzing several options, even ones that are obviously unethical, one can gain insights that can be applied to less clear-cut situations. The fundraiser should be able to imagine different potential outcomes to ethical dilemmas in order to resolve them. "Making good ethical decisions involves many imaginings: imagining a range of future alternatives; imagining what each alternative means for the individuals, the organizations, and the communities involved; imagining the organization and the individuals not as static, but as changing and growing; and imagining the current dilemma as one phase of that growth" (Fischer, 2000, p. 8). Ethical rules, including those that come from religious and cultural traditions, are an important part of ethical decision making.

Fischer also talks about philanthropy as a gift economy—her second framework. The most important aspect of a gift economy is that "the exchange is not *quid pro quo*, and while reciprocity is expected, the return is not given directly to the original giver" (Fischer, 2000, p. 11). A donor gives to an organization not in order to receive a direct market exchange in return, but perhaps to repay something that the donor had received in the past from another source. "While fund raisers in philanthropic nonprofits spend time in both market and gift economies, their primary purpose is to keep the spirit of the gift alive, to sustain and enhance the cycle of giving" (Fischer, 2000, p. 16).

According to Fischer, fundraisers have three basic value commitments: organizational mission, relationships, and personal integrity. "The fund raiser, acting with integrity, has the task of creating and maintaining a supporting network of relationships in order to further the mission of the organization" (2000, p. 21). Fundraisers often face ethical dilemmas when their daily decisions do not align with the mission of their organization, when there are issues with workplace relationships, or when personal integrity is challenged. Fischer developed a chart based on these three basic value commitments to assist fundraisers with making ethical decisions (see **Table 11-1**). The chart organizes the envisioned alternative actions and how they may affect organizational mission, relationships, and personal integrity of the decision maker.

Given an ethical dilemma at work, how might a development officer use this chart to help figure out the most appropriate decision? Here is an example. Suppose a development officer, Mr. Jones, is working with a major gift prospect, Ms. Murphy, about naming a particular room in a new building in memory of the prospect's deceased great-aunt, Ms. Smith. They have developed a

Table 11-1 Ethical Decision-Making Chart

Alternatives	1	2	3	4
Organizational Mission				
How does this alternative promote or detract from the organization's mission? Basic philanthropic values?				
Relationships				
How does this alternative affect long-term relationships with colleagues, donors, volunteers, and community members?				
Personal Integrity				
In what ways does this alternative help or not help you develop into the person you want to become? How does it strengthen or weaken your own integrity?				

Source: Fischer (2000). Reprinted with permission of John Wiley & Sons, Inc.

great relationship through this process, and Ms. Murphy asked Mr. Jones to come to her home to discuss the project. At her home, Ms. Murphy pulls out a very old portfolio from her ancient trunk. In it is a copy of a book written by Mr. Smith, the husband of Ms. Smith. She hands it to the development officer and tells him to keep it as a memento of the project. Mr. Jones accepts it, but has second thoughts after coming back to the office and discovering that the inside of the book cover was signed by Teddy Roosevelt. It might just be worth a lot more than the original $15 price of the book that Mr. Jones had noted on the back outside cover.

Mr. Jones sits down with his boss, Ms. Franklin, and they discuss carefully several alternatives, which are considered in the context of the story narrative and the concept of the gift economy. First, Mr. Jones might simply return the book and tell Ms. Murphy that he could not accept it. Second, Mr. Jones would keep the book and thank Ms. Murphy for it with both a phone call and a handwritten note. Third, Mr. Jones would suggest making a special display case for the book and inside signature at the entrance to the room that will be memorialized for Ms. Smith. There may be other ideas. Each alternate path would be fleshed out with answers to the questions from the chart. Once the chart is completed, the participants look for which solution provides the best alternative. Through the conversation and analysis a solution usually becomes clear.

NONPROFIT ACCOUNTABILITY TO STAKEHOLDERS

With all of the negative press surrounding corporate scandals such as those at Enron, Arthur Andersen, and other organizations, the American public has become increasingly aware of the buzzword "accountability." Accountability applies to business practices at nonprofits as well as corporations. Scandals, fraud, and embezzlement are not unique to for-profit corporations, as we have seen in the case of William Aramony of the United Way.

What Is Accountability?

According to Marenakos (2005), "Accountability is all about being answerable to those who have invested their trust, faith and money in you" (p. 2). Accountability, or conducting business in a manner that keeps an organization's reputation beyond reproach, is good practice and ultimately good for all stakeholders.

As mentioned briefly in Chapter 6, the U.S. Senate completed extensive work with the charitable sector to develop a law pertaining to accountability. The Panel on the Nonprofit Sector was an independent effort by charities and foundations to ensure that the nonprofit community remains a vibrant and healthy part of American society. Formed in October 2004 as a reaction by leaders in the nonprofit sector to the increased scrutiny of the U.S. Senate Finance Committee, the panel prepared recommendations for Congress to improve the oversight and governance of charitable organizations. The panel presented its final report to Congress in June 2005, and hundreds of nonprofit organizations signed on to the report in an effort to standardize accountability practices.

In the introductory letter of the report, "Strengthening Transparency, Governance and Accountability of Charitable Organizations," the co-conveners of the panel, Paul Brest, president of the William and Flora Hewlett Foundation, and M. Cass Wheeler, chief executive officer of the American Heart Association, wrote,

Accountability is crucial to our sector. Charitable organizations are an indispensable part of American society, offering relief from disasters, nurturing our spiritual and creative aspirations, caring for vulnerable people, protecting our natural and cultural heritage, and finding solutions to medical and scientific challenges. But they can fulfill these missions only by maintaining the trust of the public. Meeting the ethical standards that will justify this trust requires a series of ongoing commitments. (Independent Sector, 2005, p. 1)

The primary goals of the panel were to improve transparency of charitable organizations, enhance governance in charitable organizations, and strengthen government oversight of charitable organizations. The recommendations presented to Congress included the following categories: acceptable standards for board size and governance, compensation of board members and nonprofit executives, employee and board travel expenses, establishing audit committees, and defining and minimizing conflict of interest.

How Nonprofits Can Achieve Accountability

According to McLaughlin (2004), a consultant at Grant Thornton in Boston, nonprofits can take several action steps to reach accountability. McLaughlin's four principles, or "SOCK," are:

Systems: procedures and technologies that produce predictable results
Oversight: financial reporting and good governance structures
Culture: intangible qualities that reflect the values of the organization
Knowledge: professional financial expertise, along with a well-trained board and staff

McLaughlin further mentions some of the ways that nonprofits can translate these principles into actions:

- Establishing an audit committee
- Establishing internal controls
- Establishing a code of ethics
- Reporting finances on IRS Form 990
- Full disclosure of finances and governance information—including posting information on the organization's Web site

See **Exhibit 11-2** for further suggestions for Ethics Management.

Exhibit 11-2 Ethics Management

There are eight key guidelines for managing ethics in the workplace:

1. Recognize that managing ethics is a process.
2. The bottom line of an ethics program is accomplishing preferred behaviors in the workplace.
3. The best way to handle ethical dilemmas is to avoid their occurrence in the first place.
4. Make ethics decisions in groups, and make decisions public, as appropriate.
5. Integrate ethics management with other management practices.
6. Use cross-functional teams when developing and implementing the ethics management program.
7. Value forgiveness.
8. Note that trying to operate ethically and making a few mistakes is better than not trying at all.

Source: McNamara (2005, pp. 8–9).

PAID SOLICITATION

An ethical issue facing the field of fundraising involves the practice of paid solicitation. The AFP Fundraising Dictionary Online (Levy, 1996–2003) defines a solicitor as "a person, paid or volunteer, who asks for donations on behalf of an organization or cause" (p. 111). Many in the field of fundraising frown upon the paid solicitor, believing that in all too many cases, donors are unaware that a significant portion of their donation will never reach the charity itself. Kelly (1998) points out: "Solicitation firms do not serve new, small, and unpopular causes, which is economically logical given the for-profit motives of the firms. Those for whom it would be difficult to solicit money are not viable clients. Rather, clients of paid solicitors are charitable organizations seeking gifts for which no investment is required" (p. 283). Many organizations who hire paid solicitors "have decided that any return, even 10% of the dollars generated, is profitable and, therefore, acceptable" (p. 283).

Not all feel the use of paid solicitors is unethical, however. Paid solicitation is a reality that is legal and a useful business strategy as long as there is no fraud involved. According to the December 2004 Massachusetts Attorney General's Report on Telemarketing for Charity,

> While some charities use their own staff to conduct fundraising campaigns, most find the use of professional solicitors to be a more effective way of raising funds while also getting their message out to the public. In addition, many smaller charitable organizations

may not have enough employees or volunteers to conduct their own solicitation drive, and thus it is only through the use of a professional solicitor that they may effectively publicize their causes while concurrently raising necessary funds. (Office of the Attorney General, 2004, p. 3)

CONFLICTS OF INTEREST

For fundraisers, conflicts of interest are conflicts in which their own personal concerns interfere with their ability to use good judgment on behalf of their organization (Fischer, 2000, p. 168). Two common conflicts involve commission-based pay and finders' fees. Major fundraising associations clearly discount these practices as unethical. The AFP code states that members shall be compensated by salary or set fee, not by percentage-based compensation or commission. These prohibitions do not restrict an organization from giving annual raises for excellent performance of fundraising staff.

Another controversial practice involves substantial financial gifts given to the fundraiser him- or herself, in addition to or in lieu of gifts to the organization. Hall (2004) notes that "it is not unusual for donors to develop a strong attachment to fund raisers . . . who solicit them" (¶ 8). This attachment occasionally leads to gifts made directly to the fundraiser. No law prohibits a fundraiser from accepting personal gifts from donors, as long as undue pressure was not applied (Hall, 2004). More and more charities are asking their fundraisers to regularly review and sign their code of ethics that clearly indicates that the acceptance of personal gifts, above a specified dollar amount, is unethical.

ETHICAL AND LEGAL ISSUES RAISED BY COMMERCIALISM IN SCHOOLS

Schools are increasingly reaching out to businesses for sponsorship dollars, a fundraising practice that raises several ethical and legal issues. According to Molnar and Reaves (2001), "Since 1990, commercializing activity in schools has risen 473 percent" (p. 20). It is a tempting fundraising model. Public schools have many pressing needs, and corporations can afford lucrative sponsorships through vending contracts and soft-drink sales.

Ethical issues arise when schools reach out to corporations for private funding. Many advertisers clamor for the opportunity to have a "captive" audience among the student population, especially during formative years. It is a prime opportunity for corporations to build brand loyalty early. Some of the issues that schools should consider include:

- Forcing kids to view advertising throughout the school day
- Marketing unhealthy foods and beverages, with the possibility of contributing to childhood obesity
- Using kids as market research subjects
- Pushing a particular brand without the express consent of parents

On a federal level, the Better Nutrition for School Children Act of 2001 gives more authority to the U.S. Department of Agriculture and less to junk food and soda corporations. This act is a key element in the oversight of commercial activity in school systems. However, administrators of school systems need to also be aware of the ethical issues involved in commercial sponsorship versus widespread community fundraising.

PRIVACY AND CONFIDENTIALITY

Due to their importance, tenets related to privacy and confidentiality are virtually always included in fundraising code-of-ethics statements. The AFP Code of Ethical Principles and Standards of Professional Practice are unequivocal: "Members shall not disclose privileged or confidential information to unauthorized parties" (2004).

Fischer (2000) wrote that although privacy takes several forms, the root notion of privacy is being able "to control who has access to our thoughts and feelings, to our bodies, and to various pieces of information about us. . . . Confidentiality is the guardian that protects these forms of privacy" (p. 145). Maintaining trust is paramount in the relationship between an organization and its various stakeholders. Privacy and confidentiality are expected, and therefore, great damage to the relationship is possible when a fundraiser, either knowingly or inadvertently, commits a breach of either.

RELATIONSHIPS OF TRUST

All notable literature about fundraising, since the late 1800s until current times, highlights the development of relationships between fundraisers and their donors as the primary tenet of any successful fundraising campaign. Within the rubric of developing solid relationships is the development and maintenance of trust. There are numerous reasons why a donor might donate to a specific charity, yet repeated examples show us that trust must be present to continue the donating relationship. This includes trust that the donation will be used for its intended purpose, trust that information will be kept private and confidential, trust that the fundraiser will not be swayed by conflicts of interest, and trust that fundraisers and the organizations they represent will abide by their codes of ethics (see **Exhibit 11-3** through **11-5**) and practice ethical decision making at all levels.

Exhibit 11-3 The Independent Sector: Statement of Values and Code of Ethics

The IS believes that each organization in the independent sector should have a formally adopted code of ethics and finalized this statement in January of 2004 to be used as a starting point for nonprofit and philanthropic organizations to use in developing their own codes. The statement has ten main principles as listed below.

I. Personal and Professional Integrity
All staff, board members and volunteers of the organization act with honesty, integrity and openness in all their dealings as representatives of the organization. The organization promotes a working environment that values respect, fairness, and integrity.

II. Mission
The organization has a clearly stated mission and purpose, approved by the board of directors, in pursuit of the public good. All of its programs support that mission and all who work for or on behalf of the organization understand and are loyal to that mission and purpose. The mission is responsive to the constituency and communities served by the organization and of value to the society at large.

III. Governance
The organization has an active governing body that is responsible for setting the mission and strategic direction of the organization and oversight of the finances, operations, and policies of the organization. . . .

IV. Legal Compliance
The organization is knowledgeable of and complies with all laws, regulations and applicable international conventions.

V. Responsible Stewardship
The organization and its subsidiaries manage their funds responsibly and prudently. This should include the following considerations:

● It spends a reasonable percentage of its annual budget on programs in pursuance of its mission;
● It spends an adequate amount on administrative expenses to ensure effective accounting systems, internal controls, competent staff, and other expenditures critical to professional management;

- The organization compensates staff, and any others who may receive compensation, reasonably and appropriately;
- Organizations that solicit funds have reasonable fundraising costs, recognizing the variety of factors that affect fundraising costs;
- Organizations do not accumulate operating funds excessively;
- Organizations with endowments (both foundations and public charities) prudently draw endowment funds consistent with donor intent and to support the public purpose of the organization;
- Organizations ensure that all spending practices and policies are fair, reasonable and appropriate to fulfill the mission of the organization; and,
- All financial reports are factually accurate and complete in all material respects.

VI. Openness and Disclosure

The organization provides comprehensive and timely information to the public, the media, and all stakeholders and is responsive in a timely manner to reasonable requests for information. All information about the organization will fully and honestly reflect the policies and practices of the organization. Basic informational data about the organization, such as the Form 990, reviews and compilations, and audited financial statements will be posted on the organization's website or otherwise available to the public. All solicitation materials accurately represent the organization's policies and practices and will reflect the dignity of program beneficiaries. All financial, organizational, and program reports will be complete and accurate in all material respects.

VII. Program Evaluation

The organization regularly reviews program effectiveness and has mechanisms to incorporate lessons learned into future programs. The organization is committed to improving program and organizational effectiveness and develops mechanisms to promote learning from its activities and the field. The organization is responsive to changes in its field of activity and is responsive to the needs of its constituencies.

VIII. Inclusiveness and Diversity

The organization has a policy of promoting inclusiveness and its staff, board and volunteers show diversity in order to enrich its programmatic effectiveness. The organization takes meaningful steps to promote inclusiveness in its hiring, retention, promotion, board recruitment and constituencies served.

IX. Fundraising

Organizations that raise funds from the public or from donor institutions are truthful in their solicitation materials. Organizations respect the privacy concerns of individual donors and expend funds consistent with donor intent. Organizations disclose important and relevant information to potential donors. . . .

(continues)

Exhibit 11-3 (*continued*)

X. Grantmaker Guidelines

Organizations that are grantmakers have particular responsibilities in carrying out their missions. These include the following:

- They will have constructive relations with grantseekers based on mutual respect and shared goals;
- They will communicate clearly and on a timely basis with potential grantees;
- They will treat grantseekers and grantees fairly and with respect;
- They will respect the expertise of grantseekers in their fields of knowledge;
- They will seek to understand and respect the organizational capacity and needs of grantseeking organizations; and,
- They will respect the integrity of the mission of grantseeking organizations.

Source: Independent Sector (2004).

Exhibit 11-4 Donor Bill of Rights

PHILANTHROPY is based on voluntary action for the common good. It is a tradition of giving and sharing that is primary to the quality of life. To assure that philanthropy merits the respect and trust of the general public, and that donors and prospective donors can have full confidence in the not-for-profit organizations and causes they are asked to support, we declare that all donors have these rights:

I.
To be informed of the organization's mission, of the way the organization intends to use donated resources, and of its capacity to use donations effectively for their intended purposes.

II.
To be informed of the identity of those serving on the organization's governing board, and to expect the board to exercise prudent judgement in its stewardship responsibilities.

III.
To have access to the organization's most recent financial statements.

IV.
To be assured their gifts will be used for the purposes for which they were given.

V.
To receive appropriate acknowledgement and recognition.

VI.
To be assured that information about their donations is handled with respect and with confidentiality to the extent provided by law.

VII.
To expect that all relationships with individuals representing organizations of interest to the donor will be professional in nature.

VIII.
To be informed whether those seeking donations are volunteers, employees of the organization, or hired solicitors.

IX.	**X.**
To have the opportunity for their names to be deleted from mailing lists that an organization may intend to share.	To feel free to ask questions when making a donation and to receive prompt, truthful, and forthright answers.

DEVELOPED BY	ENDORSED BY
American Association of Fund Raising Counsel (AAFRC)	(in formation)
Association for Healthcare Philanthropy (AHP)	Independent Sector
Council for Advancement and Support of Education (CASE)	National Catholic Development Conference (NCDC)
Association of Fundraising Professionals (AFP)	National Committee on Planned Giving (NCPG)
	Council for Resource Development (CRD)
	United Way of America

Exhibit 11-5 Code of Ethical Online Philanthropic Practices

Network for Good exists to foster the effective and safe use of the Internet for philanthropic purposes. In its effort to promote high ethical standards in online fundraising and to build trust among contributors in making online transactions and contributions with the charity of their choice, this code is being offered as a guide to all who share this goal. Contributors are encouraged to be aware of non-Internet related fundraising practices that fall outside the scope of this Code.

Ethical Online Practices and Practitioners will:

Section A: Philanthropic Experience
1. Clearly and specifically display and describe the organization's identity on the organization's Web site;
2. Employ practices on the website that exhibit integrity, honesty, and truthfulness and seek to safeguard the public trust.

Section B: Privacy and Security
1. Seek to inspire trust in every online transaction;
2. Prominently display the opportunity for supporters to have their names removed from lists that are sold to, rented to, or exchanged with other organizations;
3. Conduct online transactions through a system that employs high-level security technology to protect the donor's personal information for both internal and external authorized use;
4. Provide either an "opt in" or "opt out" mechanism to prevent unsolicited communications or solicitations by organizations that obtain e-mail addresses directly from the donor. Should lists be rented or exchanged, only those verified as having been obtained through donors or prospects "opting in" will be used by a charity;

(continues)

Exhibit 11-5 (*continued*)

5. Protect the interests and privacy of individuals interacting with their Web site;
6. Provide a clear, prominent and easily accessible privacy policy on its Web site telling visitors, at a minimum, what information is being collected, how it is being collected, how it can be updated or removed, how this information will be used and who has access to the data.

Section C: Disclosures

1. Disclose the identity of the organization or provider processing an online transaction;
2. Guarantee that the name, logo, and likeness of all parties to an online transaction belong to the party and will not be used without express permission;
3. Maintain all appropriate governmental and regulatory designations or certifications;
4. Provide both online and offline contact information.

Section D: Complaints

1. Provide protection to hold the donor harmless of any problem arising from a transaction conducted through the organization's Web site;
2. Promptly respond to all customer complaints and to employ best efforts to fairly resolve all legitimate complaints in a timely fashion.

Section E: Transactions

1. Ensure contributions are used to support the activities of the organization to which they were donated;
2. Ensure that legal control of contributions or proceeds from online transactions are transferred directly to the charity or expedited in the fastest possible way;
3. Companies providing online services to charities will provide clear and full communication with the charity on all aspects of donor transactions, including the accurate and timely transmission of data related to online transactions;
4. Stay informed regarding the best methods to ensure the ethical, secure, and private nature of online ePhilanthropy transactions;
5. Adhere to the spirit as well as the letter of all applicable laws and regulations, including, but not limited to, charity solicitation and tax laws;
6. Ensure that all services, recognition and other transactions promised on a Web site, in consideration of gift or transaction, will be fulfilled on a timely basis;
7. Disclose to the donor the nature of the relationship between the organization processing the gift or transaction and the charity intended to benefit from the gift.

Source: Network for Good (2008).

REFERENCES

Anderson, A. (1996). *Ethics for fundraisers.* Bloomington: Indiana University Press.
Association of Fundraising Professionals (AFP). (n.d.). A donor bill of rights. Retrieved December 10, 2008, from http://www.afpnet.org/ka/ka-3.cfm?content_item_id=9988&folder_id=898

Association of Fundraising Professionals. (AFP). (2004, October). AFP code of ethical principles and standards of professional practice. Retrieved June 22, 2006, from http://www.afpnet.org/ka/ka-3.cfm?content_item_id=1068&folder_id=897

Ethical code. (n.d.). Retrieved December 11, 2008, from http://www.imaginecanada.ca/node/21

Fischer, M. (2000). *Ethical decision making in fundraising.* New York: John Wiley & Sons.

Fogal, R., & Burlingame, D. (1994). *Ethics in fundraising: Putting values into practice.* San Francisco, CA: Jossey-Bass.

Hall, H. (2004, October 15). When gifts get personal. *Chronicle of Philanthropy.*

Independent Sector. (1991). *Obedience to the unenforceable.* Washington, DC.

Independent Sector. (2004). *Statement of values and code of ethics for charitable and philanthropic organizations.* Retrieved June 26, 2006, from www.independentsector.org/PDFs/code_ethics.pdf

Independent Sector. (2005). *Strengthening transparency, governance and accountability of charitable organizations.* Retrieved August 1, 2005, from www.nonprofitpanel.org/final/Panel_Final_Report.pdf

Kelly, K. S. (1998). *Effective fund-raising management.* Mahwah, NJ: Lawrence Erlbaum Associates.

Levy, B. R. (Ed.). (1996–2003). *The AFP fundraising dictionary online.* Retrieved January 4, 2007, from the Association of Fundraising Professionals Web site, www.afpnet.org/content_documents/AFP_Dictionary_A-Z_final_6-9-03.pdf

Lindahl, W. E. (1997, Winter). Ethical issues in fundraising. *Nonprofit Management and Leadership, 8*(2). San Francisco, CA: Jossey-Bass.

Marenakos, L. (2005). *Accountability matters.* Charleston, SC: Blackbaud.

McLaughlin, T. (2004, November 9). *Simple steps to achieve greater accountability and stewardship.* Boston: Grant Thornton, LLP.

McNamara, C. (2005). *Complete guide to ethics management: An ethics toolkit for managers.* Retrieved June 1, 2006, from http://www.managementhelp.org/ethics/ethxgde.htm

Molnar, A., & Reaves, J. A. (2001). *Buy me! Buy me! The fourth annual report on trends in schoolhouse commercialism: Year 2000–2001.* Tempe, AZ: Education Policy Studies Laboratory.

Moss, D. (1995, June 23). Charity embezzler gets 7-year term. *USA Today.*

National Council of Nonprofits. (2004). Sample whistleblower policy. Retrieved December 11, 2008, from http://www.councilofnonprofits.org/?q=whistleblower

Network for Good. (2008). Code of ethical online philanthropic practices. Retrieved December 10, 2008, from http://www.fundraising123.org/article/ephilanthropy-code-ethics

Newsmakers. (2007, August 15). Brian Gallagher, President and CEO, United Way of America. *Philanthropy News Digest.* Retrieved August 7, 2008, from http://foundationcenter.org/pnd/newsmakers/nwsmkr.jhtml?id=186800002

Office of the Attorney General, Commonwealth of Massachusetts. (2004, December). *Attorney General's report on telemarketing for charity.* Boston: Author.

United Way. (n.d.). *Accountability.* Retrieved June 26, 2006, from http://national.unitedway.org/about/accountability.cfm

United Way of Central Virginia. (n.d.). *Frequently asked questions.* Retrieved June 26, 2006, from www.unitedwaycv.org/pages/questions.htm

United Way of Snohomish County, Washington. (2003). *A brief history.* Updated September 2, 2003. Retrieved June 26, 2006, from http://www.uwsc.org/history.pdf

chapter twelve

Organizational Issues in Fundraising

Fundraising is a broad process that requires organizational infrastructure to succeed. Someone needs to be assigned to do the prospect research, develop the plans for fundraising, cultivate and meet with donors, send out the direct mail and write proposals for corporate and foundation prospects, ask major individual prospects for gifts, provide recognition and stewardship, and finally evaluate the operation and provide feedback to constantly improve the process. How to best organize, budget, and staff the fundraising operation are the key issues in setting up and maintaining an appropriate infrastructure. We begin by considering the typical organizational structure of a development office.

ORGANIZATIONAL STRUCTURE

The development or fundraising activity is not an isolated function of a nonprofit organization. In military terms, the head of this office is not in a "line" position. The development office is not a machine that cranks out money—off to the side somewhere and isolated from the mission of the organization.

Instead, the lead fundraiser is in a "staff" position. The development office works as an extension of the CEO, executive director, or president of the organization. The function of fundraising can actually extend across many positions within the organization. For example, every time a program staff member interacts positively with a client, he or she may be providing the reason a donor would want to support the organization. Or the staff accountant, in preparing the endowment reports or processing a donation of stock, may actually be helping in the fundraising process. The development office then acts as a leader and coordinator of the fundraising process—which actually extends across almost every aspect of the nonprofit organization.

What does a typical development office look like in a nonprofit organization? How does development fit within an organizational chart? **Figure 12-1** shows an inverted U-form functional structure. This chart is one example of where development may fall within an organization's structure.

As Figure 12-1 shows, the "manager of fundraising" (usually called the "director of development") works right under the CEO and board of directors, while at the same time she or he works alongside divisions such as finance, purchasing, services, and human resources. Fundraising is both supportive and administrative in the typical structure of an organization. It is integrated and relates to every division within an organization's entire structure. This highly charged relationship within the organization's structure has

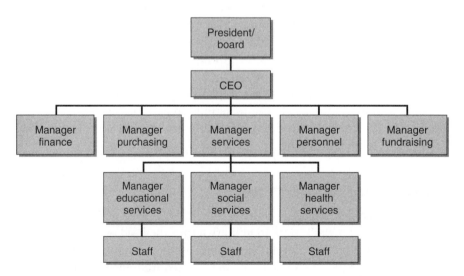

Figure 12-1. Organizational chart. *Source:* Anheier (2005, p. 158)

led to much research and discussion of best practices so that development may serve the organization's best purposes, while simultaneously functioning as the professional arm it is meant to be.

Depending upon the size of the organization and the organization's budgetary needs, a typical development office (or subset of development that is subdivided across several areas of an organization, such as a hospital or university) will usually consist of a combination of professionals and support staff. Most often there will be a director of development, who relates the most to the CEO of the organization and interfaces with the board of directors. This individual is in communication regularly with these key individuals on issues related to the strategic plan of the organization—especially the board of fundraising component of the plan. This person finds out what direction the directors and CEO would like to see the organization move toward and also finds out what programming changes or developments are taking place, thereby giving direction to the development office. The director of development will also provide direction to the board of directors and the CEO in terms of cultivation, solicitation, and stewardship of key major donors to the organization. This arrangement has the potential of creating role confusion; hence all participants need to be clear about the roles and willing to be flexible as the roles change.

The role of the director of development is a visible role that holds the responsibility of maintaining relationships with the board of directors, who are often donors to the organization, and positioning the organization within the community it serves. In addition to staying in touch with upper management, the director is a public relations person and is often the second face or voice of the agency when dealing with corporate sponsors, foundation directors, or individual donors. The director of development will often work hand in hand with upper management to maintain and cultivate the relationships associated with these significant funding sources.

Reporting to the director of development are typically individuals who specialize in an area of fundraising related to the largest source of revenue for the organization. For example, in a very large mega-church setting, professionals may specialize in annual giving or major gifts, as individuals are the largest source of donations for religious organizations. Alternatively, in an arts organization where a good amount of revenue comes from the corporate and foundation area, there might be a manager or director of corporate and foundation relations. In a division within a university setting, for example, there might be a professional charged with alumni reunion giving, special giving, or campaign giving who is responsible to manage those larger gifts and individual donor relationships. In a social services organization, there may be an individual specializing in government grants.

In support of the above professionals, a development office will often employ development associates. The role of development associate varies from organization to organization. There is one exception. Most organizations have donor-database software that is crucial to the function of development. The electronic database maintains personal files and giving history related to individuals, foundation grants, and corporate sponsorships in some instances. The development associate is charged with maintaining these files and keeping the database current and accurate so it can be utilized for campaigns as they arise, such as annual funds or special events where mailing lists become essential to the success of how much revenue any given appeal can generate. The development associate will also be responsible for acknowledging gifts and researching potential additional sources of income, whether from individuals or other areas of funding that are significant to their specific organization. In larger organizations, a whole cadre of staff with specialized titles may handle these functions.

The nonprofit sector has so much variation in size and scope that the actual configurations of development offices vary tremendously in size and function. A small organization might have one director of development and one development associate. A large organization might have a whole sub-department of five to eight people maintaining the donor database, entering gifts, and providing reports to the rest of the unit. The average development office usually has two professionals and two support staff. A large, complex nonprofit organization may have over 100 staff members. For these organizations the most important question is whether or not to centralize or decentralize the fundraising structure.

Centralization Versus Decentralization

A person who is in the fundraising profession for any given period of time will most likely at some point work for either a health care organization or university, as these are two of the most corporatelike nonprofits within the field and employ the largest percentage of fundraising professionals. The issue of centralization versus decentralization of fundraising efforts is crucial to large nonprofit organizations and is the context for the research in this area.

Hall (1992) takes a close look at this issue in her article "The Decentralization of Development: Impact on Power, Priorities, Faculty Perceptions." In particular, she considers "the decentralization of the development function in research universities and the impact decentralization has on the balance of power among the university's academic leaders, on the ability of the university to set its own priorities, on the communication between academic units and the central development office, and on the relationship between the faculty and the development officers" (p. 569).

It holds true that the issues Hall uncovers in her exploration of this issue in the university setting translates into issues that large nonprofits face across the board, be they hospitals, arts organizations, service organizations, or any organization that is larger in scope and has to contend with a wide variety of needs and program budgets, along with multilayered aspects of management. At the core of whether or not to centralize or decentralize development's function is the issue of power.

Hall defines the differences between centralized and decentralized offices as the following:

> In a centralized system, all of the development officers are staff to the vice president for development. They are supervised in the central development office and paid by the central development office budget. Development officers work not for any academic unit, but rather on university-wide priorities, which include the academic units. In a decentralized system, at least some of the academic units have development officers whose primary responsibility is to raise money for the academic unit. All of the AUDO's [Academic Unit Development Officers] are supervised exclusively by their deans and paid exclusively through the academic unit budgets. The university also has a vice-president for development and central development staff who work on university-wide priorities. (pp. 570–571)

As we can see from this definition, a centralized office primarily focuses on university-wide priorities, while a decentralized structure allows development officers to focus on the individual needs of the academic unit they are responsible for in raising funds.

Hall goes on to suggest another method of structure, a "hybrid system" that, while unique, encompasses some structural elements of both a centralized and decentralized development office. Hall defines a hybrid system as:

> Any system that fits neither the description of a centralized system nor the description of a decentralized system. Generally, in a hybrid system the development officers have a dual reporting relationship

with both the dean and the vice-president for development. They often receive line supervision from the central development office and programmatic supervision from the dean. The cost of operating the academic unit development office is often jointly budgeted by the academic unit and the central development office. (p. 571)

In this model, we begin to understand how layered the function of development becomes. In a hybrid system, the development officers not only are responsible to their individual academic units but also share in the responsibility of fundraising for the university's priorities as a whole.

Hall goes on to state, "Decentralization can shift the balance of power in the university" (p. 572). In fact, "a dean with full-time staffing for development is likely to be more methodical in implementing effective development procedures and will raise more money" (p. 572). In a 1989 survey, Hall found that "the amount of private support for an academic unit increases the dean's power among other deans. According to 75 percent of the respondents, the level of private support increases the dean's power with the president" (p. 573). Again, we see how crucial this issue is to the placement of the development office within a nonprofit organization. When one department, or academic unit in this case, is seen as more powerful than another, is the mission of the organization truly being advocated and is progress a possibility? While "decentralization makes it easier to establish a development strategy that recognizes and utilizes the strengths of each group" (p. 576), Hall points out, "faculty, according to development officers, tend to be interested in obtaining funding primarily for status-quo activities" (p. 577). In a centralized system, the outlook is not all that brighter. Hall states, "Information is a resource," and "one dean told me that in his opinion the problem was that centralized, to a large degree, meant secret" (p. 579). Again, the issue of communication surfaces loud and clear. The further Hall examines the options of these two types of development function and organizational placement, the more evident it is what is at the heart of the matter: internal perception of development, how development communicates within the organization, and whether or not either structure brings the fundraising function closer to its point of genesis, to stay in touch with and promote the mission of the organization.

Communication seems to be the most greatly challenged in a centralized system. Hall articulates, "The central development officer is at a considerable disadvantage in trying to establish an effective working relationship with faculty because of the size and diversity of institutions" (p. 579). Hall is quick to point out the importance of communication across divisions in a large organization: "Cooperative activities begin with frequent interaction and conversation. Ideas for joint projects grow out of lunchroom discussions and hallway meetings. Failure of centralized development systems to engender such cooperation is, at least in part, the result of the isolation of central development officers and faculty from one another" (p. 578). Indeed, such a scenario is likely in any large organization. Where one division works apart from the very programs and people it is responsible for, isolation occurs and progress is hindered at best.

Where is the best place for development within a nonprofit? Hall suggests a hybrid system with elements of central development, where answering to the president and CEO are in order and the mission is adhered to, while simultaneously taking some of the decentralized aspects into account to allow for greater internal communication. Hall found that:

> Academic officers and development officers have the fewest criticisms of internal communication in development systems that require development officers to report jointly to the vice-president for development and a dean. The case study interviews indicated that development officers in such hybrid systems carried information between the central development office and the academic unit. Since they were directly affiliated with both offices and had access to information in both, they became pipelines for sharing the resource rather than resource gatherers for either. (p. 580)

We can see that the hybrid system, with its streamlined approach to communication and strategic fundraising, is probably the best way to propel a large, complex organization to its greatest potential to gain funding and consequently further its mission.

Tracking System Infrastructure

If communication within an organization is so important to success, how should it be done? A basic strategy for communication among staff within an organization regarding status of relationships between the organization and its donors involves setting up a donor tracking system. Ann Fitzgerald (2002) explains the reasons for having such a good tracking system:

A good system:

- Improves ability to communicate with donors and respond to *their* needs and interests
- Ensures that the fundraising effort provides maximum value to an institution's objectives
- Allows the department to comply with legal and accounting requirements
- Maximizes staff resources and fundraising opportunities
- Gives staff flexibility and time to be creative
- Minimizes administrative work
- Reduces stress (you can find things when you need them) (Fitzgerald, 2002)

In starting a sound fundraising campaign, regardless of the method utilized, development is charged with administrative and organizational issues that are central to any efficient fundraising team. It all begins with organization and communication. The key strategy is having a sound, effective system in place to support the efforts of a development office.

What needs to be tracked in such a system? Most important is the key contact information on prospects and donors: name, address, phone numbers, and e-mail address. Second, the donation records need to be included as well. Data involve dates, amounts, type of gifts, pledge information, and planned giving details. Third, contact information for major gift prospects is essential for any organization that has more than an annual giving program. The more people involved in fundraising, the greater the need becomes to keep track of prospect contacts, including the date and description of the action. Generally speaking, for most organizations, all the other possible information in a database would be considered very helpful, but not essential. These data may include the following: employer information, family information, prospect coding, educational information, and marital information.

Software systems that include a robust and usable reporting function are essential. Success at reporting from the system comes in part from maintaining the accuracy of the data. If fields are not up to date with correct information, the reports will not reflect reality. Providing enough data-entry staff is not sufficient either; it must be complemented by the mindset of the development professionals focused on sending in new information to the staff in charge of the database.

BUDGETING AND RESOURCE ALLOCATION

Budgeting for fundraising should be determined through a reasonable and thoughtful process involving the appropriate staff and considering the relationship of the budget to projected fundraising success. Unfortunately, in many organizations the overall budget level and the specific line items within the budget are not set in this way. Often the budget is set based on last year's budget or last year's fundraising success. Often the wrong people are involved in the process—a budget analyst may be making these decisions in a vacuum or the CEO may be simply creating the budget based on intuition alone. Occasionally, the budget is set low to prevent the reporting of high fundraising expenses on IRS Form 990—even when a larger budget would bring in a much higher level of net gift returns.

Getting an organization to change its ways of budgeting for fundraising is not always easy. Years ago, as I was taking on a new assignment as the head of fundraising for an academic unit within Northwestern University, I met with the CFO of the unit to discuss my budget. I had prepared a report that supported the concept of a higher level of investment in fundraising producing a wildly higher level of corresponding gifts. I went through the report and explained my plan. The CFO sat there listening. After a long pause he simply stated that he appreciated the proposal but that my budget would be equal to the amount of unrestricted gifts raised in the previous year. Case closed. To be fair, within two years I worked to develop trust with the CFO, showed success in fundraising, and finally was rewarded by getting an additional fundraiser (and corresponding increase in the budget) based on an expanded fundraising plan.

So what is the best process for setting the development budget? The key driver is to understand that there is a relationship between fundraising effort and fundraising results, keeping all other variables constant. The effort of course can take various forms. It might involve exclusively professional staff funded with the budget directly; it might involve the extensive use of volunteers—perhaps involving the board members taking a lead role. The first step in the budgeting process would be to come up with three to five different "effort scenarios" based on different-sized budgets. There might be organizational constraints that force the maximum budget level to stay within a certain amount. Is there an internal bound on the budget level that going beyond just would not be considered possible by the organization? If so, then the scenarios should stay within that maximum amount. The middle scenario would represent a status quo budget, essentially set at last year's amount. Then the development staff would consider how to increase the effort (either one or two levels of increase) and how to decrease the effort (either one or two levels of decrease). The results of this step would be a spreadsheet describing the basics of each scenario along with the resulting budget amount. **Table 12-1** provides a fictionalized example.

The next step in the process involves getting the right people at the table to discuss the expected gift revenue resulting from each scenario. The key is to have a combination of high-level decision makers and those at the ground level in the fundraising operation. The combination will help to develop trust in the process by the leaders of the organization and an understanding of the broader concerns of the leaders by the development staff. Perhaps the CEO, the board chair, the director of development, and another professional fundraiser would be the team. They would first look at historical information (a chart of budget levels and resulting gifts from as many years as possible) and would have a general discussion of the relationship between budget and results. This might

Table 12-1 Effort Scenarios

Very Low Effort	Low Effort	Same as Last Year's Effort	High Effort	Very High Effort
$70,000	$200,000	$320,000	$505,000	$570,000
Mail once to 10,000 prospects	Mail once to 20,000 prospects	Mail twice to 20,000 prospects	Mail three times to 20,000 prospects	Mail three times to 40,000 prospects
Eliminate the Major Individual Officer	½ FTE Major Individual Officer	One FTE Major Individual Officer	1½ FTE Major Individual Officers	2 FTE Major Individual Officers
Eliminate the special event	Cut back on special event dinner—cheaper venue	One special event dinner	Bigger production of the one event dinner	Two special events
Eliminate Foundation Officer/Board handles	Eliminate Foundation Officer/Board handles	½ FTE Foundation Officer	1 FTE Foundation Officer	1 FTE Foundation Officer
Eliminate staffing of computer systems/Web—volunteer handles	½ FTE Staff to computer systems/Web	½ FTE Staff to computer systems/Web	1 FTE Staff to computer systems/Web	1 FTE Staff to computer systems/Web

Table 12-2 Net Gifts Raised for Each Effort Scenario

Very Low Effort	Low Effort	Same as Last Year's Effort	High Effort	Very High Effort
$70,000	$200,000	$320,000	$505,000	$570,000
$110,000 Projected gifts	$235,000 Projected gifts	$520,000 Projected gifts	$830,000 Projected gifts	$1,205,000 Projected gifts
$40,000 Net gifts	$35,000 Net gifts	$200,000 Net gifts	$325,000 Net gifts	$635,000 Net gifts

include discussion of delay factors involved in seeking major gifts, where the effort in one year might not result in gifts until years later (see **Exhibit 12-1**). Then they would estimate the gift income projected for each scenario. Once the projections are made, they would look at the net gifts raised for each scenario. **Table 12-2** extends the process in our fictionalized example.

The table creation process will provide a context for discussion by the team. Each person will be given the opportunity to participate in the debate regarding the level of budget, and a voting process could be used to fix the table estimates. Once the table is completed, the best scenario will hopefully become clear to the group. The CEO would make the final decision based on the input from the team.

The next step in the process would be to develop a more specific detailed budget for the approved scenario. The director of development would look at the personnel, benefits, computer, special events, mailing, and printing lines that make up the detailed budget. They would try to stick very close to the

Exhibit 12-1 Adding Fundraising Staff

One of the difficult issues for small organizations is deciding when to add an additional fundraiser to the staff, perhaps to work with major gift prospects and donors. The costs are quite high ($60,000 to $90,000, not including benefits) and results, unfortunately, are dependent on the prospect pool, the success of the organization, as well as the skill and determination of the person who might be hired for this position. Banking on results from any "rule of thumb" is risky. The delay factor for major gifts further complicates the process. Can the organization absorb the cost for a few years while the fundraising process grinds along at a slow, deliberate pace? There is no easy answer. The key would be to get the board to understand the issue and be willing to perhaps front the expense for a three-year test period. The huge potential reward of building a major gift program makes this an important issue for organizations attempting to stretch and grow.

total amount used in the budget planning process. Once the detailed budget is developed, the CEO would approve the budget and include it (both expenses and projected revenues) in the budget for the organization. The board then would approve the complete organizational budget, including the fundraising component.

Once an organization has successfully developed a more formal and thoughtful budgeting process it may want to consider going a step further and incorporate resource allocation into the budgeting process. Fundraising involves a variety of techniques. Which combination of techniques will produce the greatest amount of support? In our fictional budgeting example the techniques highlighted were: direct mail, major individual giving, foundation giving, special events, and Internet fundraising. How do you make sure that when you create a budget at a certain level that you have most effectively allocated effort across the various fundraising programs?

The resource allocation process actually follows the basic concept for determining the overall development budget level. For a complete description of a resource allocation process, see my book *Strategic Planning for Fund Raising* (1992). See **Exhibit 12-2** for an example of my model's predictive capacity. Here I will just consider the basic concept as illustrated in the following discussion, which continues the fictional budgeting example.

Suppose our budgeting process selected the "high effort" level of a $505,000 budget. How might that be best allocated to raise the most money for the coming year? To do this the development team will need to do some projections by fundraising technique. For the direct mail program consider three (or five) different scenarios. For the major individual fundraising consider three (or five) scenarios. Likewise for all the remaining fundraising programs. This is easier than you think, since you have already thought about the different scenarios as you developed the different budget levels. You simply need to create a cost estimate for each scenario within the fundraising programs and an estimate of how much might be raised at each level.

Do not consider any overhead that will be needed in the budget regardless of the funding levels for particular programs. In our example, we might find that $50,000 is fixed. This represents the basic office expenses just to run a development operation, regardless of the techniques used. That leaves

Exhibit 12-2 Resource Allocation

Lindahl's model for resource allocation (1992) predicted that Northwestern University could have raised an additional $16.4M in 1987–1988 beyond the base case of $63.7M if $2.5M in fundraising costs were better reallocated across the range of possible fundraising techniques and markets.

$455,000 to allocate among the fundraising programs: direct mail, individual major, foundation grant seeking, special events, and Internet fundraising.

Table 12-3 shows the estimates needed before moving to the next step in the process—only the three most costly of the five possible levels are considered.

Table 12-3 Cost and Gift Estimates for Each Effort Scenario*

Very Low Effort	Low Effort	Same as Last Year's Effort	High Effort	Very High Effort
		Mail twice to 20,000 prospects $40,000 Cost	Mail three times to 20,000 prospects $50,000 Cost	Mail three times to 40,000 prospects $100,000 Cost
		$85,000 Gifts	$100,000 Gifts	$250,000 Gifts
		One FTE Major Individual Officer	1½ FTE Major Individual Officers	2 FTE Major Individual Officers
		$70,000 Costs	$100,000 Costs	$140,000 Costs
		$200,000 Gifts	$300,000 Gifts	$500,000 Gifts
		One special event dinner	Bigger production of the one event dinner	Two special events
		$100,000 Costs	$125,000 Costs	$150,000 Costs
		$125,000 Gifts	$150,000 Gifts	$175,000 Gifts
		½ FTE Foundation Officer	1 FTE Foundation Officer	1 FTE Foundation Officer
		$30,000 Costs	$60,000 Costs	$60,000 Costs
		$60,000 Gifts	$200,000 Gifts	$200,000 Gifts
		½ FTE Staff to computer systems/Web	1 FTE Staff to computer systems/Web	1 FTE Staff to computer systems/Web
		$30,000 Costs	$70,000 Costs	$70,000 Costs
		$50,000 Gifts	$80,000 Gifts	$80,000 Gifts

* The first two levels of possible funding for each fundraising program were not considered so as to simplify the analysis.

Using Excel to create a spreadsheet, all of the 243 scenarios (five programs with three levels for each program, or $3 \times 3 \times 3 \times 3 \times 3$) are entered one per row and sorted by net gifts. The columns would have the following labels: Direct Mail Costs, Direct Mail Gifts, Individual Major Costs, Individual Major Gifts, Special Event Costs, Special Event Gifts, Foundation Costs, Foundation Gifts, Internet Costs, Internet Gifts, Total Costs, Total Gifts: Net Gift. The scenario with the largest net gifts within the bounds of the budgeted amount ($505,000 minus $50,000 = $455,000) will be selected. In our example, the following allocation scenario provides the largest net gifts:

Direct Mail Cost: $100,000
Individual Major Cost: $140,000
Special Events Cost: $125,000
Foundations Cost: $60,000
Internet Cost: $30,000
Total Costs: $455,000
Total Budget (with $50,000 overhead): $505,000
Total Gifts: $1,150,000
Net Gifts: $645,000

Comparing the best allocation with the original allocation (from the budgeting exercise above) we find a net gain in gifts of $320,000 ($645,000 new net gifts minus $325,000 original net gifts). This is without spending a single additional dollar—simply reallocating resources. Certainly as this method is applied to real situations, the actual gain will depend on many different variables. The theoretical improvement in performance, however, provides an incentive for allocating resources as thoughtfully as possible within the fundraising budget.

HUMAN RESOURCE ISSUES IN FUNDRAISING

Fundraising positions span many different functional areas. In larger organizations different people would be assigned to the different areas. But in smaller organizations the staff (often just one or two persons) would be expected to handle the variety of responsibilities in these positions. The functional areas can be subdivided into four main categories. The first would be support staff that understand and work with databases, gift processing, computer reporting, direct mail production, prospect research, and special events logistics. Second would be the communications specialist. This person must be an excellent writer and would be assigned to grant writing for corporations and foundations, case statement development, and Web site design. Third would be those with direct personal contact with the donors and prospects. This could be a major gift officer or other person assigned to personal cultivation, solicitation, and stewardship of gifts from individuals, corporations, and foundations. Finally, the fourth category of function is management of the fundraising process. The manager would be looking at the process more broadly to make sure the resources are adequately allocated and the staff hired and assigned to the correct tasks. This person would usually have a title such as "Director of Development" or "Vice President for Development for Institutional Advancement." Careers in development can progress among all of these functional areas, although executive or managerial-level positions will rarely be given to staff without some experience working directly with donors and prospects.

Salaries for fundraising professionals have gone up over the past few years. The average salary for U.S. respondents to the 2008 AFP Survey "increased to $72,683 in 2007—a two percent increase from the average in 2006. Average salaries for Canadian fundraisers increased . . . to C$74,376—a four percent increase" (AFP, 2008, May 12). The report goes on to discuss the top reasons for seeking another job. They were: (1) to earn a higher salary, (2) my values and the organization's values are not the same, (3) frustration with the work environment, (4) personality conflicts with my coworkers or manager, (5) to get more time to spend on personal/family activities, (6) to engage in more interesting or challenging work.

Duronio and Tempel (1997) identified characteristics of fundraisers that help to define the profession. The survey of 955 female and 793 male fundraisers included the following findings:

- More than eight of every ten respondents worked in another field before fundraising.
- Most common previous professions were education, advertising and promotions, and general business.
- The typical female respondent was white, 42 years old, had a B.S. in education, and earned less than $40,000.
- The typical male was white, 45 years old, had a graduate degree in business or education, and earned $40,000 to $60,000.
- Overall, the field is maturing compared with evidence from the 1980s.

They also asked respondents to identify the personal characteristics, skills, and professional knowledge of the best fundraisers they personally knew, rather than theorizing what the "ideal" fundraiser would look like. According to the authors, the most common responses are listed here:

- *Personal characteristics:* Commitment to cause/organization, integrity, and honesty.
- *Skills:* Organizational, communication, writing, making the ask, and effective listening.
- *Professional knowledge:* All areas of fundraising (but especially planned giving), tax/legal knowledge.

The actual number of fundraisers in the world is unknown but could be estimated to be at least 100,000 individuals. The field is growing each year, and with the number of new nonprofit organizations being formed each year, the number of fundraisers should grow correspondingly. Those interested in entering the field have several routes to choose from. First, they could start as a low-level development staff member and work their way up the ranks to eventually become a director of development. Or they could take noncredit workshops and other training in the field (e.g., The Fundraising School at the Center on Philanthropy at Indiana University) in order to be able to transfer skills from the for-profit world into the nonprofit world of fundraising. Finally, several masters' degree programs, such as the ones at North Park University (www.northpark.edu) and at New York University (www.nyu.edu) provide specialized for-credit educational experiences that prepare a person to enter the fundraising field.

Hiring

Currently there is a great demand for experienced fundraisers in the United States. Hence those hiring rarely get to choose someone who fulfills the entire list of desired requirements for a fundraising position. Salaries have also escalated over the past few years, and many smaller organizations are unable to keep pace. An approach that may prove useful is to take someone with excellent basic skills—someone who writes well; relates well to others; is persuasive, hard working, smart, and organized—and train him or her about the process and techniques of fundraising (see above for examples of educational programs).

Once candidates for a position are identified and the interview process starts, it helps to understand the particular questions and appropriate answers for those involved in the fundraising profession. First, consider whether or not the candidate has a heart for the mission of the organization. Has he or she volunteered for other organizations with a similar mission? Can the person talk convincingly about the lives of clients being transformed by the organization? Although mission match is not the only criteria, it is the base criterion for the hire. Don't hire someone lacking passion for the mission—even if the person seems perfect in all other ways. It won't work in the long run. Second, try to determine whether or not the candidate has the communication skills necessary for development work. Can the person speak clearly and logically? Is he or she an exceptional writer? Development work involves extensive writing. Third, consider whether or not the candidate has self-confidence and is a self-starter. Can the person handle rejection? Since typically only a portion of those asked for gifts will give them, fundraising demands a positive attitude about work and life in general.

Finally, when talking to an experienced fundraiser, it is essential to listen carefully as the candidate describes his or her involvement in the fundraising process. Be cautious of a candidate who takes complete credit for each gift that was raised under his or her watch. Fundraisers do not raise gifts in a vacuum. It is most often a team effort. A successful fundraiser builds and maintains relationships between a donor and the organization, not just between the fundraiser and the donor. Candidates who talk about a team—rather than an individual—effort to raise gifts will help to identify themselves as people who will be more collegial in the new job as well. Teamwork is important to the fundraising effort.

Compensation

A compensation issue specific to fundraising revolves around whether or not to pay commissions or bonuses for gifts raised by those in the development office. Employees in for-profit companies are used to rewarding the sales staff by providing commissions for each sale. A sales manager may wonder why commission-based compensation in fundraising is not allowed by the major fundraising associations in their ethics statements. For example, the AFP Code of Ethical Principles and Standards states that "members shall not accept compensation or enter into a contract that is based on a percentage of contributions; nor shall members accept finder's fees or contingent fees" (2007). Why the restriction? The main argument is the inability to assign fair credit for the transaction to any one individual. Suppose Mr. Jones was solicited by fundraiser Ms. Smith and the organization received a gift of $100,000. Can we attribute this gift to the work of Ms. Smith? If we do, we may miss the involvement of many others. Here is just a start to the possible list:

- The executive director met with Mr. Jones a month ago to describe the various projects being developed at the organization.
- The head of the direct mail program solicited Mr. Jones for over 20 years, and Mr. Jones responded with annual gifts from $50 to $5,000.
- The head of the project, who actually worked outside of the development office, went with Ms. Smith to the solicitation event and gave a great description of the particular project that eventually was funded.
- A volunteer originally told the organization about Mr. Jones and encouraged the first contact 25 years ago.
- The prospect researcher discovered that Mr. Jones recently sold stock in a publicly traded firm where he was an officer. The value reported to the Securities and Exchange Commission was $2,000,000.

As you can see, giving a percentage reward to one person on the team doesn't make sense. So even though a commission-based system might encourage greater effort, it is simply unethical for someone to take credit for the gift. The only one who should take credit for the gift is the donor!

So what can be done—ethically—to reward fundraisers who are making a positive difference and are involved in successful solicitation, active cultivation, and meaningful stewardship? The AFP Code of Ethical Principles and Standards (AFP, 2007) allows bonuses or performance-based compensation, provided "such bonuses are in accord with prevailing practices within the members' own organizations and are not based on a percentage of contributions." This approach provides a way to reward high performance generally for those doing well in their positions.

Relationship to Executive Director

The relationship between the lead fundraiser in an organization and the executive director is key to successful fundraising. There needs to develop a trust between these two individuals as they work to develop strong relationships with donors and prospects. In many ways the reporting structure is a bit odd. The director of development works for the executive director, yet the director of development gives the executive director (and perhaps board members as well) directions for who, where, and when contact needs to be made with the donors in the organization. This role reversal can cause a tension in the relationship if the two people are not careful. Meeting regularly, communicating at an honest level, and sticking to a mutually developed fundraising plan can help to further the working relationship.

Klein (2007) clarifies what the most common reasons a productive relationship between the director of development (DOD) and the executive director (ED) fails to happen. It is when the ED

- fails to maintain appropriate skills as the organization grows over the years,
- has been on the job too long and lacks enthusiasm for the task,
- is defensive and cannot take criticism,
- is afraid to ask for money,
- controls the board and limits the board members' interest in fundraising,
- is threatened by the knowledge of the director of development,
- works constantly, never takes vacations, and expects the staff to do the same, or
- thinks the director of development should be the one to just go out and get the cash.

In contrast, an ED may have difficulties with the DOD. The following are the most common reasons I have discovered going the other direction. The DOD

- may not take the initiative to make things happen,
- goes around the ED and develops strong relations independently with the board members,
- asks for short-term gifts rather than take a long-term strategy with donors so as to best prepare for the next job change instead of meet the needs of the organization, or
- may have been on the job too long and lack the enthusiasm needed to engage a familiar donor base.

A good relationship between the DOD and ED requires a good understanding of the responsibilities of each party. Clarifying exactly the role each should play helps to set the basis for the entire relationship. Open and honest communication will go far in making sure this key relationship is strong and healthy.

Performance Evaluation

Nonprofit accountability is demanding better tracking of success across the organization, including within the development office. But evaluating performance of fundraising staff can be a challenge. Staff with little direct donor contact are easier to evaluate, while those development officers whose success is tied to donors' giving are the most difficult to evaluate. The main issue for those with direct responsibility for major gifts is the balance between looking at the results in terms of dollars raised versus quantity and quality of effort. The earlier discussion regarding the problem of giving credit to the fundraiser for gifts raised provides a basis for the problem of performance evaluation. If credit for gifts cannot easily and fairly be assigned to particular staff, how can the use of the total gift levels to assess performance be justified? The only solution is to build a performance evaluation system based more broadly on other criteria.

The other criterion in use today is tracking the quantity and quality of contacts with donors. Each time a donor or prospect is visited personally or called for more than a superficial reason, the fundraiser records a summary of the event either into a computer system or manually in a "trip" or "visit" report. Then a process is set up to give credit for the number of visits or calls and the quality of the calls. Obviously, quality is open to interpretation. But without some indication of quality, the evaluation system would encourage many potentially meaningless contacts with donors. This certainly would defeat the goal of rewarding success.

Some organizations have set up fairly elaborate point systems that give particular points for visits, for phone calls, for number of proposals submitted, adherence to budget, percentage solicited that result in gifts, and whether or not key leaders were brought in to engage with the donors. Staff falling below some standard would be counseled and mentored so as to bring their points up during the following time period. Fundraisers would have bristled at such scrutiny 20 years ago, but today this reporting requirement and tracking system is becoming more routine.

The professionalization of the evaluation process makes sense within the broader movement of the entire field to the status of a profession. Fundraising has grown as a profession over the past 20 years. There is a collection of knowledge central to the practice, there are university-based degree programs associated with the field, there is a certification system (CFRE, Certified Fund Raising Executive) available to practitioners through the AFP, and there is a code of ethics that binds the members of this profession. The coming 20 years will show the further movement to a true profession—a profession that will combine a growing theoretical base with informed practice.

REFERENCES

Anheier, H. K. (2005). *Nonprofit organizations: Theory, management, policy*. New York: Routledge Taylor & Francis.

Association of Fundraising Professionals (AFP). (2007). *Code of Ethical Principles and Standards*. Retrieved March 27, 2008, from http://www.afpnet.org/ka/ka-3.cfm?content_item_id=1068&folder_id=897

Association of Fundraising Professionals (AFP). (2008, May 12). *Charitable fundraising salaries increase across North America* [Press release]. Retrieved July 31, 2008, from http://www.afpnet.org/ka/ka-3.cfm?content_item_id=24480&folder_id=2326

Duronio, M., & Tempel, E. (1997). *Fundraisers: Their careers, stories, concerns, and accomplishments*. San Francisco, CA: Jossey-Bass.

Fitzgerald, A. (2002). *Systems for fundraising success*. Presented at the 25th Annual Resource Bank Meeting, April 11–12, 2002. Philadelphia, PA. Retrieved February 5, 2006, from http://www.heritage.org/About/Community/fundraising.cfm

Hall, M. R. (1992). The decentralization of development: Impact on power, priorities, faculty perceptions. *Teachers College Record, 93*(3), 569–582. Retrieved April 24, 2006, from the Academic Search Premier database.

Herman, R. D., & Associates (Eds.). (2005). *Jossey-Bass handbook of nonprofit leadership and management* (2nd ed.). San Francisco, CA: Jossey-Bass.

Jalandoni, N. T., Lamkin, L. M., Pollak, T. H., & Weitzman, M. S. (Eds.). (2002). *The new nonprofit almanac and desk reference*. San Francisco, CA: Jossey-Bass.

Kelly, K. S. (1998). *Effective fund-raising management*. Mahwah, NJ: Lawrence Erlbaum Associates.

Klein, K. (2007). *Fundraising for social change* (5th ed.). San Francisco, CA: Jossey-Bass.

Lindahl, W. E. (1992). *Strategic planning for fund raising*. San Francisco, CA: Jossey-Bass.

Raymond, S. U. (2004). *The future of philanthropy economics, ethics, and management*. Hoboken, NJ: John Wiley & Sons.

Salamon, L. M. (1997). *Holding the center, America's nonprofit sector at a crossroads*. NY: The Nathan Cummings Foundation.

Index

Italicized page locators indicate a figure; tables are noted with a *t*.